LEARNING BEYOND THE CLASSROOM

Education has become one of our major preoccupations, vital to young people's life-chances, central to any strategy for economic prosperity and social cohesion. But the challenges facing young people as they become adults are more complex and demanding than ever before.

Rather than continuing to pour money and effort into making schools and colleges more effective as institutions, Tom Bentley argues that we should focus on the connections between schools and society, relating education more closely to the challenges of adulthood. To be truly effective, education must give young people exposure to a wide range of contexts and role models for learning, along with experience of genuine responsibility. It must avoid containing them in the single, increasingly outdated context of the conventional classroom.

Learning Beyond the Classroom reviews projects from the UK and other countries which represent the seeds of a new approach. It explains how such an approach can be used to address some of the most pressing challenges for education: promoting active citizenship, developing employability and tackling chronic underachievement.

Tom Bentley argues that, in an increasingly complex society, we cannot rely solely on dedicated teachers to deliver the understanding and personal qualities young people will need to thrive. Effective education will have to extend beyond the classroom, using a broader range of resources – cultural, social, financial and physical – than we usually associate with education services.

Drawing on a wide-ranging review of educational innovation and on contemporary analyses of economic, social and technological change, *Learning Beyond the Classroom* shows that creating a revolution in education requires us to think far more radically about the role of young people and the kinds of learning opportunities we offer them. It sketches a new landscape of learning: a vision of education which combines the rigour and depth of the best professional instruction with the flexibility and motivational power of community-based, collaborative learning.

Tom Bentley is a senior researcher at Demos, the independent think-tank, and an adviser to David Blunkett MP, Secretary of State for Education and Employment. He was born and educated in East London and at Oxford University. His research areas include: young people, education, the future of work and the combating of social exclusion.

LEARNING BEYOND THE CLASSROOM

Education for a changing world

Tom Bentley

London and New York

First published 1998
by Routledge
11 New Fetter Lane, London EC4P 4EE

Simultaneously published in the USA and Canada
by Routledge
29 West 35th Street, New York, NY 10001

Typeset in Garamond by Routledge
Printed and bound in Great Britain by Page Brothers (Norwich) Ltd

British Library Cataloguing in Publication Data
A catalogue record for this book is available from the British Library

· *Library of Congress Cataloging-in-Publication Data*
Bentley, Tom
Learning beyond the classroom / Tom Bentley.
Includes bibliographical references and index.
1. Educational change–Great Britain. 2. Education–
Aims and objectives–Great Britain. 3. Active learning–Great Britain.
4. Continuing education–Great Britain. 5. Educational sociology–Great Britain.
6. Educational planning–Great Britain. I. Title.
LA632.B47   1998
370'.941–dc21   98–19892

ISBN 0–415–18259–x

CONTENTS

PREFACE

This book combines three things. First, it presents a general argument about how change in society is creating new educational challenges. Second, it presents examples of how educational innovators are beginning to meet those challenges, forging new forms of practice to supplement and enhance basic provision. Third, it analyses the implications of wider change and lessons from practice for the way that our education systems work in the future.

Education systems stand at a crossroads. On the one hand we are pushing a decades-old infrastructure to satisfy more demand, meet higher standards and deliver ambitious objectives. On the other we are creating a new set of institutions, with radically different characteristics, to meet the emerging challenges of lifelong learning. We must attempt to resolve the tension between these approaches if we want today's school students to become successful lifelong learners.

Achieving this requires far-reaching change, both to education systems and to our ideas of what education is for. But the agenda I set out is not a detailed blueprint, nor a utopian wish list. The argument is grounded in existing, practical examples. The seeds of solutions are already beginning to grow, and the current system can be progressively transformed by a process of evolution and innovation.

The projects I describe are constantly developing: testing their effectiveness, learning from failure, extending and refining their provision and their objectives. This learning process is vital to the next stage of development in education. Local innovation and imagination must be supported by clear frameworks, rigorous standards and adequate resources.

Perhaps the most important recent development is the National Framework for Study Support, which will help create out-of-hours study centres in thousands of schools over the next three years. But support structures for active, community-based learning are only a foundation on which to build. The rest is a challenge for the whole of society: to recognise the need for change, and learn to do things differently.

Tom Bentley
August 1998

ACKNOWLEDGEMENTS

I owe many people a great debt for their contribution to this book.

The work has its origins in the *Forum on active learning in the community*, chaired by David Hunt (now Lord Hunt of Tamworth), whose foresight, enthusiasm and generosity played a vital role in establishing the momentum and potential of the project. The work of the forum and initial research leading to this book were made possible by a generous grant from the Calouste Gulbenkian Foundation. Thanks go to the other members of the forum: Michael Barber, Tom Shebbeare, Rebecca Gray, Howard Green, Geoff Thompson MBE, Dick Whitcutt, Sir John Smith, Selina Garner, Peter Mandelson, Jenny Shackleton and Deborah Jenkins. Jim Cogan and Michael Norton both played a vital part in establishing the Forum and in developing the ideas. Thanks also to Dave Turner, who has done as much to turn these ideas into practice as anybody else, and to Jane Buckley and Jennifer Mullis.

Several people generously gave me detailed and thoughtful comments on drafts or draft chapters. They are Howard Gardner, Charles Handy, John MacBeath, David Hargreaves, Ian Christie and Marianne Talbot. Their help was invaluable. I have also relied on the support and ideas of several other people, including Geoff Mulgan, Perri 6 and Charlie Leadbeater. Simon Retallack gave me able support with background research. Thanks also go to the whole of the Routledge team. Needless to say, any remaining errors and weaknesses in the text are my responsibility.

All my colleagues at Demos deserve thanks for their friendship, patience and good ideas. Without their support, and the environment for working and learning that they help to create at Demos, I would not have been able to produce this work. Thanks to Lorna Clarke-Jones for her unique contribution, and to the other friends who supported and encouraged me while I was writing – especially Leandra Box, Debbie Porter and Véronique Pain.

Finally, and most importantly, thanks to Richard and Penny Bentley: for their wisdom and experience, and for their unfailing love and support. As a learner, I owe them everything.

1

INTRODUCTION

The things you learn in school are to do with education and to get jobs.
You're not really using them in actual real life.

(18-year-old, Birmingham)

This book argues that if we want education to be effective in the next century, adult society must take up an active partnership with the people who so far have been largely left out of the debate: with young people themselves. It argues that there are two crucial tests of an effective education system: how well students can apply what they learn in situations beyond the bounds of their formal educational experience, and how well prepared they are to continue learning and solving problems throughout the rest of their lives. To do this, education must be both broader and deeper. Broader, because it must include a wider range of learning experience, experience of roles and situations which mirror those we value in society. Deeper, because it must nurture a greater understanding in young people: understanding of themselves, their motivations and goals in life, and of the subjects and disciplines they study.

The implication of these two tests is that education must become more open, using a range of resources much wider than public infrastructure, taxpayers' money, contracted parental obligations and the skills of increasingly worn-out professionals. It must be able to use human, financial, social, cultural and informational resources from the whole of society to stimulate and develop young people's ability to learn and understand for themselves. This learning will not take place only inside schools and colleges, but in communities, workplaces and families. It requires a shift in our thinking about the fundamental organisational unit of education, from the school, an institution where learning is organised, defined and contained, to the learner, an intelligent agent with the potential to learn from any and all of her encounters with the world around her.

Without such a change the education system will be unable to meet the demands of the twenty-first century. More than this, I argue that the current system is already failing to provide the preparation that young people need in order to thrive. Our assumptions about what education is for, and about how it

1

works, must change. This might seem surprising. Over the last twenty years, education has become one of our most urgent priorities as a society. Participation and attainment have risen, and public spending has increased. We probably know more about how the system is performing than ever before. But despite this, we are reaching the limits of what the current system can do. Even if it manages to achieve ambitious targets for numeracy, literacy, basic skills and qualifications, it will not meet the needs of its students unless it changes more radically.

The most important reason for this argument is the nature of change in wider society. Over the last twenty-five years, the ways we live, work and communicate have been transformed, and the changes will continue. Learning is only effective when it relates meaningfully to a wider social context, and for us the context is changing dramatically. One of the clearest illustrations of this change is the way in which young people's role in society has become such a potent and frequently debated issue. Is young people's behaviour getting worse? When do they stop being children and become adults? Is drug-taking a normal part of their lives? Will they be able to support the needs of an ageing population? Are they damaged by family breakdown? Who is responsible for young people, and when?

At the heart of these questions is a curious paradox. Living in a time of rapid and unsettling change pushes us to think harder about young people. On the one hand, we are spurred to guard and control them more tightly, trying to protect and pass on what we value and ensure that they do not fall prey to risks and threats. On the other, we want them to be creative and enterprising, to learn from the mistakes of previous generations and to solve problems where we have failed, such as sustaining the natural environment and creating meaningful work for everybody. We are torn between the desire to prepare young people properly for an uncertain future, and the recognition that we do not have all the answers for them. Added to this is the fact that younger people tend to adapt on their own, embracing many changes quite spontaneously, and producing cultures and ways of thinking which can seem alien and threatening to those of us who are more set in our ways.

Education is no stranger to this paradox. On one hand we hear political rhetoric converging around the need for a 'flexible', 'high-skill' workforce, able to thrive in a labour market where the pace of innovation continually rises, and where jobs for life are disappearing. On the other we are concerned that young people learn the values and obligations of citizenship, that they learn right from wrong, and that they achieve standards set for them by adults and experts. We want them to understand the essence of what is valuable in a world increasingly characterised by diversity, mobility and choice.

This seems much harder at a time when the old structures and norms which supported duty and traditional ways of living are breaking down. National institutions have steadily lost the trust and esteem of citizens. Marriage is less popular and less successful. Traditional elites have felt their positions threatened by unforeseen change. Education, the preparation of young people for the challenges and responsibilities that they will face in adult life, becomes at once more important and much more difficult.

The first big question to be faced is the place of education in an information society. The changes of the last two decades have been fuelled by one basic transformation: the fact that information can be collected, synthesised and communicated with more speed, precision and power than we have ever known before. Information and communications technologies are shaping every sphere of our lives, from personal relationships to the structure and content of work, economic investment to leisure, human reproduction to patterns of transcontinental migration. With these capacities has come a growing appreciation of the extent to which we are connected and interdependent (Mulgan, 1997). To make sense of these connections, to turn them into opportunities rather than threats, we must use information to create, share and use knowledge. The explosion of information means that much of it is useless and trivial, requiring us to sort and synthesise, to spot connections that matter, to distinguish meaningful messages from the noise that surrounds them. This is another reason why education is so important. To make full use of the resources that an information society offers, we must be able to handle the overload, to develop capacities which can make sense of it all without screening out things that might be valuable.

The ubiquity of information and knowledge in society poses a stiff challenge for education systems. If people can gain access to knowledge on demand through the internet, the Open University, interactive television or firm-based universities, what is compulsory education there for? The days when state education provided the main opportunity for most people to learn effectively have gone. The private sector in Britain already spends more on education and training than the public sector. Public education systems must not only provide good-quality learning in themselves, but also full access to the knowledge resources offered elsewhere. Such resources are constantly growing and shifting, requiring educators to adapt more rapidly and responsively than ever before.

The second question is about values. In any society, the function of education in the first two decades of life has been partly to develop in young people the values, attitudes and understandings which society holds dear. Even in secular, supposedly 'value-neutral' systems, the liberal virtues of individual freedom, tolerance, mutual respect and fairness have been implicitly cherished. Education helps to glue society together, transmitting common values and cultural heritage, promoting messages about what members of society owe to each other. But when the world is connected in countless, unprecedented ways, when peoples and cultures travel with increasing lightness and speed, and societies are becoming more porous and mixed, how can education act as a common core? The proportion of ethnic minorities in Britain is predicted to double over the next twenty years to more than 10 per cent.

We are learning that the value differences between generations, in Britain and elsewhere, are increasingly sharp. When value changes come from all directions, formed and shaped by complex, fluid processes, can education hope to frame and instil a common core by making decisions at the top of the system and then transmitting them down the chains of command? Will it be able to keep up, to stay relevant to the needs and concerns of the people it is supposed to serve?

This question brings us to the third major challenge for education. How can it motivate young people to concentrate, work purposefully and learn for themselves? The information age provides a dazzling array of distractions and alternative pursuits with which formal education has to compete. A recent study found that two-thirds of people aged between 16 and 25 believe that schools do not prepare people for real life. How can education convince its students that what it offers is worth having? Information penetrates our lives with increasing power, whether we like it or not – a fact that is illustrated by the debates about internet pornography, teen magazines and the influence of television. Equipping and motivating young people to learn, not just in the first two decades but for the rest of their lives, is an urgent priority. But the tools with which we control their behaviour and their access to previously guarded information seem increasingly ineffective. The problem brings us back to our starting paradox. How do we instil in young people what we really value, passing on the wisdom that society has managed to accumulate, while simultaneously equipping them to solve problems and meet challenges which older generations do not know how to solve?

In this book I argue that the seeds of solutions to this paradox are already here. In the worlds of work and relationships, we are beginning to understand that high performance flows, not from the rigid imposition of external structures and constraints, but from the distribution of responsibility and a commitment to honesty, transparency and shared goals. When these conditions are met, the true constraints on performance and fulfilment begin to appear, and the means to overcome them can be created. My analysis is rooted in projects which are pioneering new, effective approaches to learning and educational achievement.

At the core of the argument is the idea that our conception of knowledge must shift to include, alongside knowledge of what to say, how to say it, and knowledge of oneself, the *ability to do* (Drucker, 1993: 24). In Chapter 2, alongside indicators of underachievement and distress among young people, I examine evidence that many of them are unable to apply what they learn at school in situations where it might actually be useful. The way that education is organised encourages an artificial distinction between knowing and doing. This is also a historical divide, between knowledge and manual workers, and between academic and vocational education. But the distinction between formal, theoretical knowledge and practical skill is being eroded by the fact that the systems by which we organise life increasingly incorporate technology which can process information, 'the action of knowledge upon knowledge itself' (Mulgan, 1997: 20). Learning how to apply knowledge in unfamiliar situations is more and more important. It requires practice in environments which closely resemble those in which we will eventually do so for real. And yet schools and classrooms resemble less and less the situations in which the rest of us live, work and learn. I argue that, for young people, who want to be a part of society from an increasingly early age, learning environments should as far as possible be those in which adults demonstrate their ability to do, as well as to know in more abstract ways.

Despite our efforts so far, formal education is not equipping young people with the resources they need to thrive in adulthood. As one young man in a recent study by the Industrial Society put it, 'I think a lot of the time at school . . . they teach you knowledge but they never teach you how to learn.' Chapter 2 looks at the dimensions of this failure. They include the brittleness of understanding which conventional educational success often inculcates, lack of readiness for the world of work, growing psychological distress, the failure of relationships, and political alienation. When set against the challenges that we face, from the demands of personal relationships to the threat of global warming, these problems are grounds for serious concern.

The beginnings of solutions to these challenges are already here. First, they flow from recent advances in our understanding of intelligence and the ways in which humans learn. Intelligence is both broader and more flexible than educationalists and psychologists have assumed in the past. In particular, the idea that we can be *emotionally* intelligent opens up a whole new range of educational opportunity. The habits of thoughtfulness and emotional self-management established in childhood and adolescence will have a profound influence on a person's success and wellbeing for the rest of their lives. Opportunities to develop emotional competence are a crucial part of the new landscape of learning.

I then look at a number of projects and initiatives which, in various ways, are taking up the challenge of learning out of school. Some are based in schools and connected to the curriculum, while others are completely independent. Some are very new, while others are more established. Their focus varies widely, but they are all contributing to the goal of opening up learning, making a wider range of resources available to young people, and helping them to become active, self-managing learners. Much of this work is new, and its long-term impact has not always been evaluated, although there is clear evidence of effectiveness in some projects. In Chapter 5 I examine some of the common characteristics of successful 'active learning projects', and the ways in which they contribute to young people's development and understanding.

From this point, I look at how the active learning embodied in our range of examples can be used to tackle three of the most important concrete challenges facing our education system: learning citizenship and morality, developing employability, and tackling underachievement and exclusion. I argue that, in each of these areas, the solutions lie in involving young people in a much wider range of contexts for learning, and in giving them real responsibility for what they are doing, while retaining an emphasis on rigour and achievement which is found in the best academic education. At each stage, I set out the major changes in context – in employment and the economy, in social values and morality, and in the cultural and economic factors which influence educational attainment. The arguments imply that we should think of young people not as 'pupils', in the sense of a transparent space into which information can flow, but as 'intelligent agents', that is, as active learners who have the potential to make *all* of their encounters with the world more intelligent. Because the kinds of learning that I describe take place as much outside the classroom as in it, the argument means that, over time, schools will become *neighbourhood learning centres*, offering learning opportunities to a wide range of people in their local areas. Their provision will be more diverse and more flexible, offering services to adults as well those of school age. Schools will become brokers as well as providers, forging partnerships with employers, voluntary and religious organisations, parents and young people, to extend and enhance opportunities for learning.

At the heart of the argument is the recognition that learning can take place in any situation, at any time, and that to improve the quality of education we must overcome the historical mistake of confusing formal, school-based instruction with the whole of education. This does not mean that learning is easy. Developing understanding and the capacity to thrive is challenging and difficult, and to do so successfully requires discipline, rigour and consistent effort. But if we continue to focus our efforts to improve the abilities of young people on the institutions which contain them, we will soon reach the limits of progress. If we want a quantum leap in educational performance, we must be prepared to think more radically, and to develop young people's capacity to learn *in* society, rather than at one remove from it.

The last chapters of the book examine the implications of the argument for the way we organise and think about education as a whole. I argue that systems of assessment must become both more broad-ranging and more coherent, using more information and involving learners more actively in assessing themselves, as well as drawing on the judgement of a range of experts and authorities in the field.

Young people are not empty vessels waiting to be filled with the wisdom of ages. From the earliest age they begin to convert their experience into assumptions and theories about the world. Their learning should incorporate and reflect these assumptions, and challenge them to become deeper and more sophisticated. But too often, school-based instruction encourages them to place what they learn in a narrowly-bounded category, failing to give them the means with which to compare it to the other assumptions and experiences that make up their world view. Overcoming this failure is partly a question of good teaching, but it also depends on direct experience: the chance to test out formal knowledge in a range of circumstances, to observe other people using such knowledge in varied and valuable ways, and to learn how conflicting perspectives can be reconciled.

Developing understanding in this way, I argue, depends on our ability to create *learning relationships*: patterns of interaction which are meaningful because they facilitate the exchange of knowledge and insight, and the synthesis of such knowledge into wider understanding. If learning takes place in a wide range of contexts, we need to focus on the connections *between* people and contexts which support effective learning. Rather than thinking of these factors as characteristics of institutions, as we are used to doing with schools, we should see them as factors which support learning relationships.

This argument does not seek to denigrate the value which schools and teachers currently help to create. Many schools already excel at learning relationships. Centres of learning excellence have a vital place in the vision that emerges from this book. But reform must focus as much on the connections between educational institutions and the communities in which they sit as on the internal effectiveness of the institutions themselves.

The aim should be to make the most of the resources available to support learning, by making their provision more flexible, open and responsive to the needs of each individual learner. But it is impossible to do this while adults and professions retain tight control over exactly where, and how, each individual learns. Motivating young people to take their place in the world with intelligence and consideration for others depends on allowing them to take responsibility for what they do. But responsibility cannot be exercised without real choice. This, perhaps, is the greatest risk attached to changing our view of education in the ways that I argue we should: it requires us to take more notice of, and be more responsive to, what young people say about themselves, about us, and about the quality of their learning. If we want young people to be responsible, and to absorb what society values, they must be able actively to engage with it. Taking such a step is certainly a risk, but only when it has been taken will we truly have made the transition from an information society to a learning society.

2

THE CHALLENGES

I guess I could call myself smart. I mean I can usually get good
grades. Sometimes I worry though, that I'm not equipped to achieve
what I want, that I'm just a tape recorder repeating back what I've
heard. I worry that once I'm out of school and people don't keep
handing me information with questions . . . I'll be lost.

(Emily, 15)

Our growing preoccupation with education has produced a wide range of
responses. In the UK, participation in higher and further education has
increased dramatically. Standards of attainment in schools have, on the whole,
risen: more pupils gain qualifications at ages 16 and 18. Control of education
has been centralised. The National Curriculum and the introduction of league
tables have made some aspects of performance more transparent. Performance
targets, based on National Curriculum testing, have come to dominate the
policy agenda, along with a higher-profile inspection system. Pre-school
learning and childcare are being expanded. A new framework of vocational
qualifications has been introduced, and apprenticeships have reappeared,
albeit in limited form. Education has experienced wave after wave of reform,
and the pace is unlikely to slow. In the business world, attention has turned to
how the combined knowledge and experience of a firm's employees and associates can best be used. 'Knowledge management' and 'the learning
organisation' have become buzzwords, spawning a whole new generation of
management theory and 'how to' manuals. Energetic efforts are being made to
promote 'lifelong learning' and to provide the resources and opportunities for
people to improve their employability by taking career breaks, re-skilling, or
updating their knowledge in a particular area. School systems across the world
are compared and contrasted, and the role of education and skills in economic
growth is fiercely debated.

But if the basic function of education is to prepare young people to meet
the challenges of adult life, too often it is failing. While overall attainment in
the UK has gradually risen, along with participation in post-compulsory
education, there is evidence that those at the trailing edge of attainment have

been doing worse than before. Even among those who do succeed in getting formal qualifications and finding work, young people often find themselves unprepared for the challenges and demands they will encounter in life after school. A growing number of studies suggest that even those with sophisticated formal knowledge of a subject can be bad at using it in unfamiliar surroundings or to solve novel, complex problems. This inability to transfer knowledge from one domain to another points to a lack of real understanding, a crucial failure in a world where problem-solving and transferable skills are at a premium. More broadly, evidence suggests that many people are not coping well with the tasks and challenges of ordinary life. This includes the inability to save money for the future, to understand and persevere in relationships, to plan and manage a career, to recognise and carry out obligations as a citizen, and to cope with stress, change and insecurity.

Some might argue that it was never the purpose of schooling to prepare people for such a wide range of challenges: family and friends are the primary sources of learning about life, and it is unrealistic to expect formal institutions to take on such a broad remit. There is some truth to this argument, and education institutions will never be able to do the whole job. But we must recognise that, in any society, education must have a general aim: to equip its pupils with the tools and capacities to succeed in life. Forgetting this can lead to a gap between ends and means, allowing us to devote too much time and energy to the means, without thinking so much about whether they serve the overall end. In order to avoid this, it is worth thinking briefly about the nature of the challenges that young people will face.

These can be grouped in order of generality, from the global to the personal and intimate. Global challenges sometimes seem to defy any possibility of solution, let alone of finding ways of educating people to solve them. They range from preserving the planet as an environment in which humans can survive to preventing the ravages of war, poverty and disease across the world. At a time when wealth, information, people and environmental pollution cross the globe faster and in more complex ways than ever before, these challenges are unprecedented. At a societal level there are problems of similar complexity – finding forms of political decision-making that serve every citizen, stimulating and regulating economic activity to ensure that people are able to satisfy their material needs and find gainful work, sustaining and developing forms of community and association which give people sufficient security, fulfilment and support, managing the framework of law and protecting weak and vulnerable members of society. At the next level are the localised challenges of running organisations and shared spaces so that they are effective and inclusive, allowing people to interact safely and creatively, formalising arrangements that work well without stifling innovation. At a more intimate level are the challenges of family life: providing for dependants, succeeding in long-term relationships and coping with insecurity and hardship. Finally, there are the deeply personal challenges of making successful

9

life-choices: finding work, deciding where and how to live, choosing between different career paths, understanding oneself and achieving one's ambitions, and coping with the inner stress and insecurity that modern life can generate.

The scale and complexity of these challenges is daunting. While it is important to be clear about them, we should also recognise that many people are surviving and thriving in all sorts of circumstances, that the seeds of solutions are being generated all the time. More than anything else, these challenges show how the world is changing, and point to the need for education to change with it. At each stage of the argument this book will seek to explain the key changes affecting young people – in the worlds of work and relationships, in organisations and politics, in values and relationships – in order to show how the kinds of learning I argue for relate to the future rather than the past.

The evidence of failure is clear in many areas.

Basic educational failure

The schools system in the UK still produces too many young people with no formal qualifications and an alarming lack of basic competence. Twenty per cent of the British working population has no qualifications (DfEE, 1997); 8.8 per cent of boys and 6.5 per cent of girls leave school with no GCSE or equivalent qualifications. The Basic Skills Agency recently estimated that a quarter of those under twenty-five have limited mathematical competence and a fifth lack basic literacy skills. Meanwhile, in 1996 only 41.3 per cent of boys passed GCSE in English language. While over two-fifths now pass five GCSEs at grades A*–C, only one-third pass five that include maths and English. School exclusions have more than tripled over the last five years, with pupils from some ethnic minorities disproportionately at risk. Eighty per cent of pupils excluded from secondary schools and 92 per cent of those excluded from primary schools are boys. Currently, only around a third of those permanently excluded from school find their way back into mainstream education. Such failure is closely linked to a drastic reduction of life-chances for many young people: unemployment (seven out of ten habitual truants leave school without any exam passes), crime (school non-attenders are up to three times more at risk of being involved in crime – 30 per cent of prisoners were truants), problem drug use, and often homelessness. The causes are complex, influenced by factors external to schooling, such as poverty, low parental supervision, family breakdown and conflict and the influence of peer groups. But the experience of education inevitably plays a part. Many of the young long-term unemployed are deeply ambivalent about returning to education, and often openly hostile. Pupils who are labelled as disruptive or under-achievers at an early stage of their education are often treated as a problem to be contained from then on. The pressure of school league tables may have added to the incentives for schools to focus on those with a reasonable chance of doing well, to the cost of those left behind. Teachers with large classes and large workloads can find it difficult to provide the care, encouragement and stimulation required to help these pupils achieve, especially when one or two disruptive pupils in a class can deny everybody else the chance to learn effectively. But there is little doubt that this early experience of failure contributes to the problems of crime, unemployment, anti-social behaviour, alienation and fatalism among young people that have received so much media attention and caused so much concern in recent years. The Metropolitan Police recently estimated that children between the ages of 10 and 16 commit 40 per cent of street robberies, a third of car thefts and 30 per cent of house burglaries in London, and that most of these offences are committed during school hours. Hundreds of thousands of young people are at best only marginally connected to the formal economy, their contact limited to occasional or temporary work, leaving them dependent on benefits and the informal economy for survival, isolated both from opportunities for development and from peers and role models who might act as a positive influence.

Relationships

There is also significant evidence that many young people are failing in their relationships. Marriage is down, divorce is up. Lone parenthood has also grown, placing exacting demands on many inadequately prepared young mothers and fathers. Among those with the fewest prospects in other areas of life, relationships are often unstable, unsatisfying and unproductive. Evidence from the British Household Panel Study shows that those with low levels of employment security are least likely to be in stable, long-term relationships (Wilkinson, 1996). Many young people see little point in getting married, or if they do, more and more often it ends in separation and failure. But this is not just a problem for the disadvantaged. Relationship breakdown is part of a much wider cluster of social trends affecting the whole population. It is difficult to separate cause from effect in this area: are young people having more problems with relationships partly because more of them experience family breakdown during childhood, or because of much broader changes in society? It is probably safe to say that marriage is less valued than in the past, and that there are highly complex historical forces at work, but there is clearly an urgent need for young people to be better prepared for the world of relationships – to think in the long term, to make choices that they can stick with, to recognise the dangers ahead, to be aware of themselves and able to recognise and meet the needs of others. Perhaps most importantly, young people must be able to resolve personal conflict successfully. Research has shown that successful and long-lasting marriages are not those with the lowest level of conflict between spouses, but those in which conflict is resolved effectively. Central to this task is the ability to communicate, a vital tool for helping young people gain control over their lives as well as for successful relationships.

Yet homeless young people, the unemployed and younger teenagers who are off-site secondary pupils are particularly isolated and unhappy with communication (Catan *et al.*, 1996).

Saving for the future

Personal savings are a crucial indicator of people's readiness to face the future, to cope with unexpected crises such as temporary spells of unemployment, and to plan career breaks for parenting or adult learning. Britain has always had a relatively low level of personal savings, partly because of our historical tendency to tie up our assets in home ownership. It is a serious problem, which governments have so far failed to solve through tax breaks and financial incentives. It is especially serious for young people because they cannot count on collective welfare provision in the way that their parents might have: saving for retirement and insurance for long-term care will be essential to avoiding poverty in old age and dependence on limited state resources. Rising life expectancy and the growing number of older people living alone add to the challenge. The signs are that many young people are not investing enough in their future, and are not making provision early enough. Thirty-six per cent of people aged 16–24 have no savings or financial investment products (compared to the national average of 26 per cent), while the majority of the rest (48 and 41 per cent respectively) only have up to £200 saved or invested (Jupp, 1997). One recent Mintel survey found that, on current rates of saving and provision, the clear majority (57 per cent) of 20–29-year-olds would have a difficult or poverty-stricken retirement. Thirty-one per cent would only be able to expect their income in retirement to be equivalent to between 25 per cent and 40 per cent of their final earnings. Twenty-six per cent will be able to expect a pension on retirement representing less than 25 per cent of their final earnings. As Ben Jupp's work has shown, many would like to save more but do not manage it, finding themselves caught in cycles of consumption which leave behind little with which to plan for the future (Jupp, 1997). As with relationships, this is partly a problem of being unable to take a long-term view. Many of the social and cultural forces acting on young people seem to encourage short-term, immediate gratification and little consideration of long-term interest. Crucial decision points are often recognised as such but not taken, put off until another time.

Employability

Despite the growing debate over young people's readiness for work, and the number of initiatives and programmes aiming to improve employability, there is still considerable evidence that many young people are ill-prepared for the changing world of employment. One estimate recently put the cost of low employability at £8 billion every year (Industry in Education, 1996). In the 1996 Skill Needs in Britain survey, 40 per cent of employers thought that there was a significant gap between the level of skills of their 16–19-year-old employees and those skills they needed to meet current business objectives. Of those reporting such a gap, the most common problems were in: management skills (66 per cent), general communications skills (65 per cent), computer literacy (64 per cent) and personal skills (61 per cent). Employers demand that, alongside formal qualifications and basic skills, young people should have the *qualities* that make them effective workers. These include reliability, initiative, flexibility, communications skills and, crucially, the capacity to collaborate successfully with a range of different partners. Changes in the organisation of work demand greater self-reliance and flexibility: it is no longer the norm for a graduate or school-leaver to enter one organisation and remain with it for most of their career. The growth of small businesses and self-employment also demands skills of self-management and self-organisation. Young people need to be prepared for more career choices, a less fixed working environment, often within the service sector – work which demands much greater interpersonal skill than traditional manufacturing or clerical jobs. Across the range of employment, creative and critical thinking and the capacity to innovate have become more important as new technologies and markets present new opportunities, and as established ways of getting things done become less effective in the face of social change and increased competition. Many young people are thriving in this environment, but many are not. Some do not even get started because their lack of qualifications means that they cannot jump the first hurdle of employers' recruitment processes. Others find it difficult to make the right choices, or to think strategically about the job that they are in and where it might take them. Many of the young unemployed seem stuck in an 'expectations gap', looking for work in declining industries and expecting wages that they are unlikely to find. Others do not have the skills to manage themselves and their own learning, and find themselves stuck in a cycle of insecure, low-paid work which leads nowhere. Others may find their way into rewarding, demanding work and then discover that the pressure and stress of long hours and fierce workplace competition limit their ability to thrive in other areas of their life, leading to dissatisfaction, strained family relationships and stress-related illness.

Citizenship

As in many historical periods of change, young people's sense of morality and citizenship is currently provoking much concern, influenced by the high-profile media coverage of juvenile crime and disorder and continuing problems of public order, property crime and violence in many British cities and housing estates. Such concern is cyclical, and can be traced through history from ancient Greece, through the Middle Ages, to the late Victorian period. But, whether or not it has been overblown by moral panic and media

13

debate, there is a real problem of alienation and disaffection, especially with formal politics and institutions. One indication of the scale of political alienation is voting turnout. Only 57 per cent of voters aged 18–25 actually voted in the 1992 election. Research by Helen Wilkinson and others has shown that interest and engagement in mainstream party politics is lowest among this age group. In one survey, a third of 18–34-year-olds said that they saw themselves as being 'outside' the system, and less than a sixth of 18–25-year-olds saw themselves as having a duty to vote (Wilkinson and Mulgan, 1995). Similarly, trust in politicians and in national institutions, which has fallen steadily over the last ten years, is lowest among young people. A recent British Social Attitudes survey found that only 5.4 per cent of 18–24-year-olds were very proud of the way democracy works in Britain (the figure for over-fifty-fives is 68 per cent) (SCPR, 1997). Another study found that only 12 per cent of 12–19-year-olds admitted 'a great deal' or 'quite a lot of interest' compared with 32 per cent of adults. More than a quarter of teenagers said they had no interest at all. Young people have always shown less interest in politics than their elders, but the gap seems to have widened sharply over the last ten years, suggesting that the current generation of young people may genuinely be more politically disengaged from the mainstream than earlier ones (Roberts and Sachdev, 1996). There is also considerable evidence that young people do care about social, environmental and political issues. Young voters, for example, are more likely than any other age group to say that particular issues would change the way that they vote. They are more likely to belong to an environmental organisation than to a political party. Recent research has also shown the extent of voluntary activity and practical altruism among young people, which is far higher than some commentators might expect. But there is no doubt that many young people feel alienated and distanced from the values and institutions of mainstream society.

Wellbeing

There is also hard evidence that young people's subjective wellbeing is under growing threat, that they are finding it harder to cope with the stress and anxiety that modern life generates (Rutter and Smith, 1995). One 1992 report estimates that up to 20 per cent of children in the UK suffer mental health problems, and that emotional and conduct disorders affect 20 per cent of adolescents (NCH, 1996). The OBCS disability survey discovered mental health problems in 25 per cent of the child population; 7 to 10 per cent of the child population had moderate to severe problems (Carnegie UK Trust, 1997). Another study found that 10 per cent of 15-year-old boys and 18 per cent of 15-year-old girls had psychological or emotional problems of some significance, rising to 33 per cent of 18-year-old boys and 42 per cent of 18-year-old girls (West and Sweeting, quoted in Carnegie UK Trust, 1997: 44).

A similar range of surveys show increased risk of depressive disorders among younger age-groups (Rutter and Smith, 1995). About 5 per cent of teenagers are seriously depressed and twice that number show significant distress. Professor Ian Goodyer, of Cambridge University, found 3 per cent of school-age students suffer from a major depressive disorder – a further 10 per cent are likely to have suffered such a disorder in the previous year (Rutter and Smith, 1995). Depression is found in about 10 per cent of 11–16-year-old girls (Carnegie UK Trust, 1997).

Similarly, the increase in suicide over the last thirty years has been confined to adolescents and young adults. Suicide among 18–25-year-old men doubled between 1979 and 1990. Suicide is now the second most common cause of death for 15–34-year-old men. In 1992 more young men took their own lives than were killed on the roads. Annually in the UK about six in every 100,000 boys and between one and two in every 100,000 girls commit suicide. Rates of suicide are substantially higher among males than females, although there are some indications that it might rise for young women as they increasingly enter the labour market and face the same kinds of pressures and choices as their male peers. Similar patterns can be found from examinations of eating disorders, self-harm and alcohol and drug misuse.

The failure of educational success

Alongside all these problems – the wider issues and challenges which young people face in life beyond school, and the failure of those who never really succeeded in education – there is worrying evidence that schooling does not always work effectively even for those who do pass exams and launch a career, because their understanding is not sufficiently deep for them to be able to use it under unfamiliar conditions. The pace of social, economic and technological change demands that each person must be able to use their available resources creatively, critically and rigorously to meet the problems or challenges they encounter. More and more, it is the transfer of knowledge and understanding that counts, and it is not clear that those who can learn enough to pass written exams are being equipped with the self-awareness, mental discipline and depth of understanding needed to use their knowledge to best effect. One of the most powerful advocates of this argument is Howard Gardner, whose book *The Unschooled Mind* presents an impressive body of evidence demonstrating that people with apparently sophisticated knowledge of a subject will often fail to apply it successfully when they encounter problems whose form or context is unfamiliar to them (Gardner, 1991). People revert to basic, intuitive understandings of the world which Gardner shows to be rooted in early childhood, and which have never been successfully challenged or overridden by schooling. In difficult or unfamiliar circumstances, these powerful intuitions surface, producing basic errors and misunderstandings among those who, according to their educational track record, should have little problem meeting the challenge.

The evidence presented by Gardner is difficult to ignore. The failures occur in a broad range of disciplines and school subjects, and among adults as well as children. In the sciences, Gardner describes the basic *misconceptions* which remain implicit in people's problem-solving strategies, despite formal knowledge of the appropriate scientific laws. One study asked university students to identify the forces acting on a coin which has been tossed straight up in the air and has reached the midpoint of its trajectory. In answering the question, 90 per cent of engineering students who had not yet taken their mechanics course, and 70 per cent of those who had, answered incorrectly, insisting that there were two forces acting on the coin, one upward and one downward, when in fact once the coin is in the air the only force acting on it is gravity. These answers were given by students perfectly able to quote the requisite laws of gravity and motion, and who had extensive formal knowledge of the physical issues in question. As Gardner says,

> Nearly all students without formal science training and a disconcertingly high percentage of those with such training offer explanations that are at variance with simple and well-established laws of motion and mechanics.
>
> (Gardner, 1991: 155)

Other research shows the fragility of mathematical understanding, most often expressed in 'rigidly applied algorithms'; mathematical rules which are applied rigidly and inappropriately without sufficient consideration of their role or the circumstances under which they apply. For example, in one study, college students were told that there were six times as many students at a university as there were professors. When asked to calculate the number of professors or students and given the number of one or the other, most produced the correct answer. But when asked to write down a formula which expressed the proportions of students and professors, using 'P' for the number of professors and 'S' for students, most got it wrong. The study established that this was often because the students could not handle the idea that 'P' or 'S' referred to the number of professors or students, rather than to a concrete entity. This was true even when students had learned and could recite the phrase 'X refers to the number of some entity'.

In other areas – economics, statistics, history, humanities and arts subjects – similar basic errors are common among graduates and university students, as well as among school pupils. They often amount to oversimplifications and stereotypes, which are consistently applied despite formal teaching supposed to challenge and undermine them. Such errors include: referring frequently to a random 'primary rule', such as the idea that the more that something is produced, the lower its price must be, which overrides other considerations also learned by students but not properly employed in the reasoning process; or the systematic tendency to underestimate the importance of situational factors and overestimate the effect of internal dispositional factors in producing historical explanations; or the failure to understand the importance of interpretation in history, treating it as the task of arranging a series of agreed facts in a simple chronology. One study found that, when people were asked to estimate the number of African countries represented at the United Nations, the number in the answer was related to the place of the question in the test – the lower the question number, the lower the estimate of countries, and vice versa.

Another study by Jonathan Baron found that people of all ages carry a series of robust biases in their thinking, including sticking with the *status quo* once it has been chosen, attention to irrelevant factors, and throwing good money after bad because they already have resources sunk in a project, despite having fresh information about how new money could be spent more effectively. As Gardner says, such biases 'tend to disappear only when individuals have gained a great deal of firsthand experience with situations that run counter to the bias or stereotype' (Gardner, 1991: 172).

All these examples display evidence of a mismatch between different kinds of knowledge, and a failure of the kind of understanding which can bridge the gap between abstract and concrete, between intuitive understandings and more formal or symbol-led reasoning. Since schooling largely takes place in the context of abstraction and simulation, of pupils learning about things by replicating them, reading in books or listening to teachers, and then practising simulated problems, they present a serious challenge to the value of the outputs, or end products, of formal education. The challenge is perhaps best summed up by Paul Cobb's story of a young girl being asked to add 16 and 9. When she did the sum by counting on nine from sixteen, she produced the correct answer. But when given the problem in written form she failed to carry over the 1 and produced an answer of 15. She remained convinced that both answers were correct, one for the worksheet problem and the other for adding nine biscuits to sixteen more. As Cobb says,

> For her, school arithmetic seemed to be an isolated, self-contained context in which the possibility of doing anything other than attempting to recall prescribed methods did not arise.
>
> (quoted in Gardner, 1991: 164)

Such stories illustrate, rather than demonstrate, the problem. But these are not just isolated examples. The evidence presented in Gardner's *The Unschooled Mind* (1991) shows that these cases reflect widespread misunderstanding and an inability to grasp concepts, principles and techniques beyond the relatively narrow range of contexts in which they have been learned. The explanation stems from the fact that children do not enter schools as blank slates, their intellects perfectly ready to be filled with knowledge. There are different ways of knowing, different kinds of understanding which need to be

17

synthesised and integrated as knowledge grows. Young children are constantly building up pictures of how the world works, based on a deep, intuitive interpretation of experience. Such pictures and theories remain strong in all of us unless they are properly meshed with other kinds of knowledge primarily expressed through systems of symbols, whether these be words, mathematical equations or anything else.

Developing literacy in symbolic notational systems is the principal task of all education systems. But the evidence suggests that, all too often, competence in such systems is not properly integrated with the other ways in which young people come to know about the world. Knowledge and techniques learned in school do not connect sufficiently with the problems and roles for which they are used in the rest of society. The depth of understanding required to produce correct test answers too often fails to reach that which is necessary to make productive use of that knowledge in other kinds of situation. Another illustration of the difficulties pupils have in connecting wider experience to school-based learning is provided by Jean Rudduck from her studies of students' perceptions of school:

> I enjoy going out and that but when you come back doing things like hydrogen . . . God, it's hard. Because now we use diagrams like – you know, them round balls that are joined together. I don't know what they are called. We are using them now and I find it right difficult with that.
>
> (female student, 14, in Rudduck *et al.*, 1996)

The capacity to integrate, to make knowledge coherent and consistent across the range of our experience and actions, is not sufficiently developed by mainstream education, constrained as it is by curriculum and time demands, limited resources and a reliance on text-based assessment. The contexts in which curriculum-based knowledge are used and displayed become bound up with the situations and routines of school. The connections between different opportunities, both to learn and to demonstrate understanding, are too weak to become meaningful or useful. Mary Alice White has given us a clear description of why this should be for young people:

> imagine oneself on a ship sailing across an unknown sea, to an unknown destination. An adult would be desperate to know where he is going. But a child only knows he is going to school. . . . The chart is neither available nor understandable to him. . . . Very quickly, the daily life on board ship becomes all important. The daily chores, the demands, the inspections, become the reality, not the voyage, nor the destination.
>
> (White, 1971: 340)

18

The conclusion that such evidence points to is that the most detailed formal knowledge is without value unless you can understand what it is for and what you can do with it. Conventional school-based learning, it seems, too often fails to mesh the knowledge in the curriculum with the contours of wider experience. This fact offers a warning to educational reforms which focus too heavily on producing 'correct answers' in narrow contexts. In trying to improve pupils' ability to pass tests, we may lose sight of the end to which their learning should be geared. That end should be the development of understanding which can be applied and extended by taking it into the spheres of thought and action which, in the real world, demand intelligent behaviour. It is only when we are ale to do this that learning can actually add value to our lives.

3

SEEDS OF SOLUTIONS:
THEORIES

How should we respond to this situation? What resources could we use to ensure that young people are better equipped to thrive in this new environment? The conventional response, although it contains many different strands and some fierce debates, is to assume that we should make education more effective by having more of the same: greater participation in pre- and post-compulsory education, higher-quality teaching of our standardised curricula, and greater commitment to education by pupils and parents. While education spending has steadily risen in real terms, successive governments have sought to resist the idea that there is a straightforward link between educational performance and public spending. This is not just a political imperative. Education, like healthcare, is one of the core 'knowledge industries' in a knowledge economy. As we learn more about how people learn, and as information and knowledge become used more intensively in every sphere of life, demand for education rises continuously. Even though education is consistently rated by the public as one of the highest priorities for government spending, people are also resistant to tax rises, and the search for further resources becomes continual. Student contributions to university tuition fees, and private sponsorship of education initiatives, are just two examples in the UK. As with almost all public services, the big challenge for education has become to improve the effectiveness of services so that increased public investment really makes a difference.

The emphasis of reform has therefore been on accountability and value for money, on improvement targets, comparison of performance, and greater control of the techniques used to achieve specified outcomes within a standardised framework. Much of this is valuable, and should facilitate better teaching, greater accountability, better results and clearer dissemination of success. In short, this approach has sought to improve the efficiency and effectiveness of the educational machine, sometimes adding new gears and levers, sometimes trying to improve the overall quality of the product, but always aiming to improve the overall productivity of the system by reorganising and lubricating its internal workings, redesigning the process from the outside. But the problem is that some of the assumptions underlying this approach seem increasingly out of step with the ways in which the external environment has changed, and with some of the responses we are seeing elsewhere. Even more importantly, they run the risk of ignoring new insights into the nature of learning itself. If the core assumptions about what education is trying to achieve, the organisational framework within which it takes place, and the forms of understanding and ability which people can acquire become too fixed or narrow, then it is unlikely that education will achieve its full potential, however much effort or money is spent on it.

This chapter sets out the major advances in our understanding of intelligence and learning, which may help us to frame our approach to some of the challenges described in Chapter 2. As Professor John MacBeath of Strathclyde University recently wrote, 'Learning is a subject about which we have probably learned more in the past decade and a half than in the previous 200.' What we have learned has helped to overturn the historical idea of intelligence, formed around the beginning of the century, which has dominated educational thinking and practice for many decades.

The core assumption underlying theories of intelligence during most of the twentieth century has been that there is a single, underlying factor which determines a person's level of general intelligence. This factor, known as 'g', is assumed to have been determined by the relative power of the brain and the central nervous system, and its capacity to retain and process information. Much of the research on intelligence has focused on trying to analyse and measure the neural capacities which support g, while others have looked for the genetic origins of these capacities, in order to discover the extent to which intelligence may be inherited. According to this view, intelligence is understood as an internal characteristic of individuals, which can be scientifically measured as such. However, a growing number of researchers and scholars, supported by a growing body of evidence, have undermined this assumption.

The starting point for our new framework is Howard Gardner's theory of multiple intelligences, or MI theory, first set out in his book *Frames of Mind* (Gardner, 1983).

Gardner, in investigating the range and nature of intelligence, produced a step-change in the way we think about it. His argument, supported by numerous studies, shows that intelligence is far more diverse and broad-ranging than had previously been assumed. This theory means that our traditional ways of measuring intelligence, which grew out of the desire to produce quick, standardised tests and a generalised quotient which could be easily applied to whole cohorts of people, are of only limited accuracy and usefulness.

At the risk of describing it too briefly, MI theory makes two fundamental claims. The first is that intelligence is grouped into eight broad clusters which can be determined more or less independently of each other. They are:

1   logical–mathematical intelligence
2   linguistic intelligence

3 spatial intelligence
4 bodily–kinaesthetic intelligence
5 musical intelligence
6 interpersonal intelligence
7 intrapersonal intelligence
8 naturalistic intelligence

Gardner argues that everybody possesses these eight kinds of intelligence: that they are a new conception of what it is to be human, essential properties of the mind. His second claim is that each of us has a different blend of the eight. This second claim has far-reaching educational implications, which we will come to later in the chapter.

Gardner's division of intelligences rests on two main foundations. First, it reflects neural configurations uncovered by studying cognitive development in a wide range of different populations including, notably, those with particular talents who do not fit the conventional model of the 'intelligent person': prodigies, 'idiot savants' (people whose general reasoning capacity is for some reason severely impaired but who display amazing talent or ability in a particular domain, such as art or mathematics). Second, the division follows socially useful lines – in the world of vocations and occupations, specific individual intelligences are displayed by those who are prodigious or expert in a particular domain: linguistic intelligence by announcers, writers and actors, spatial intelligence by architects, sculptors and sailors, interpersonal intelligence by politicians, professional negotiators, clerics and so on.

This does not mean that the clustering of intelligences is purely subjective. Each reflects a careful and rigorous balance between evidence on the biological origins of problem-solving ability and the ways in which such abilities are expressed and developed in the world. To identify each 'intelligence', Gardner used evidence from a range of sources, including studies of the cognitive development of normal and gifted children, studies of the breakdown of cognitive skills following brain damage, studies of exceptional populations such as prodigies, idiot savants and autistic children, evolutionary and cross-cultural accounts of cognition, information about the correlation of results across different psychometric tests, and measures of the transfer and generalisation of ability across different tasks. In addition, each intelligence must have an identifiable core operation or set of operations. None the less, the definitions of intelligence set out by MI theory reflect the ways in which we define ability in the real world, rather than purporting to describe a general, neutral quality. It is important to recognise that, according to Gardner's view, intelligence is partly defined by what we value in society. As Gardner has said, each of the eight could be subdivided into several core components, and the list of intelligences could conceivably be far longer. Each intelligence represents a cluster or family which can be further explored and, perhaps, developed.

MI theory recognises that any occupation or task will involve a combination of these intelligences, but argues that every individual has a differently balanced portfolio of abilities, which requires careful nurture and attention to develop talents to their full potential. There are many things that we would want all young people to learn during their education. But if each of us has a different blend of intelligences, not only will we be more suited to some kinds of knowledge and understanding than to others, we will also be more suited to some kinds of *learning* than to others. In other words, our routes to understanding will vary with our balance of intelligences, and an education which was effective in promoting understanding should be able to offer different routes to different learners. In particular, Gardner argues that we must pay more attention to the different *entry points* which can lead to understanding. The five entry points which Gardner advances are: the narrational or storytelling approach; the logical quantitative approach, using numbers or logical reasoning; the foundational or philosophical approach, using basic or fundamental questions as a starting point; the aesthetic approach; and the experiential approach, where learners approach understanding by actually performing activities relating to it.

This new picture of intelligence has fundamental implications for the ways in which we think about schooling. School education, while employing all of a child's portfolio of intelligences in some way, focuses on a relatively narrow range of core competences, centred around the linguistic and logical–mathematical intelligences. This is primarily because the transmission of knowledge takes place through linguistic and logical reasoning, through talking, thinking, reading and writing, and because testing of educational attainment is most often done with standardised, paper-based examinations. Given the evidence so far of the limitations of our current educational arrangements, we should think hard about how the organisation of learning might better reflect the range of human potential and ability, and whether we can be more effective at assisting young people in reaching genuine, deep understanding of those subjects which they already study.

Howard Gardner's work on intelligence has probably been the most influential of the last twenty years, but Gardner is one of a number of scholars who have helped to broaden our understanding of what intelligence is. Another is the Yale psychologist Robert Sternberg, who has worked to understand the actual mental processes which are drawn on by standard intelligence testing, such as the solving of analogies. This work soon took Sternberg beyond what is measured by conventional tests, to explaining two other dimensions of intelligence – the 'practical' ability to adapt to varying contexts and situations, and the ability to display 'creative' intelligence by creating routines for familiar activities and becoming better able to deal with novelty. In a similar way, Stephen Ceci of Cornell University has gone beyond the conventional framework by investigating the importance of environment and intellectual development to the definition of intelligence. Ceci argues, like Gardner, that there are multiple forms of intelligence underlying standard IQ scores, and that the environment in which a person develops has a crucial influence on the ways in which their abilities develop. He argues that g, the single underlying general intelligence factor, is an inadequate explanation of the root of intelligence (Ceci, 1996). Similarly, Michael Cole has presented compelling evidence of the role that context and environment have in influencing test scores, particularly for students from different social and cultural groups (Cole, 1996).

The second major contribution to our new picture was brought together and crystallised by Daniel Goleman, author of the best-selling book *Emotional Intelligence* (Goleman, 1996). The book synthesises a mass of research on the functioning of the brain which shows the influence of emotions on individual performance and interpersonal relationships. In many ways, as Goleman explicitly states, the theory develops Gardner's categories of interpersonal and intrapersonal intelligence. This work effectively ends the rigid historical distinction between reason and emotion, showing that in practice the two are inseparably intertwined. Goleman shows that emotions have a central role in determining our success in life. The crucial emotional centres of the brain play an integral and essential role in managing our behaviour. Emotional stimuli can short-cut the more rational processors of the neocortex, producing quick responses and swamping all other thoughts and considerations. Often this is useful, for example allowing swift reactions to threatening situations. But all too often emotional responses swamp more considered or subtle responses, producing hasty or crass action which serves the individual badly, and alienates or angers others.

The psychologists who first articulated the theory of emotional intelligence, Peter Salovey and John Mayer (1990), set out five major domains:

1   knowing one's emotions
2   managing emotions
3   motivating oneself
4   recognising emotions in others
5   handling relationships

As with Gardner's multiple intelligences, each of us holds a different balance of these five, and our strengths and reputation among others will vary accordingly. But Goleman shows that emotional intelligence is perhaps more important than any other factor, such as social class or raw IQ, in determining a person's life-chances; their success at work, the quality of their relationships, their personal wellbeing. Goleman's book shows the crucial importance of young children's emotional development and documents how the different aspects of emotional intelligence come into play in different situations. He pinpoints the role of personal qualities such as empathy, optimism, self-awareness and the social arts of communication, leadership, negotiation and social analysis, and explains many of the strategies and insights that can defuse rage, help overcome melancholy and depression, and enhance relationships. The analysis applies to all spheres of life: to medical care, marital, parental and working relationships, management, professional conflict resolution and coping with the effects of severe trauma or stress. It is important to point out that we should not confuse emotional intelligence with an automatic tendency to do good, or to act widely. Sensitivity to emotions in ourselves and others can still be used for negative ends: for example to manipulate and control. But for our purposes there are two crucial insights from Goleman's work.

The first is that even severe emotional problems and trauma can be tackled through emotional relearning. Goleman presents strong evidence to show that, with time and careful support, children and young people can learn to reduce the effects of traumatic experience – of abuse, violence or neglect – by learning to recognise the source of their distress, rehearsing and revisiting the experience, and developing other, more positive components of their emotional portfolio. The effect of such experience is to reduce the level of activity in those parts of the brain on which severe trauma is imprinted, and make it less likely that such experiences will short-circuit the brain and allow the memory and fear of trauma to dominate experience and behaviour.

Second, and perhaps most important, 'temperament is not destiny'. Despite the fact that our emotional profile reflects, at least to some extent, our biology, or the wiring of our 'emotional circuitry', there is clear evidence that our innate dispositions to shyness, optimism, melancholy or boldness can be moulded and developed. For example, development of social intelligence can be a spontaneous antidote to shyness and timidity – as a child becomes more competent at dealing with others, timidity can be left behind. As Goleman says, 'There is a range of possibility even within genetic constraints.' This is because of the way that the brain develops during childhood and puberty, and the opportunity for emotional learning that this presents. We are born with many more neurons than the mature brain will retain – at different stages in life the brain goes through a process of 'pruning', where it loses those connections which are least used, and retains those which have been most utilised. Between birth and the age of six, the brain establishes new connections between neurons at a rate of 2.5 trillion a year, or 4.7 million new connections each minute (Goodwin, 1988). This means that childhood and adolescence represent crucial opportunities to help shape the portfolio of emotional capacities:

> The habits of emotional management that are repeated over and over again during childhood and the teenage years will themselves help mould this circuitry.
>
> (Goleman, 1996: 226)

Goleman argues that emotional illiteracy is a preventable deficit which produces huge costs in later life. The evidence that he presents shows that specific kinds of emotional learning, many of which take place in the family or peer group, but also in schools, can play a significant part in helping young people to know themselves and those around them, to recognise emotional risks and problems, and to address them before they become chronic. Emerging educational work in emotional development, such as the Self Science project, and research into the factors which put young people most at risk of dangers such as child abuse, alcohol and drug misuse, teenage pregnancy and severe depression, all show emotional intelligence and literacy to be at the core of successful prevention.

Developing emotional competence has often been seen as a task of parenting and family life, and not the responsibility of formal education. This is partly right: the family is the crucible of all learning, and plays a vital role in developing intra- and interpersonal capacities among children. But schools are still the places where children begin to form relationships with others beyond their immediate family, and where they learn to work with and understand the needs of people who are relative strangers. Emotional literacy and competence are still developing as components of education. Different approaches are being invented, developed and evaluated. But the evidence from the relatively few systematic studies so far is that such learning does have an observable effect on attitudes, behaviour and the quality of relationships within schools. Developing emotional literacy is obviously a crucial part of preparing young people to survive and succeed in adult life, and Goleman's work provides powerful evidence that schools can play an important part, though not an exclusive one, in supporting it.

The final contribution to our framework comes from the work of another Harvard psychologist, David Perkins (1995). Perkins's work, which has its roots partly in the study of artificial intelligence and the ways in which people reason, examines the definitions of intelligence made over the last hundred years, and proposes a new view of intelligence which also rejects the idea that intelligence is a fixed or unitary quality. He demonstrates that, to a significant degree, the capacity for intelligent behaviour can be *learned*.

Perkins argues that the underlying bases of intelligence, over which researchers have debated for more than a century, are not necessarily mutually exclusive. His argument is that, although the basis of intelligence is partly neural, so that our capacity for intelligent behaviour in different domains is rooted in the structure and processing of our brains, this neural capacity is really only the platform for the development of intelligence. Rather than dividing intelligence only along social and neural lines, Perkins suggests a broader division between three foundations of intelligent behaviour: neural intelligence, experiential intelligence and reflective intelligence.

Neural intelligence refers to the underlying neural factors which contribute to intelligent behaviour, stemming from the 'efficiency and precision of the neurological system'. This is the basis for 'natural' talent in a particular field, and provides the raw processing power which is a prerequisite for intelligent thought. However, Perkins argues that 'mental power' alone is an inappropriate way of thinking of intelligence – while neural factors make some contribution to general intelligence, education and other factors can make a significant impact on general intelligence, and it has proved impossible to identify clear causal connections between variations in the brain and variations in intelligent behaviour.

Experiential intelligence is that derived from direct, context-specific knowledge, the kind of knowledge displayed by a chess master or a professional musician, or any person who has built up a pool of expertise based on extensive experience of thinking and acting in particular situations over a period of time. Perkins argues that this kind of knowledge makes a crucial contribution to intelligence which an account of 'general' IQ would miss. People only develop mastery in two or three fields at most, whatever their general IQ. Accumulated knowledge, rather than IQ, corresponds most closely to a person's ability in the workplace, and IQ in any case reflects a substantial amount of 'crystallised intelligence', which by definition reflects prior learning.

Perkins defines reflective intelligence as 'the contribution to intelligent behaviour of strategies for various intellectually challenging tasks, attitudes conducive to persistence, systematicity, and imagination in the use of one's mind, and habits of self-monitoring and management'. Reflective intelligence derives from our capacity to take a mental step back and observe our own efforts to solve a problem or achieve a goal. As Perkins says, it effectively constitutes a control system, which can be greatly developed by learning, acting upon our thinking and doing. It involves critical self-review, the cultivation of dispositions which support intelligent behaviour, and the use of mental *strategies* to solve unfamiliar problems or get round obstacles. Numerous studies have shown that people who use mental strategies significantly add to their capacity for intelligent behaviour, even among those with high IQ and high levels of experience. Reflective intelligence gives us a bird's eye view of our own learning, allowing us to question our own approach to a situation, helping us to cope with novelty and to be aware of our own natural biases of thought and action. Such strategies are essential to intelligent behaviour, because the challenges that we confront in our lives are not exclusively driven by predictable patterns. Especially when the external environment is changing unpredictably, but in any case as we progress through life, we need the capacity to stand back, to generalise from our experience, and to try out different approaches in careful, systematic ways. Perkins shows that, while some people are more naturally able to do this, it is also a capacity that can be learned, with significant results for overall problem-solving ability.

These three kinds of intelligence combine in ways which produce a whole greater than the sum of its parts. Neural intelligence can help a person acquire knowledge faster than she otherwise might, accelerating her accumulation of experiential intelligence. Developing intuitive, experiential recognition of patterns and knowledge of procedures in a particular field also frees up neural capacity for other kinds of learning, while the use of reflection and mental strategies can help ensure that her accumulation of knowledge from experience is as systematic and fruitful as possible. The three kinds of intelligence can amplify each other's effects and compensate for each other in challenging situations. For example, reflective use of problem-solving strategies can at least partially compensate for an absence of experience, as well as speeding up the accumulation of relevant knowledge in a domain in which the learner is a novice.

These major contributions to our understanding of intelligence have fundamental consequences for the way we think about preparing young people for successful, fulfilling adult lives. They show that our conventional conception of schooling, its purposes, methods and scope, are in fact limited to a relatively narrow range of capacities, outcomes and types of challenge. This is not to say that the full range of intelligence as set out above does not come into play during a young person's school career; many teachers and parents are aware of the need for young people to develop problem-solving and mental management skills, and even more recognise the capacity for self-awareness and positive relationship skills. Similarly, the development of a broad range of intelligences such as musical, bodily–kinaesthetic and spatial intelligence is addressed in the school curriculum, although usually in specific, segmented subject areas such as physical education. But the basic thrust of school education is to develop a narrower set of core competences, based around the linguistic and logical–mathematical intelligences, laid down in a prescribed curriculum framework, and assessed mainly through standardised written tests which favour particular kinds of ability and, as we have seen, do not always demand a deep understanding of the subject.

As we saw in Chapter 2, the challenges that young people will face during their adult lives are far broader, richer and more uncertain than the ones which education explicitly prepares them for. They are also less predictable, because the structure of society and organisations, the applications of technology, the values and aspirations of people and the threats to wellbeing and survival are changing so rapidly. It would be easy to argue that it is not the job of an education system to cultivate all these different kinds of knowledge and disposition, to prepare people for such an awesome range of situations. To be effective, formal education should have clear and limited aims; overload is a recipe for failure; teachers are already stressed and overworked. But the implications of such an argument are short-sighted and fatalistic. The purpose of education systems is to prepare young people in appropriate ways for the challenges and responsibilities they will face throughout their lives, and if society is changing, so should the way in which we introduce young people to it. Similarly, there is nothing to say that the only way to improve the quality and effectiveness of an education system is to pump more resources into the same basic structure, expecting it to cope with new and increased demands. Part of the aim of this book is to show how education can be transformed using resources that we already possess, by connecting it to the knowledge, experience and creative potential which often surround schools in local communities and workplaces.

Our new understanding of intelligence demands that education, when conceived of as a preparation for life, reflects a far broader range of potential and ability than it currently does. It should nurture and cultivate many different kinds of intelligence, rather than just one. It should assist young people in developing the means to manage and understand their emotions, so that they are able to cope with stress and trauma and create lasting and fulfilling relationships. It should also equip them with the capacity to reflect on their own learning, to understand its relevance to their lives beyond school, and to wider, more long-term goals. It should enable them to learn and devise strategies for solving problems and coping with unfamiliar situations, to recognise the opportunities and resources in any environment, to utilise those resources to the full, and to collaborate effectively with others to achieve both shared and individual goals. Our new understanding also shows that such capacities can often be learned: that the question is not whether or not you have the ability, but to what extent you can learn it, and where your distinctive talents, needs and interests lie. In short, while the challenges of life may seem more complex and daunting than ever before, there are ways in which we can learn to meet them. The next chapter describes an emerging body of practice which has begun to take up some of these challenges.

4

ACTIVE LEARNING IN PRACTICE

So much for theory. These developments in what we know about intelligence and ability help frame our debates on education and young people, and point the way towards new ways of organising learning and teaching. But new research and theory often take a notoriously long time to reach the everyday world of schools, teachers and pupils. What about the practice? This chapter describes initiatives and projects which encourage or provide active, community-based learning. Many of them have emerged over the last twenty years, often at the margins of the education system. They are the result of grassroots collaboration between the voluntary sector, educators, parents, employers and young people themselves. Other projects have been more structured and large-scale. Many of these initiatives provide evidence of clear benefits for the young people who take part in them. Others, however, have not been independently evaluated because they are too new or too small. I will argue that they represent the seeds of a new approach which, in time, could help to transform education.

The common characteristic of these initiatives is that they aim to supplement or enhance mainstream educational provision, creating new opportunities to learn and providing new human, social and financial resources to support young people's educational development. They have widely varying aims, methods and structures. To get an overview, we can group them into broad categories, setting out their aims, range and scale, and looking at some of their results.

Places to learn

Several major initiatives, now beginning to be integrated into mainstream provision, have aimed to expand the supporting infrastructure of learning by creating opportunities for young people to pursue self-directed learning out of school hours.

The largest of these is the Prince's Trust Study Support programme, which has brought together many different organisations to create study support centres across the country. Study Support aims to provide a framework within which many different educational programmes and learning opportunities

30

can be made available. The context is less controlled and rule-driven than school, but nevertheless provides:

- structured learning opportunities;
- instruction and expert support; and, crucially,
- safe, attractive places which young people can use to develop their own motivation and learning skills.

Since 1991 the Trust has supported the establishment of hundreds of study support centres. It is now establishing a national network, bringing together organisations with similar aims to:

- provide effective and coordinated out-of-school learning opportunities;
- promote innovation; and
- assess the value and effectiveness of different approaches and efforts.

It has embarked on a three-year programme of research to develop rigorous measures of the value that can be added by study support, and the best ways to assess, evaluate and develop self-directed learning activities (Tower Hamlets, 1993). The basic premise underlying this approach is that, while good schools make a difference to learning, achievement depends as much on developing the capacity to be a responsible, independent learner who can make full use of a wide range of resources. The Study Support programme has taken up the challenge of making meaningful connections between the different strands of learning which all young people experience:

- formal, curriculum based learning in school or college;
- learning within the home and family; and
- the informal learning which comes from peer groups, contact with adults outside the family, and broader social experience.

Other programmes have developed similar opportunities for other age groups. For example, Education Extra supports and develops opportunities for children to pursue learning activities outside school hours, while the Kids' Club Network focuses more on pre-school provision. Many individual schools have developed breakfast and homework clubs, summer school programmes and parenting centres, all of which aim to broaden the resources and opportunities available for learning so that young people can pursue it more widely, rather than in the more restricted context of the school day and year. Many Education Business Partnerships have also dedicated themselves to developing study support, often in partnership with the Prince's Trust, local employers and youth organisations. Specific centres may develop innovations or programmes which have distinctive value, but the overarching aim is to act as hubs for diverse networks of opportunity, resources and support.

One of the furthest developed examples of study support in action is the Tower Hamlets Summer University, a two-month programme of activities which brings together several thousand young people to pursue an array of learning activities from sports to literacy, photography and media to computer studies. The university has quickly developed a strong reputation among young people in an especially deprived area of London, producing a range of certification and qualifications, reducing youth crime and helping to strengthen a culture which values learning, and is helping radically to improve formal educational attainment in the borough (Tower Hamlets, 1997).

Also in this group of initiatives are the schools partnerships developed by Business in the Community, such as Compact and Compact Plus, which seek to increase the human and financial support available to young people and schools in return for a commitment to achieve specified goals such as improved attendance, academic attainment and records of behaviour.

Promoting innovation

Other educational organisations are more explicitly committed to understanding and promoting innovation in educational research and practice. Education 2000, a charitable trust established in 1983, runs practical, community-based projects in the UK aiming to develop effective educational practice. It is also a partner in the transnational 21st Century Learning Initiative which aims to:

- synthesise and disseminate innovation and best practice in education around the world; and to
- encourage radical reform of education systems to reflect new understanding of learning.

Another example of commitment to innovation is ANTIDOTE, founded in 1996 to stimulate debate on the place of emotional literacy in public life, in particular in education and the school curriculum.

Finally, one of the most exciting projects dedicated to new methodologies of learning and teaching is Birmingham's University of the First Age (UFA), dedicated to providing accelerated learning opportunities to Birmingham's school students. Drawing on Howard Gardner's theory of multiple intelligences, UFA provides 'multi-sensory' learning courses in a range of subjects, working intensively during school vacations and following up with distance learning resources which students work on during the rest of the year, contacting tutors by fax and email.

Civic engagement

The third major group of initiatives contains those which seek ways of engaging young people in the communities and institutions around them. Volunteering,

32

of course, is thousands of years old, but over the last twenty-five years many new organisations have sought to develop volunteering opportunities for the young. The two largest initiatives in the UK are Community Service Volunteers (CSV) and Prince's Trust Volunteers, both of which have become major national providers and coordinators of volunteering opportunities for young people. CSV runs a wide range of programmes, including:

- using university students to help school pupils with literacy;
- volunteering opportunities in the community; and
- six- or twelve-month voluntary placements.

Prince's Trust Volunteers have developed a more focused programme for young people aged 18–25, with the aim of developing particular skills and qualities, broadening social experience and awareness, and building the confidence and self-esteem of participants. They have so far run courses for over 25,000 volunteers. Teams of volunteers undertake a series of challenges over a twelve-week course, learning to work together to achieve common goals, focusing on their own personal development and on effective collaboration. Teams typically include a mix of students and employed and unemployed young people. Team leaders are recruited from employer organisations, with the aim of gaining valuable experience for themselves, as well as developing the capacities of their teams.

Alongside these major providers are the more traditional youth service organisations, the uniformed organisations such as the Scouts and Guides, which often provide valuable opportunities for young people to develop skills and qualities which will serve them well in later life. However, the ethos and identity of such organisations are often very specific, and their programmes highly structured. For many young people, for whatever reason, fitting into an organisation such as this does not appeal. Some may find that, where other aspects of life are characterised by choice and freedom, the structures and disciplines involved in the uniformed organisations are not as attractive as they might once have been. For others, often those who face greater disadvantage and fewer positive opportunities, the tradition, authority and discipline are too much to cope with.

There are literally hundreds of organisations coordinating or providing voluntary activities for young people, and it would be impossible to cover them all. But aside from the largest providers, several younger organisations are developing new approaches to social engagement, and hold great potential for broadening young people's social experience and integrating their needs and interests with those of others.

These include Changemakers, which gives young people opportunities to create their own community projects, collaborating with peers, teachers, youth workers and others in their communities to achieve positive social outcomes. Working through team-based projects, young people explore what community means to them, identify a community need and then design and manage action to meet the need. A wide range of projects has included fundraising for local charities and hospitals, campaigns to improve the local environment or against racism in sport, and helping to provide study support for younger children. While students are guided in working out the implications of their chosen projects, and thinking through the strategies and resources needed to complete them, their choice is open. It is up to the participants themselves to decide on an objective and how best to achieve it. The basic assumption of the Changemakers approach is that creating positive change in your local community is a crucial part of the development of personal effectiveness and active, responsible citizenship. During and after their projects, young people are encouraged to reflect on what they achieved and how they did it, the reflections centred around a set of twelve 'enterprise skills' needed to carry out a successful project. These are:

1 Assessing strengths and weaknesses
2 Seeking information and advice
3 Making decisions
4 Planning time and energy
5 Carrying through an agreed responsibility
6 Negotiating successfully
7 Dealing with people in power and authority
8 Solving problems
9 Resolving conflict
10 Coping with stress and tension
11 Evaluating your performance
12 Communicating (verbally and non-verbally)

Other initiatives follow a similar approach. Barclays New Futures, for example, gives grants to schools to pursue a 'social challenge', providing resources, support from corporate advisers and an evaluation framework to help structure and assess projects. FOCUS, another young voluntary organisation, organises vacation courses and school-based programmes which support young people to run their own projects in collaboration with peers, young people from other schools and adult volunteers from their local communities. Projects range from running activity afternoons for local elderly people to much more ambitious and large-scale events. FOCUS staff organise a framework for the activities, brokering relationships between schools, employers and voluntary organisations, organising holiday courses, and facilitating action planning, monitoring and evaluation.

Tackling marginalisation

Many youth organisations work in similar ways, but with a more specific objective: to promote social integration and develop the motivation and life-skills of young people at risk of marginalisation and educational failure. As concern has risen over the growing exclusion of young people from mainstream society, and from opportunities to work and to sustain healthy personal, parenting and civic relationships, there has been a groundswell of initiatives looking for approaches which help to integrate them, improve their access to opportunity, and motivate them to work towards positive goals rather than being caught in vicious cycles which often result in crime, problem drug use, homelessness, isolation and dependence on the illegal economy.

These include the Youth Charter for Sport (YCS), an organisation born out of the social problems of inner-city Manchester, which has worked to connect young people's talents with the status and influence of sporting personalities and the resources and social concerns of companies. YCS combines a ground-level presence and concern with the everyday risks facing young people, with a wider commitment to raising their profile and creating positive opportunities. It uses the prestige and status of leading sports personalities to attract business sponsorship and support, and to offer young people guidance and support through a 'social curriculum' which emphasises an ethic of responsibility and sporting excellence.

Another initiative trying to reach young people who are distanced from mainstream education is Youth Works North East, an inter-agency partnership coordinated and evaluated by the Social Welfare Research Unit at the University of Northumbria. This initiative has worked:

- to develop youth work practice with disaffected young people; and
- to improve understanding of the skills and competences which disaffected young people most need, and the professional skills required to nurture them.

One of the results has been a set of learning resources aiming to provide young people with incentives and structures for positive learning activity in the community, while retaining the space for them to make such activity their own. A series of 'Rap Packs', covering issues such as crime, drugs, parenthood and truancy, are used to facilitate discussion, reflection and action by young people themselves. Another major strand of this programme is the 'Keyfund', which allocates £1000 for each local project to fund groups of young people in community-based projects. Young people, in dialogue with project leaders and other adults, apply for funding to run small-scale projects which they have designed and planned themselves. The aim is to foster a series of generic skills including:

- decision-making;
- coping with stress and tension;
- solving problems; and
- evaluating performance.

This flexible framework and funding base has produced a number of projects with positive social outcomes, both for the young people concerned and for others in their communities. As the descriptions of youth workers testify, the results have often been positive:

> The group started off doing a minimal amount of work but by their third application they were talking as if it were their project, they had done far more work and they entered into the negotiation process . . . with far more confidence.

> . . . the difference is amazing . . . when you think back to that first meeting . . . chaos . . . now they come in, sit down, discuss what needs sorting, arrive at decisions, they're dead business like . . . you can see them growing . . .

Other initiatives have developed out of the growing need for effective local crime prevention. One of the most impressive is, slightly confusingly, also called Youth Works, the result of collaboration between Marks and Spencer, the Groundwork Trust and Crime Concern. Youth Works has established detached youth projects on deprived housing estates, combining activities and resources with opportunities for young people to define their own needs and plan their own projects. Evaluation has shown that they can have a significant impact on crime in and around the estates, as well as providing opportunities for positive progression for the young people involved. Another crime prevention partnership is Youth Action Awards, run by Crime Concern and Prudential, which challenges young people to design their own projects focused on a specific crime prevention goal. The London Borough of Merton has also produced a sophisticated resource pack to engage young people in reflection on the issues of crime prevention, and is using it to support local projects aimed at empowering young people to tackle crime in ways which they feel are important and realisable.

There are also many organisations, such as INCLUDE (formerly Cities in Schools), which work to prevent permanent school exclusions by offering individualised support to students and parents, brokering solutions other than exclusion with schools, and providing 'Bridge' courses for older teenagers who have already lost touch with the education system. Other examples include The Weston Spirit, Youth at Risk, Youth Clubs UK, NACRO Schools and Brathay Hall, Fairbridge and projects run by individual Training and Enterprise Councils and Careers Services. All are working in similar ways to create opportunities for young people at risk of marginalisation and to develop their abilities and motivation. Much of this work is still identified with the 'youth' sector, but it is beginning to spread into other fields, helping to erode the barriers between community-based learning and the formal education sector.

Improving employability

Employability has been one of the most important vehicles for developing links between schools and other organisations. Many organisations and employers run large programmes promoting work experience and developing employability. One of the largest is the Trident Trust, which now organises work experience for over 160,000 young people every year. Through its Skills for Life programme it has developed an integrated approach to providing students and school pupils with practical learning experience and personal development. The programme also aims to relate these activities to relevant National Curriculum areas.

The Trust acts as a broker and facilitator between schools, employers, community organisations and colleges, helping to provide the knowledge and resources needed for successful partnerships, to provide quality assurance for work experience placements, and to support students, schools and other partners to evaluate progress and achievement by young people. It has also piloted its own accredited certificate, in partnership with the RSA. Trident Trust has become one of the leading organisers of work experience for young people, and as such has made a major contribution to the infrastructure of partnerships between young people, schools and outside institutions. The skills on which it focuses are similar to many other initiatives seeking to develop the qualities and capacities not covered by formal, exam-based learning. These skills, frequently called core or key skills, include:

- communication and interpersonal skills,
- relationships;
- problem-solving; and
- skills of self-managed learning.

Trident programmes, as with many other new learning initiatives, focus on the process of action planning, which is crucial to the effectiveness of all learning initiatives, especially those which aim to support young people in creating their own projects and positive learning outcomes.

A much newer initiative is Pathways to Adult Life, developed with the London Enterprise Agency in partnership with employers and the Department for Education and Employment (DfEE) in a number of schools across England. This programme was developed as a management tool for schools, to create learning activities which improved pupils' awareness of and readiness for the challenges of adult life, in particular the world of work. Its overall aim is to enhance 'whole person development' within the National Curriculum, recognising the need for a more holistic approach to young people's preparation for adult life. Pathways to Adult Life also recognises the constraints that schools face in incorporating new initiatives into an already packed curriculum. The result is a set of tightly focused management tools which provide a framework for schools to develop learning activities related to:

- identified curriculum subjects;
- pupils' awareness of the world of work; and
- whole-school planning of these areas of learning.

It has been used by many of its pilot schools as a vehicle for improving overall standards of pupil attainment, most often from the curriculum base of Personal, Social and Health Education (PSHE) and careers guidance. Similar to many of the initiatives described above, Pathways to Adult Life aims to be a tool of *connection*, particularly between what happens within school and the wider world. As one headteacher put it,

> Pathways . . . has encouraged many staff to see beyond the boundaries of their subject. It has brought many more students into contact with the world beyond school. It has allowed staff and the local business community a greater insight into each others' ways of working and an appreciation of each others' problems.

Another scheme, KAPOW!, founded in the US and now growing in the UK, targets a younger age group. It uses corporate volunteers to visit classes of 8–12-year-olds and deliver sessions on work-related issues such as career and vocational awareness, self-awareness, interdependence and decision-making. The programme also includes a worksite visit for pupils. While modest in scope and too new for detailed evaluation of impact, KAPOW! once again focuses on increasing contact between pupils and adult role models, and on giving young people direct experience of the organisational context of work. It also brings other adults into schools, making the boundaries between the school and other institutions more porous, and attempting to facilitate the transfer of knowledge and understanding between contexts.

Another major employability initiative, founded over thirty years ago, is Young Enterprise, a national organisation which supports teams of young people to establish a commercial company over the course of a school year. Supported by over two thousand businesses, the organisation brings together teams of students with corporate volunteers who advise them on their projects. Evaluation has shown high rates of approval among young people, parents, teachers and advisers. The programmes are viewed as both enjoyable and highly useful by all involved, and encourage:

- awareness of the commercial world;
- development of personal motivation and self direction; and
- other personal qualities increasingly valued by employers.

There are hundreds of other initiatives aimed at improving employability, run by employers' groups, individual companies, local voluntary organisations, TEC and Careers Services and Education Business Partnerships.

Mentoring

One of the most significant areas of growth in the last decade is mentoring projects, designed to create supportive individual relationships between young people and adults who support and encourage their progress. Mentoring schemes have spread quickly, stimulated by companies, Education Business Partnerships, voluntary organisations, some local education authorities and now by a National Mentoring Network. Business in the Community's Roots and Wings programme has established mentoring projects in a number of inner-city areas. One exemplar in the field is the Dalston Youth Project (DYP), established by Crime Concern in Hackney, one of the most deprived areas of Britain. DYP runs intensive programmes for young people at risk of educational failure and frequent criminal offending. Combining after-school learning activities and youth work support with school liaison, parental involvement and the creation of one-to-one mentoring relationships between young people and volunteer adults, DYP has shown itself to have a significant impact on:

- school attendance and positive transition from school to further education or training; and
- the offending and arrest rates of its participants.

Alongside its programme for older teenagers, it has recently begun a cycle aimed at preventing school exclusion among younger teenagers. Its value lies in the flexible combination of resources which it provides, of which the nurture of positive, voluntary mentoring relationships is a crucial part.

Promoting participation

Another strand of innovation, grounded in the debate over children's rights and the implications of the UN Convention on the Rights of the Child, has been to extend young people's opportunities for democratic participation. This has taken place both within existing institutions and in new organisations run by or with young people, with the aim of raising the profile of young people and developing their capacities to participate in and take responsibility for democratic decision-making.

One strong area of development has been in local government, where several local authorities have developed strategies for improving young people's participation in the management of services which affect them. Save the Children has led much of this work, for example developing participation projects with Birmingham City Council.

Other voluntary organisations providing young people's services have also developed new approaches to participation. YMCA England, for example, ran a Peer Education project, supporting young people to develop presentations and learning resources on important issues and to use them with young people from other projects. Other voluntary organisations, from the Woodcraft Folk and the IBIS Trust to Centrepoint, the young people's homelessness agency, have also developed peer education programmes.

One of the major engines for developing democratic participation in schools has been Schools Councils UK. Student councils have existed for many years, but many fail to achieve their full potential, often because they have not been fully integrated into the decision-making structures of school manage-ment. At their best, however, they can do much to enhance the participation of pupils in important decisions, and contribute to the ethos of effective schools. They act as an agent of communication and connection between the interests and perceptions of pupils and the decisions and priorities of teachers, staff and managers. The last decade has also seen the blossoming of regional youth councils across many parts of the country, debating youth issues and acting as advocates to a range of organisations over specific issues.

Two particular organisations have attracted recent attention, both organ-ised and run by young people. The Participation Event Group (PEG) began in 1996 by organising a conference attended by young people and youth profes-sionals from across the north of England to debate the issues of young people's participation. Following the success of the conference, PEG has established itself as a base for networks of activity across the region, producing a newsletter and supporting local groups. A similar organisation, named Article 12 after the article of the UN Convention which lays down the right of young people to participate in decisions affecting them, was established in London in 1996. Its aim is to promote young people's participation across a national network. While many of these organisations do not have a formal educational focus, the core of their activity is effective learning, about the issues and questions affecting young people, the responsibilities and processes of decision-making, and effective communication and relationships.

Finally, Children's Express, the news agency for young people, has quickly established a strong presence in the UK since it arrived in 1995. Children's Express has become a major force in the US, winning a string of media awards and developing a national network of bureaux. It works by establishing bases for young people to research and develop stories on issues which concern them, and by selling the finished stories to newspapers, journals and broad-casters. Children's Express stories regularly appear in national broadsheets, television and radio stations, and they have also produced a special edition of

the *Architect's Journal*. By building young people's responsibility and participation into every level of its organisation, Children's Express has become an
exemplar of positive achievement and professionalism. Its ability to motivate
young people, to raise the profile of issues affecting them, and to stimulate
high-quality collaborative learning, shows the potential of community-based
projects which focus on the needs and perceptions of young people themselves
while stimulating an environment in which their abilities and aspirations can
be dramatically raised.

There are many other youth organisations and school-based initiatives
working along similar principles to those profiled in this chapter. Some are
based around arts and culture, such as the London International Festival of
Theatre, some in environmental education, such as Learning through
Landscapes and Going for Green. Some are very new, and do not have established track records, while others have already demonstrated their effectiveness.
Overall they vary widely in aims, scope and methods. But between them they
possess the seeds of a new approach to learning, helping to develop skills,
personal qualities and dispositions which conventional schooling often strug-
gles with, and serving to connect the acquisition of knowledge and
understanding with the contexts and situations in which they might be
displayed or employed. The next chapter examines some of the positive
general characteristics that they share; the components of successful active
learning programmes.

41

5
WHAT MATTERS MOST
Key characteristics of active learning projects

The projects and initiatives described in Chapter 4 cover a vast area. It would be hard to find a set of characteristics or principles which they all share, or to reduce their value to one set of core principles. It is probably more useful to think of them as a *family*, comprising many different shapes, sizes and activities, but also sharing many underlying characteristics, with complicated, criss-crossing networks of similarities, differences and common bonds.

This chapter examines some of the most important shared features of active learning projects. Its purpose is to draw out the most important principles for understanding how active learning can work, to help give a practical foundation for understanding its future development. Many of the features we describe might seem to be in tension with others, but this is not necessarily an inconsistency. As I will argue, successful learning comes from making tensions creative, by identifying, managing and seeking to resolve them. Eliminating all tension or conflict from an activity helps to deaden it, closing it off from the forces which influence and motivate it. If the tension is too high it can produce panic, anxiety and failure. But removing all tension induces complacency and boredom, limiting and devaluing achievement as a result.

Achieving the right balance between the different forces influencing the learning process, between internal discipline and external demand, between goal and current reality, between control and freedom, is a theme to which we will return. Reaching such a balance in any learning programme is a continuous challenge, which can only be achieved with reference to the specific circumstances of the project and the needs and abilities of its participants; but understanding the underlying principles of active learning is a precondition of success, helping to create the dynamic processes and environments in which learners can develop the understanding, awareness and dispositions to learn effectively in all areas of their lives.

This chapter does not present the kind of conclusive evidence which educational researchers and inspectors increasingly demand. This is for various reasons. First, not all of the projects mentioned have undertaken the kind of independent evaluation required to draw out conclusive evidence. Second, many of their characteristics are still not susceptible to the kind of evaluation which produces data-driven performance. Very often it is the *qualities* of a project, and of its relationships, which help to distinguish it, making it attractive and accessible for young people. This chapter should therefore not be taken as an attempt to provide conclusive proof of their effectiveness. Instead, its aim is to clarify and explain what underlies their particular activities and aims, to help set an agenda for their development. With this in mind, we can examine their most important features.

Clearly-defined objectives

The place to start is always with objectives. Misunderstanding or vagueness about what you are trying to achieve can be fatal to the success of any project, and even with relatively open learning activities this is still the case. Every one of the initiatives profiled in this book works hard to establish clear goals, and then to identify the strategies by which to achieve them. In one sense this is obvious – few of us would like to think of ourselves launching into a task or activity without understanding what we are trying to achieve, but in fact it happens all too often. This is partly a problem of explanation and transfer. Teachers may know what they are aiming for, and pupils usually have some idea. But all too often there is a wide gap between these different perspectives. When working to the demands of a predefined programme of study it is especially easy for professionals to work towards objectives which are clear in their minds, but not necessarily in those of their students.

With schooling this is a particular danger because in most societies it is compulsory. School is something you start doing at an early age and follows a pattern with which you become very familiar very quickly. Whether you like it or not, school is something you have to do, and the potential for losing track of what you are trying to achieve is considerable. Similarly, for hard-pressed teachers concerned about discipline, timetables, examination results, it can be easy to lose sight of the need for objectives to be clear and shared. As long as enough students are able to produce correct answers, and seem to be on the right track, it can be easy to assume that they understand what they are trying to achieve.

Overall objectives will, of course, vary among a group of learners, and will almost certainly be expressed in different vocabularies. A teacher may be trying to get his or her pupils to gain an understanding of geometry at Curriculum Key Stage Two, while the pupils are trying to work out the relationship between the angles of a triangle. But, by definition, knowing what you are trying to achieve is a prerequisite for achieving it. This does not mean that learners cannot make discoveries which they did not anticipate – many of the most important scientific discoveries have been made while trying to achieve something else – but if students are unclear about what they are attempting, they will be unable to understand its significance when they get there, even if they manage to produce the 'correct' answer.

All successful active learning projects have a clear mission, or vision of what, overall, they are trying to achieve. Ideally this is something that young participants understand and subscribe to, a set of ideas which infuses their activity. But it is important to distinguish between overall mission and more specific objectives. An individual project undertaken by a small group of young people will have its own concrete purpose – perhaps to reduce the amount of litter dropped in a particular neighbourhood, to investigate the causes of air pollution, or to raise money for a planned event. On top of this particular, concrete goal will sit second-order objectives such as developing a particular set of skills or capacities, to win credits towards an award, or to publicise a neglected but important issue. As the orders of generality rise, objectives should make a clear contribution to the mission of a project. For example, to give young people experience of creating positive social change, to build confidence and motivation, or to offer positive opportunities and examples to young people at risk.

Whatever the specific content of the objectives, they should fit into a relatively clear framework which all participants clearly understand and can subscribe to. It is also important to note that immediate objectives will often change in response to experience. Changemakers projects often include failure to achieve initial objectives, and the process of reflecting on and redefining goals is integral to their value over time. Similarly, most of the ideas and suggestions thrown up by young journalists at Children's Express do not translate into published stories.

Most adults working with young people have relatively clear goals and ideas of what they are trying to do. But working towards a goal to which young people need to conform, rather than starting where they are, is a formula for disappointment. This point is emphasised by McLaughlin *et al.* (1994) in their important study of successful neighbourhood-based youth organisations in the US. They found that project leaders whose 'primary passion' is the programme or activity they lead, rather than the young people themselves, are unlikely to retain the trust or motivation of their participants. Setting, clarifying and revisiting objectives with young people, rather than for them, and responding to their identification of need and interest, is vital.

Access to a continuum of learning opportunities

Learning is a dynamic process which is ongoing; as a process, it is not divided into curriculum subjects, time periods or predefined levels of achievement. Such frameworks are often necessary to organise and assess learning, but they do not define it. In the worlds of business and personal relationships this insight is commonplace – no successful firm ever decides that it knows enough to succeed and can afford to sit back, even for the foreseeable future. No partner in a successful marriage thinks that they have finished learning about themselves, the needs of their spouse, or the nature of their relationship.

44

Active learning projects aim to embody approaches which make learning opportunities accessible, but do not limit the potential for achievement. The focus of specific projects, of course, differs enormously, but the common characteristic is that they offer open participation and a potentially unbounded progression through different stages of achievement. The focus of activity relates to wider, longer-term goals, to possible futures, as well as to the more immediate objectives of the exercise.

This openness often differs fundamentally from the organisation of more formal educational settings, which is more likely to be classified and assessed in a series of standardised progressions. Despite the best intentions, these units can become hoops to be jumped through, activities which do not offer clear ideas about where they might lead to apart from to another standardised unit. This view, often reinforced by the necessary creation of qualifications and accredited tests of competence, can work against the success of active learning projects because it limits learners' horizons.

One mark of effective active learning initiatives is that they are able to begin at a place which participants can understand, relate to, and get involved in. The participants might be disaffected, distrustful and lacking in basic skills, or they might be academic high flyers who are less confident about their ability to work with peers and achieve in the 'real world'. Criteria of success are therefore:

- to offer opportunities to which each individual can gain access;
- to ensure that the transitions from one to the other are clearly understood and supported;
- to ensure progress towards more complex or difficult tasks; which also lead to
- deeper levels of trust and responsibility.

This is one reason why active learning projects can be so successful in generating motivation: they can begin with a relatively simple challenge, and progress to more ambitious and complicated tasks and activities.

John Huskins, in his book *Quality Work with Young People* (1996), sets out a useful model of curriculum development which explains the progressive levels of involvement and decision-making. They begin with basic initial contact, followed by further meetings, establishing trust and developing open discussion with all members of a group, allowing them to express opinions, test out ideas and seek responses from others. From this base, a project can be identified and planned to meet specified needs and objectives, and the roles of different participants begin to take shape. Fuller involvement begins when group members start to assist in taking action and responsibility, to demand a role in organising the activity, and then to take full responsibility for leading and developing the project, achieving independence while maintaining contact with others who can support and assist them.

In some contexts the early stages of this process can be bypassed. Projects which are school-based, such as Changemakers, are often initiated among pupils already used to dealing with teachers and peers, so that the initial norms of contact and low-level collaboration are established. Other projects, such as Youth Works NE, target young people who may be suspicious of professionals and institutions and unused to any kind of project-based collaboration. Making initial contact and establishing trust are therefore crucial objectives. Reviewing the basis of collaboration and the roles and abilities of the participants is always useful, however, because it discourages the tendency to allocate roles and responsibilities based on prior assumptions about what individuals are able to do.

Focusing on accessibility as the starting point for a project creates a sound platform for developing active learning to its full potential. If learning is conceived as a continuous process with no fixed boundaries, this starting point can lead to complex, high-level achievement. But if the conditions of entry are too stringent, two important failures can occur. First, some people will be excluded before they even start. Second, those who are already best equipped to succeed will dominate from the start, denying others the opportunity to develop their own roles and abilities.

Real responsibility

Responsibility in successful active learning projects is distributed among all participants rather than retained by leaders and organisers. For example at Children's Express, the principle is that young people can organise things for themselves. Adults and professionals are there as supportive human resources rather than as directors, managers or controllers. The evidence from observation and from studies of such projects is that having the opportunity to take responsibility is a primary source of their motivating power for young people.

If learning outcomes are already laid down in the curriculum and the performance measurement of a school, it can seem impossible to allow pupils to make important decisions about the focus, content and style of their activity. Again, though, this approach goes against the grain of the capacities which we increasingly expect from young adults, and the qualities which they need to thrive. The results when young people are given responsibility and discretion can often be overwhelming.

For example, Bradford City Challenge has established a grants programme to support young people's independent learning activities, which is managed by a committee of elected teenagers. When the fund, of some £70,000, was established, there was concern that the young people would be unable to cope with the responsibility of such important decisions, that favouritism and inconsistency would create serious problems. Over time, the young committee members showed that they were, if anything, more rigorous and responsible about their use of the money than many adults normally are.

46

Their attention to relevant detail, and requirement of hard evidence to support applications, has amazed even those who established the fund, and it has become a significant focus of interest and activity among young people in the area. Similarly, Changemakers projects have shown that they appeal to young people of all kinds – the rebels and underachievers as well as the quiet, hard workers – and that they take on responsibility for their projects with alacrity and care.

Effective active learning projects work on the basis that decision-making should be devolved as far as possible to their participants. The framework of rules and supervision surrounding them should be clear and supportive, and opportunities for leadership should also be carefully developed so that young people feel equipped both to take on responsibility and to judge when taking an opportunity to lead is appropriate. The risk involved in allowing the freedom of decision-making is that young people may be left floundering, unsure how to proceed, prone to making hasty decisions. The best way to offset this risk is not to prescribe rules and impose decisions, but to encourage reflection and critical discussion, and to make sure that appropriate guidance is available when young people seek it. In the long term, nurturing leadership and decision-making in these ways has considerable benefits. It helps young people to develop their capacity to govern themselves. It means that their understanding of rules and constraints is based on their experience of responsibility rather than solely that of being told what to do, and it builds their readiness to use initiative and judgement in tackling problems rather than simply referring to rules or sources of external authority. All of these qualities help prepare young people to respond intelligently and responsibly to the challenges that they encounter as they reach adulthood.

Collaboration beyond the school and peer group

One of the most important features of all the initiatives described in Chapter 4 is that they cross the boundaries of contexts within which young pupil are used to acting. At the cognitive level, this is a generic characteristic of learning: the acquisition of new knowledge and understanding, and its application to new challenges. But it is also a crucial organisational feature of successful projects. One of the most telling criticisms of school education is that it can insulate pupils from the outside world, and one of the most important failures outlined in Chapter 2 is that knowledge gained in school is not transferred or applied successfully in contexts beyond the classroom.

Active learning projects can help to solve this problem by challenging young people to work effectively on projects which touch the worlds beyond their classrooms. This encourages them to consider their actions in relation to people and factors beyond the normal parameters of education. They do this in many different ways: Changemakers projects challenge pupils to identify a community issue and then to take positive action to address it; Children's

Express assignments require their journalists to identify the people and institutions they need to write balanced, informed articles; Youth Charter for Sport brings young people together with sporting personalities, business people and other members of the community to search for solutions which produce positive outcomes for everybody; initiatives to improve young people's participation in decision-making require them to meet and address the needs of other members of a community or institution; the Dalston Youth Project brings together a diverse range of financial, social, physical and human resources to provide learning opportunities and support for young people who have rejected learning within a more conventional institutional framework. Study support puts learning in a different light by releasing it from the standardised rhythms and routines of the school day. Prince's Trust Volunteers, similarly, have found that the teams who achieve most tend to be those who bring together young people not used to working together: a mixture of full-time students, employed and unemployed young people who have to reassess their assumptions and establish norms of collaboration.

The common characteristic of these initiatives is that they seek to connect resources in new ways, placing young people at the centre of networks, rather than fixing them within an institutional framework and feeding information in through its organisational structure. These networks are made of different kinds of resource: information and advice, places to use, people, sometimes money. They often overlap, and their structure will frequently shift during the course of a project, as different people come and go and new resources are factored in. But the hub of each network is the individual learner or the specific project in which they are involved.

There are three principal benefits to this approach. First, the range of resources available to a learner is potentially much greater than in a more controlled and predefined organisational setting, such as a classroom. Rather than using a textbook and a teacher as the main sources of information and support, the learner can turn to any one of the project's advisers or collaborators – to improve a corporate volunteer, a local voluntary organisation, a parent, a library – to seek the information and guidance that they need. Second, learners must find ways of marshalling and organising these resources *for themselves* in order to make best use of them. Whatever the specific content of the project, its participants must identify and utilise appropriate resources for themselves, rather than passively receiving predefined materials and using them to try to produce a 'correct answer'. In the rest of life, this is far more likely to be the way that individuals are expected to operate. This is the way that problems are solved and needs met, whether the challenge is finding employment, identifying a new business opportunity, overcoming a personal crisis, or winning funding for a new project. Third, the ways in which such projects are organised means that the learning takes place out in the open, rather than hidden within a school; its goals are authentic, taken from real-life concerns, and grounded in learners' awareness of their environment. And the process of collaboration between different individuals, often on very small-scale projects, connects the aims and practices of schools with those of the institutions surrounding them. At a basic, everyday, level, this kind of contact helps to bring together the worlds of education and employment, and to connect the processes of education with its overall goal: preparing young people to survive and to thrive in the full complexity and uncertainty of the adult world.

Concrete outcomes and celebration of achievement

Successful learning always has identifiable outcomes. They are not always predictable, but maximising the value of learning requires that we always identify its results as far as possible. For active learning projects, which do not necessarily take place within a formally accredited framework, clear identification of outcomes is even more important than in more formal curriculum subjects.

Identifying outcomes is an integral part of the planning and execution of successful projects. Outcomes are often described in terms of practical, concrete steps towards an agreed goal; raising a specified sum of money, producing a poster to advertise the project, attracting the support of a local business, borrowing the equipment needed to produce a final project report. But there are also other kinds of outcome, for learners, teachers and their communities. Individual learner outcomes might be learning how to perform a particular kind of task, or improving a performance record in a particular field – attendance, motivation, or academic performance. At the next level of generality, outcomes become more qualitative; improving one's understanding of the world of work, or of the ways in which democratic decisions are made. At group level, the outcomes are often normative, and created through the interaction of individuals in a *system* of learning and collaboration. The norms of trust, honesty and reciprocity are all sustained by successful collaboration and sharing of experience. From the basic breakdown of the stages and processes leading to a project's goal, it is possible to develop a series of outcomes which become progressively more general, contributing to overall norms of behaviour and qualitative definitions of achievement. Often a single outcome might have more than one meaning; for example, successfully finding business sponsorship for a small community project could be described as raising necessary funds, attracting external interest in the project, and developing a young person's ability to explain what they are doing and ask for support.

Different organisations tackle outcomes in different ways: some use formal accreditation or award schemes to provide a framework; others use action planning to establish the expected outcomes at different stages of the project, relating them to objectives rather than to an external structure of award and development. Some describe outcomes in specifically educational terms,

49

aiming for a positive impact on school attendance and attainment, and trying to map the connections between project-based learning and progress towards examination success. Others, such as the crime prevention projects described in Chapter 4, aim to produce positive social outcomes, reducing crime or conflict in a particular neighbourhood, developing partnerships between different members of a community.

However the learning outcomes of a project are conceived, their achievement should always be celebrated. Again there are many ways to do this, including award schemes, graduation ceremonies, presentations of work in the company of parents, peers and employers, and exhibitions of work, all of which are used by the projects we have examined. However it is done, celebration of achievement, and affirmation of the value of active learning, are crucial endorsements of the effort and ability that young people put into learning. This is not to suggest that everybody should be rewarded and praised indiscriminately; the idea is not to suggest that everybody does equally well whatever they do. Rather, it is part of the process of recognising achievement of every kind, and communicating its value. Sometimes this may be celebration of the persistence required to complete a project, but it should also be part of the process of reflection and review which accompanies all effective learning.

Regular review and evaluation

Once the aims and objectives have been set, another crucial part of the process of active learning is regular review of progress towards them. Projects which set a group of learners off in a particular direction and do not review or evaluate their achievements until they have finished, or until things begin to go wrong, will miss vital opportunities. If we conceive of learning as a continuous process which, at least potentially, has no final end point, then the beginning and end of a particular project are just points on that continuum. They are major breaks in the process, in the sense that they mark the beginning and end of a joint activity with a specific set of aims and objectives, but the activity itself should be punctuated by regular opportunities for review, reflection and evaluation.

Schools, of course, review and evaluate progress as a matter of course. But much school-based evaluation is formalised and controlled by the teacher rather than the learner. The time and effort devoted to active review and formulation of strategies for the next stage of learning is very small compared to the time spent trying to teach and learn the curriculum. All too often the emphasis is on summative assessment which seeks to aggregate and measure progress numerically, rather than formative assessment which evaluates progress in order to formulate strategies and plan the next set of objectives.

Effective active learning projects build regular opportunities for review and reflection into the process of learning. Such review is undertaken by all those involved, often with a strong emphasis on the learners coming to their own conclusions, though always with the advice and assessment of other adults and professionals. Often this review takes place within a specified framework, such as the European Quality Framework used by Barclays New Futures. This does not have to be the case, however; the framework can be constructed around the activity as part of the project planning. The crucial steps are part of a cycle of evaluation:

- to identify and agree on the objectives of a particular project;
- to agree the strategies and methods to be employed in achieving those objectives;
- to identify the roles and tasks of each member of a project team and agree their responsibilities;
- to agree key stages in the development of the project, and the evidence at each stage that objectives have been met;
- at the end of each stage, to review progress towards each objective, and the relative success of the strategies used, and the reasons for success or failure.

Following on from these conclusions comes agreement of strategies for the next phase of activity.

At each stage of this process, learners should be able to seek the views of appropriate others to add to their own assessment and develop plans for the next stage of a project. Sharply differing perceptions of what has been achieved may prompt fundamental rethinking, but collecting and comparing different assessments is itself part of the process of learning. It requires participants to explore the basis on which people make different judgements, and the extent to which what they do can meet a range of different expectations. This stands in sharp contrast to an assessment framework dominated by a single perspective, that of the teacher or external assessor.

Clear connection to other areas of learning

One of the most difficult challenges for active learning projects is to connect what they achieve to other areas of more formal learning. Achieving this transfer is by no means easy. Knowledge and understanding are often bound up in the contexts in which they are learned. Transfer, as David Perkins points out in *Outsmarting IQ* (1995), 'demands point blank attention'. In some projects the activity has obvious potential for transfer: literacy and IT skills, for example, at Children's Express; or learning about political decision-making structures, environmental and social issues. Very often learners do not associate their learning out of school with formal curriculum subjects learned in the classroom. Transfer is not a natural or automatic process, but the product of disciplined, systematic reflection.

Because school-based learning often has such a strong cultural and institutional identity, it can be especially difficult to make the crossover from other contexts. As Michael Cole (1996) has shown, demonstration of knowledge is often strongly conditioned by the cultural context in which it is applied. The vocabularies of young children can vary enormously according to their relationship to those they are speaking to and the conditions under which they are assessed. Performance is strongly related to the deep assumptions, memories and habits that we associate with different situations. But active learning projects can contribute to the capacity of learners to apply knowledge and understanding across contexts. Study support, for example, encourages the development of habits and disciplines which *support* more formal educational attainment. Evaluations of Children's Express have similarly revealed that the underlying capacities supporting attainment, such as confidence, curiosity and verbal sophistication, are identified by young journalists and editors as a positive feature of their experience. Self-reported perceptions among young journalists suggest similar changes: 'I can treat teachers as friends now' (female editor, 16); 'I have changed my English, my spelling' (male reporter, 12). Similarly, DYP intertwines the development of basic emotional and social skills and the process of defining and clarifying personal goals with gradually developed experience of mainstream educational activities: literacy classes, college 'taster courses', and so on. Pathways to Adult Life has proved most effective in schools where learning outcomes were carefully specified to reflect both curriculum requirements and the broader awareness and abilities which the framework is designed to enhance (Harris, 1996).

Active learning projects can help their participants to make connections between ways of knowing things, between situations in which they might need to learn, and between the specific content of their activities and the wider social and personal goals the participants may embrace. This strand of successful active learning is often underdeveloped. Making it happen depends not just on learners, but also on formal education: it is noteworthy that Children's Express grappled with the National Curriculum framework and decided that planning and assessing it was too cumbersome and complicated, even though its activities so obviously contribute to the goals of the English curriculum.

Effective motivation through example and respect

Finally, the adults who help to run effective active learning projects motivate their participants, not by control and compulsion, or necessarily by the promise of certificates and rewards, but by developing trusting, reciprocal relationships with them. Motivation is stimulated by activities which are inherently interesting and enjoyable to young people, and through demonstration of commitment. As one study support participant said, 'We all come because we want to – no one makes us. The older kids come, no one makes them either.' The fact that commitment is voluntary rather than forced often makes a huge difference to the perspective of a young person. It is one reason why mentoring programmes can be so engaging.

Relationships based on mutual respect support motivation in ways that frameworks based on control are unable to do. They also fit more closely with the values held by younger people. As Geoff Thompson, Executive Chair of Youth Charter for Sport, puts it, adults are no longer able to demand respect: they must command it instead. If adults can demonstrate their understanding of and commitment to the situation that young people find themselves in, and act as exemplars and role models rather than instructors, they are much more likely to support positive development over time.

This chapter has offered some key characteristics which underlie successful active learning. Many of these characteristics can be found in good schools, companies and voluntary organisations. Their definition and their validity as criteria of effectiveness will, I hope, be tested in time by more detailed evaluation. But they offer the beginnings of a framework for understanding how these projects contribute to the motivation, personal development and educational attainment of the young people who participate in them. Having looked at their characteristics, we can turn to more practical questions. How can active learning enhance our current education system? The next three chapters examine the contribution that it can make to three of our most pressing educational challenges: learning morality and citizenship, developing employability and tackling underachievement.

6

LEARNING MORALITY AND CITIZENSHIP

The world is passing through troublesome times. The young people of today think of no-one but themselves. They have no respect for age or their parents. What passes as wisdom for us is foolishness to them. As for the young girls of today, they are immodest in speech, behaviour and dress.

(Peter the Hermit, eleventh century)

School is all subjects and exams. Young people should do things which make us more aware of what's going on in the world.

(18-year-old woman, quoted in Roker *et al.*, 1998)

Everything's just flaking away. People are turning bad and every-thing's getting out of order. . . . A lot of people don't know what morality is – it's a boring way of living which is foreign to them.

(17-year-old black man, Manchester, quoted in Industrial Society, 1977)

Concern about young people's morals is nothing new. It can be traced from Aristotle through the Middle Ages and Renaissance to the Victorians and into the twentieth century. Shakespeare's *Romeo and Juliet* examined the behaviour of lawless and idle young men in the city of Verona, mirroring problems which exercised the civic leaders of seventeenth-century Florence. At the end of the nineteenth century, the psychologist William James argued that, in the absence of military combat, young men required a 'moral equivalent of war' as an outlet for their energies, to provide them with discipline and responsibility. For older generations, the challenge has not changed. They must pass on principles and practices from one generation to another, while recognising that both the context, and the outlooks of younger people, are constantly changing. This challenge is no different now than it was in the eleventh century, although we perhaps have a better chance of understanding the dynamics of change because there is so much more available information today.

The 1990s have seen a strangely familiar wave of concern about whether young people are learning right from wrong. Many factors are blamed for the apparent collapse of moral standards, from the growth of a consumer society to the influence of 'postmodernist' intellectuals. Some blame a culture of individualism, arguing that it overemphasises the claims of individual rights and encourages us to use other people as instruments of our own desires and ambitions. Others blame the media, the widening of economic inequality, or a 'me first' philosophy. Shocking individual events, like the murder of toddler James Bulger by two boys not yet in their teens and the killing of headteacher Philip Lawrence at the gates of his school, have provoked outpourings of grief, blame and anxiety. But the media debates have often generated more heat than light. For many young people there is undoubtedly a problem of disaffection, alienation and loss of trust. But there is not so much evidence that, overall, young people are unconcerned with ethical and political issues, or that they are in danger of becoming amoral.

This chapter examines the evidence of disconnection and moral decline, and of social engagement and active citizenship by young people. It reviews responses to the perceived need for moral and citizenship education and sets out an agenda for the future. I argue that, given young people's changing values and expressions of political engagement, education for citizenship and morality should follow principles of responsibility, trust and active reflection. There is an important place for instruction. Educators and parents have a moral responsibility to pass on moral values and principles. Young people also need certain kinds of knowledge and understanding, for example of political and legal institutions, and concepts such as democracy and freedom, in order to become effective citizens. However, I also argue that instruction will only be effective if it can be integrated with young people's emerging understanding and experience of themselves, and the communities that they inhabit. These communities are immediate, local and particular, in contrast to more general ideas and systems which are easily seen as remote, abstract and alien. For young people, the most obvious of these communities is the school, and I argue that as an institution this is the starting point for developing active, democratic citizenship. If values, principles, rights and duties are to be real and relevant for young people, their teaching must be combined with opportunities for active exploration and reflection of what they mean in practice.

What is the evidence of a decline in responsibility and citizenship among the young? In many Western societies there is a clear problem of political alienation. Forty-three per cent of under-25s did not vote in the 1992 UK election, and only a slightly larger number took part in 1997. Less than half as many young people feel that they have a duty to vote than do those who are over 55. Recent Demos research found that a full one-third of the younger generation were proud to be 'outside the system', and concluded that 'for many young people, politics seems to have become a dirty word' (Wilkinson and Mulgan, 1995). Trust in institutions such as the police, the judicial system, parliament, the monarchy and the church, which has fallen among people of all ages over the last fifteen years, is usually lowest among young people. Youth crime and violence are reported continuously in the media. Many people feel that the social environment is more threatening, that people are less prepared to respect each other and make an effort to help, and that it is more difficult to trust strangers. As in the past, young people are often seen as representative of these changes, displaying cultures and attitudes which are alien, hostile to tradition, and difficult for others understand.

It is certainly true that many young people feel alienated from mainstream political institutions, and that values are changing. The shift in young people's values towards greater individualism, desire for authenticity and freedom to fulfil oneself, and their rejection of imposed or traditional general rules, is becoming well-documented, associated with what Ronald Inglehart called 'postmaterialist values' (Inglehart, 1990; Hechter et al., 1993; Wilkinson and Mulgan, 1995; Jupp and Lawson, 1997). As generations grow up less preoccupied with physical and material security than were their parents, their concerns shift towards issues such as the quality of life, corporate and environmental ethics, and personal freedom to shape the way in which one lives. More basic concerns, of course, do not disappear completely, and often resurface during economic recessions. The picture which emerges from these changes is extremely complicated. It is very hard to discern whether changes in attitudes are due to overall changes in society, in which the young lead the way, or whether young people's attitudes will change as they grow older, and become more similar to those of their parents' generation (Park and Jowell, 1998). Attitudes to sexual morality, for example, have shifted very strongly between generations, and it is unlikely that young people will lose much of their tolerance as they grow older. Attitudes to mainstream politics, however, are more ambiguous. Are young people losing all trust in politicians and political institutions? Are they becoming re-engaged in a new style of politics? Are they likely to become more interested as they grow older? At the moment, it is difficult to tell.

Many people associate these changes with the idea that younger people are less moral. Their declining interest in marriage, emphasis on individual self-expression, and apparent unwillingness to accept traditional authority, can suggest that morals are less important to them. Harvard academic Peter A Hall recently examined attitudes towards moral relativism among the British, and found that younger people were far more likely to disagree with the idea that 'there are clear guidelines on what is good or evil which apply in every circumstance' (Hall, 1997). Such findings echo the arguments of commentators such as Alan Bloom, whose book *The Closing of the American Mind* (1987) documented the apparent retreat of American university students into relativism.

But while it is true that younger generations are less prepared to accept absolute rules without question, too many commentators seem to miss the fact that young people engage with moral issues all the time. Among a generation which values diversity and self-expression, the idea of moral relativism is attractive to many. Many young people *are* reluctant to accept the idea that moral judgement is anything other than personal taste. But active reflection soon reveals that, of course, there are questions and disputes in which they appeal to what is right, and seek to influence others on moral grounds. The survey evidence on moral relativism suggests not that young people believe only in individual morality as a question of taste, but that they reject the idea of a single, absolute framework for moral judgement. As Nigel Biggar has written, disagreement over a particular rule does not exclude underlying agreement on the principle which informs it (Biggar, 1997). Few people think that murder is acceptable, even if they disagree passionately over abortion. Embracing relativism is something that young people can only do when they talk in general terms, without investigating the way that morality actually impacts on their discussions, their relationships and their everyday lives.

Alongside this, as both Martin Jacques and Geoff Mulgan have pointed out (Mulgan, 1997), is the extent to which the sheer range of moral argument has broadened over the last thirty years. Debates over animal welfare, the environment, domestic violence, genetics and reproduction, the social responsibilities of corporations, have all become mainstream issues, where a generation ago they were largely confined to narrow corners of society. It is hard to avoid being confronted by moral dilemmas and conflicts in any area of life. It is more questionable, however, whether young people are adequately equipped to resolve them successfully.

There is plenty of evidence that young people are still concerned about moral, civic and political issues. The Industrial Society's 2020 Vision programme found that the social issue of most concern among 12–25-year-olds was violent crime (Industrial Society, 1997). A survey of Londoners' attitudes found that young people were the age group most concerned about the way people behaved towards each other in public spaces. A 1991 survey by the National Centre for Volunteers found that 55 per cent of 18–24-year-olds had been involved in some kind of volunteering activity over the last year, including youth organisations, community volunteering and out-of-school learning programmes. Large providers of volunteering opportunities, such as the Prince's Trust and CSV, have steadily expanded their programmes over the last decade, and found no shortage of willing young people. A recent study by the Trust for the Study of Adolescence (Roker *et al.*, 1998) found that 70 per cent of the young people interviewed had signed a petition in the last year, 59 per cent had boycotted something because of where or how it was made, such as products tested on animals, 89 per cent had given money to charity, and 48 per cent had campaigned about something happening in their local area, such as preventing building on a greenfield area or against the closure of a local railway station. Sixteen per cent had written to their MP or to local councillors. As well as this occasional involvement, more than 10 per cent were involved in regular campaigning or volunteering, including visiting the elderly, volunteer youth work, organising school campaigning groups for organisations such as Amnesty International, or volunteering in a charity shop. This pattern is replicated across the country; young people seem to be far more active than the media image of a selfish, apathetic generation might suggest, although many of those interviewed for this study also acknowledged that there could be some peer pressure not to get involved in such activities, and that this was something to be resisted: 'We can't just leave everything to someone else. If you believe in it, you gotta do it. Just ignore everyone else. Get stuck in.'

It is important to recognise the shift away from more traditional forms of engagement, and towards self-organised, issues-based activity. Very often young people seem more comfortable being involved in a single project or single-issue campaign than with the idea that they should have a general obligation to be an active citizen. Similarly, as we have seen, less than half as many 18–24-year-olds acknowledge a duty to vote as do those over 55. This is partly because direct involvement in single issues or in local projects is often perceived to have a more direct impact than, for example, joining a political party. The greater attachment to *authenticity* which the younger generation feels (Wilkinson and Mulgan, 1995) reflects a wider shift in patterns of trust and influence among the whole population (Henley Centre, 1997). Activities which individuals play a part in shaping, which are chosen rather than required, are more in tune with the changing values of Western societies. But free choice does not necessarily make them less moral. The attraction that many feel towards the idea of relativism stems partly from an important truth about morality: that ethical behaviour is only such when it is freely chosen. As one 15-year-old put it:

> It just felt right really, nothing more complicated than that. I just thought yeah I'm gonna get off my backside and do something about this because it's wrong.

This is crucial for educators and those in authority to remember when they consider moral education. There is a clear difference between prescribing and teaching the specific kinds of behaviour that some of us might like to see, and developing young people's capacities to act as moral agents. Yet much of the debate over teaching right from wrong has often obscured this distinction.

Interestingly, the TSA study (Roker *et al.*, 1998) also found a degree of ambivalence, particularly among boys and young men, in their perceptions of what 'counts' as voluntary activity. One reason for this was uncertainty about motivation; many were unsure about whether what they did counted as volunteering because there was a degree of self-interest in their involvement. Others felt that there was something embarrassing about volunteering, making it difficult to admit it to friends and family.

I work at the reading club two lunchtimes a week now. A group of my friends do it too. They didn't want to when I asked, they thought you know that it was a bit creepy. But now most of them are there more hours than I am. We all feel like we're doing something to help the younger ones.

(16-year-old boy)

But this ambiguity also illustrates an underlying confusion about what acting morally means. Many younger people absorb the implicit message that acting morally and altruistically means being self-sacrificing, rather than working for the mutual benefit of those involved. Behaviour with regard to others is rarely undertaken purely for altruistic reasons: civil society flourishes through relationships based on reciprocity.

Learning morality and citizenship

The need to ensure that young people develop the values, motivation and moral judgement to become active, responsible citizens has provoked many recent responses, and led to consultation and proposals on how citizenship might become part of the curriculum. The Advisory Group on Education for Citizenship and Democracy established by the Secretary of State for Education, David Blunkett MP, and chaired by Professor Bernard Crick, has taken on the task of establishing the case for a more coherent approach, and of recommending how this could be translated into a reshaped curriculum. The Forum on Values in Education and the Community, launched by the Schools Curriculum and Assessment Authority (now the Qualifications and Curriculum Authority – QCA) in 1996, was charged with the task of discovering 'whether there are any values on which there is common agreement in society' and deciding 'how schools might be supported in their important task of contributing to pupils' spiritual, moral, social and cultural development', a cross-curricular theme of the National Curriculum. There are many other initiatives in the UK and further afield aimed at promoting citizenship. The Institute of Citizenship Studies, for example, has initiated a number of projects including a White Paper on citizenship, essay competitions for young people, and practical citizenship education projects. The Citizenship Foundation runs projects aimed at educating young people about the legislative system, including 'mock' lawcourts and debating programmes. The Centre for Citizenship Studies in Education at Leicester University produces a series of practical resources for use in schools. The Council for Education in World Citizenship plays a similar role, seeking to inform and stimulate debate about global and international citizenship issues.

There are also many more practical, locally-based initiatives, such as Changemakers, Barclays New Futures, school and regional Youth Councils, and environmental initiatives such as Learning Through Landscapes and the Groundwork Trusts. The emphasis here is on encouraging the habits of active citizenship through local civic engagement. If citizenship is best thought of as a combination of the particular and the universal, connecting individuals through membership and engagement to a greater whole, these initiatives begin with the particular, and aim to broaden the horizons of their participants through self-organisation and collaboration.

There is already a lot happening. Thousands of individual schools have developed their own arrangements, alongside the dedicated organisations mentioned above. How should we think about a coherent strategy for developing and enhancing this body of practice?

Some approaches begin with the law and the formal framework of rights and duties which underpin citizenship. This view, for example, leads to education about parliament and the legal process, such as 'mock court' projects. Understanding the legal system is of course important, but may not be the best place to start for many young people, especially those who are at risk of ending up on the wrong side of the law. In the UK, more people think of citizenship in terms of informal civic engagement and community membership than as a set of formal rights and duties (Citizenship Foundation, 1997).

Another approach would be to attempt to teach from the basis of relatively abstract values such as democracy, freedom and duty, to instil respect for such values and to promote them in the everyday life and conduct of pupils. In one sense the Values Forum began from here, consulting a range of people and groups in society and drawing up a statement of common values that was, inevitably, fairly general. It then moved on to more practical questions of implementation, developing resources and piloting the approach in a number of schools. In the conventional model of curriculum development, the core knowledge or understanding required would be identified by experts, distilled into a common definition or content, prescribed or recommended at the top, disseminated through teaching materials and guidance, and monitored by those in authority.

But while debate and discussion of this kind is clearly very important, it carries no guarantee that its conclusions will filter through to the everyday lives of young people. As we saw in Chapter 2, 'knowing' something and being able to produce 'correct' answers under certain conditions does not necessarily mean that we can *apply* what we know to problems and choices in the rest of the world. This is a problem of transfer, from one sphere of action to another. It is also a problem of conflict between different values and value systems: the tension between different sources of authority and social pressure that we all experience when we make moral decisions. In developing resources to support pupils' moral, spiritual and cultural development, such a model has extreme limitations, and the Forum on Values in Education and the Community has recognised this. The pilot model it has developed for schools promises to be more holistic, placing less emphasis on direction and more on facilitating reflection and dialogue, clarifying and developing the various ways in which a school and its community can influence young people's values.

Education for citizenship and morality must face more than one challenge. Establishing and instilling values and principles is one, but the second, perhaps more difficult, challenge is to understand that morality is about coping with conflicting pressures, very often between two rights, rather than a right and a wrong. Rushworth Kidder has written in an illuminating way about this tension in his book *How Good People Make Tough Choices* (Kidder, 1995). He points out that living ethically often requires us to make decisions between different kinds of good: between truth and loyalty, between self and other, between the short and the long term, and between justice and mercy. His analysis leads to the advocacy of 'energetic self-reflection' to delve into our motivations and the pressures on us to behave in different ways, and to identify the principles and values by which our conduct should be guided in specific situations. The crucial point is that morality often involves painful choices, and cannot work on the basis of a single set of principles or a memorised code. As well as general principles it depends on circumstances, on judgement and interpretation, and on competing values.

This kind of tension is inherent in learning. Life requires us to cope with a series of conflicts, springing from the need to adapt in intelligent ways to new demands and opportunities, while seeking to preserve what we already value. We all struggle with these tensions. They can induce stress, confusion and uncertainty, but they are not completely negative. In fact, they help to generate both creativity and virtue, because they press us to reflect and to understand ourselves, to harmonise our world view with the realities that we encounter. These conflicts can be framed in many different ways. Here is a suggested list of some of the most important:

- rules *versus* norms
- power *versus* authority
- self *versus* other
- structure *versus* creativity
- control *versus* freedom
- familiar *versus* novel
- abstract *versus* concrete

Thinking through these tensions, and the way in which they play themselves out in everyday situations, is a useful way of thinking about learning. For example, how does a child decide between the knowledge that he should obey the rules set by his school to move between lessons as quickly and safely as possible, and the pressure arising from the norm set by his peers to dally in the corridors, chatting and catching up with his friends? In trying to solve a maths problem, how far should a pupil follow the structure set out by her textbook, and how far should she try different approaches based on past experience of what has worked, or even an apparently hare-brained idea that she has a hunch might be useful? Should one remain loyal to a friend who has entrusted us with a secret, even if we know that telling somebody else might save them from risk or harm? Effective learning is a dynamic process which finds an appropriate balance between the poles set out above, and when it is successful it makes the tensions *creative*. The result is that the tension is lessened, because the learning has helped to synthesise the different possibilities. This can contribute to an individual's deeper understanding of how to make choices, as well as to find the right answer in a specific instance. In particular, the relationship between the novel and the familiar is crucial to the learning process. Challenges and choices which are too familiar become boring and fail to stimulate concentration and/or interest. Challenges which are too difficult or unfamiliar can produce stress and anxiety, and a lack of confidence in the learner about his ability to master problems. Effective learning takes place in the zone between comfort and panic, in which a learner is engaged and stretched, but not beyond her capacity to adapt and to incorporate new information and insights.

The important point for learning morality and citizenship is to understand that making moral decisions is as much about making hard choices, and having the intellectual and emotional equipment to make them properly, as it is about knowing the rules of moral conduct. We can learn ground rules, and principles which we should usually try to follow, but there will always be cases in which the moral response is not automatic or obvious – cases where we are caught between conflicting principles, cases where diagnosis of the problem and practical interpretation of an abstract principle are difficult.

If these challenges are combined with that of applying knowledge and understanding beyond the immediate context in which it has been learned, we can see the overall challenge of moral education beginning to take shape. Understanding the framework of rules and principles which underpin morality is vital. But it only becomes meaningful when this framework is employed in the wide range of situations where moral decisions are made. One way to understand it, suggested by Geoff Mulgan, is to view these rules as a kind of grammar, in which young people must become fluent, but which have diverse and flexible applications (Mulgan, 1997: ch.8). Gaining fluency means learning one's way around the framework of rules and principles, building up knowledge of its overall shape and structure, and learning to apply it in specific instances.

This picture, I hope, shows us that the work of moral educators is far more complex than teaching a set of rules or simply prescribing values. It must include finding ways to support young people in making moral choices for themselves, in the immediate, practical situations which they encounter from day to day. Acknowledging these challenges means that *implementing* education for citizenship and morality should start from the bottom, not from the top; from the real-life experiences and concerns of young people, rather than the abstract values which society might want to instil in them.

To do this, it is useful to think about the ways in which children enter the world of relationships and values. Child psychology shows us that, from birth onwards, children engage in an exploration of the world which progresses from the immediate consciousness of self, the sensations and instincts which are felt most directly, to an emerging set of relationships with the world, including the recognition of the existence of others, beginning to grapple with and understand objects, and learning basic rules about the nature of objects and things, and the ways in which people behave. Following this comes the early understanding of multiple perspectives – that other people may see things differently – and the development of second-order thinking, the beginnings of a capacity to generalise, to move from the concrete and immediate to the abstract and general.

For citizenship we can illustrate these stages of development through a series of concentric circles (see p. 64), beginning with the self and radiating outwards through personal relationships to communities, and finally to society and the most abstract and often the most distant ring of beliefs, concepts and experiences. Of course, a young person's experience and ideas about how they relate to others would be far messier and more complex than these neat circles suggest: there are many potential conflicts between self and others, between personal relationships and the demands of communities, and between the needs and identities of communities and society as a whole. A young person's actual relationships would be closer to a network diagram, showing the different connections that they build up as their social experience broadens. But the circles are a useful way of presenting the basic stages.

Developing citizenship, according to this analysis, is a gradual outward expansion, a series of learning experiences which encourages constructive encounters with the needs, values, rights and varying perspectives of others. This process should encourage learners to understand the role they can play in influencing the social and political environment, and the ways in which they interact with other members of their communities.

In practical terms, this process should begin in families and schools, which are the earliest and most immediate communities that children become members of. Much has been written about the development of schools as communities in which all members have a share (see, e.g., Barber, 1996, and Clark, 1996). Charles Handy (1995) has argued that schools should be seen as city states, composed of citizens with their own interests, rights and responsibilities. All schools embody a set of values. In the best schools these values contribute to an overall ethos of transparency, achievement, shared responsibility and mutual respect between pupils, teachers, staff and parents. Opportunities for debate, reflection and shared decision-making are utilised from the earliest age. Some have felt threatened by this shift of power and responsibility, resisting the idea that decision-making authority should lie with the pupils it is their professional responsibility to instruct. But the positive impact on motivation, responsibility and behaviour among pupils is there to be seen.

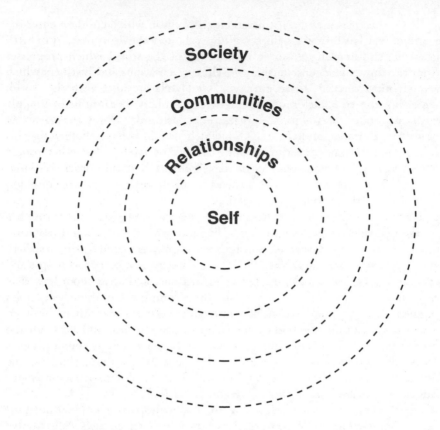

Tools for developing such an ethos include student councils, mission state-ments and behaviour policies which are genuinely the joint responsibility of staff and students. Many schools publish statements about their values and missions, especially as they become more adept at marketing themselves to parents and the outside world. But the ones which truly reflect the ethos of the school, and are understood and owned by every member, from the nursery and reception classes to the headteacher and governors, are those which have been debated and written out by everyone affected by them. For example, Columbia Primary School in London has a behaviour policy, written by its staff and pupils, and posted all over the school. It symbolises a careful process of reflection, discussion and synthesis, which has been actively considered by every member of the school community. As a piece of paper, or a set of rules, it has limited value. But as a contribution to a shared ethos, and to the strength-ening of positive norms of behaviour and the reasons which lie behind them, it is a much greater achievement. It marks a point where rules overlap with norms, and shows that responsibility for sustaining those norms lies with every individual. Some schools have extended this process even further, consulting members of their wider community on their statement of values, involving parents, employers, spiritual leaders and local residents, and extending the values and identity of the school beyond its walls.

So citizenship education begins within the school itself with the recognition that, as a member of the school community, every individual has a part to play in sustaining it. With this part come a series of rights and responsibilities. These can be expressed in formal rules of conduct and in the expectations that a pupil should fulfil in coming to school. But they are most effective when they also become internalised norms governing behaviour and relationships. Young people's ability to take an active part in these processes is strengthened, as in any other form of learning, by practice. It is a common complaint among teachers that when they have given pupils a chance to say what they want, or to make decisions for themselves, they immediately begin to behave irresponsibly, making unrealistic demands, failing to complete the tasks they set themselves, and omitting to set the ground rules they need to accomplish their objectives. But this is hardly surprising when such opportunities are isolated moments in a longer experience characterised by control and the removal of choice.

The capacity to take responsibility for oneself and to recognise the needs and interests of others is acquired progressively, through repeated experience, careful guidance and reflection. Virtue, the exercise of character and the practise of ethical conduct, is built out of experience rather than instilled as a set of rules or abstract values, and, as Aristotle pointed out, such experience comes from active participation in the rules and norms governing an institution or a community. Over time, such experience bears fruit, often in unexpected ways. An example from the primary school mentioned above, Columbia, comes from the interaction of their approach to conflict resolution and their student council. In conflict resolution, the school has been developing a method through which children are encouraged to reflect on their own behaviour and communicate their grievance directly to the peer that they have been fighting or arguing with, rather than submitting their version of a story to a staff member and then being expected to abide by the time-pressed adult's instant judgement of the merits of the case. The student council, meanwhile, has been developing its capacity to identify issues of concern to pupils, and search for solutions and new approaches. The example comes from a growing feeling that lunchtime supervisors, who are not teachers, were not dealing with playground disputes in ways which satisfied pupils. Pupils' expectations had been raised by the new approach to conflict resolution, and the ways in which the lunchtime supervisors dealt with fights and arguments seemed to be out of step. Having identified this issue, members of the student council asked for a meeting and explained the situation. One might expect that, having presented the issue, the children would expect adults in authority to find an appropriate response. In fact they went further, suggesting that the lunchtime supervisors might benefit from some training in conflict resolution, and offering to explain the problems in more detail if necessary. Having listened to the presentation, the chief supervisor considered the matter and agreed that perhaps she and her colleagues could benefit from some training. The results of the exercise included more effective resolution of playground disputes, and a general reduction in instances of fighting and bad behaviour during lunch breaks.

So, learning to be a moral agent, and to be a citizen, begins in the family and the school. But surely citizenship extends beyond these institutions? The goal of citizenship education is to enable young people to develop into active, responsible citizens in the wider world. Schools are the institutions which contain a young person's activity for most of their first two decades, but they also live in the wider world; they are members of numerous communities, and their experiences and sources of learning are far richer and more diverse than school-based learning opportunities, however good those might be. As young people grow into the wider world, it is appropriate to seek opportunities to extend their problem-solving abilities, their concern for others, and their exercise of ethical conduct beyond the school gates.

This can be done in numerous ways, some of which have already been set out above. Without prescribing how this should happen, the analysis suggests three principles:

1   The issues with which young people engage should be ones which matter to them, and which they are responsible for identifying.
2   They should be rooted in aspects of citizenship which are manifested in the *local* environment that young people encounter every day.
3   Learning about citizenship should be both active and practical. It should involve active engagement in practical activities which tackle problems or issues that young people have identified as being important.

Beyond this, the possibilities are almost too numerous to categorise; current examples include raising money for a disabled choir singer and organising for a wheelchair ramp to be built at the church where he practises; a county-wide anti-litter campaign called Green Means Clean, which lobbies local councils, produces information and awareness-raising materials, and advises local groups on strategies to reduce litter and mess; an oral history project in a former coal-mining town, where young people interviewed grandparents and other elders to find out about and record their experiences, and then produced a book based on their interviews; neighbourhood crime-prevention initiatives; campaigns against racism in football, organised with the help of Newcastle United Football Club; and projects to help younger pupils with school-work, supervising after-school clubs and providing peer tutoring and listening services. Journalism projects, like Children's Express, also involve practical citizenship. Children's Express stories involve investigating issues and questions which very often relate young people to wider communities and to society, such as children buying tickets for the National Lottery, or the prejudices surrounding young people with HIV.

It is not possible either to list the full range of projects of this kind, or to define their scope completely. That is part of the point, because they are based on the choices and motivations of young people, rather than being prescribed by adults and professionals. However, we can think about some of their components.

First, they involve collaboration. Organising such projects will always involve contacting people outside the school, asking them for information, advice or help. Working on a project team involves breaking a project down into different tasks, agreeing on who will perform each task, and planning how the different components will come together to achieve the full set of objectives. Participants must establish different roles within a team, under- stand the roles of others, and understand the norms of collaboration. They must also often seek to persuade others that what they are doing is useful, and secure appropriate help from other individuals.

Second, they require young people to set their own goals. Rather than slot- ting into a predefined framework of activity and achievement, participants must define for themselves what counts as an achievement, and then assess how far they have attained it.

Third, the process of deciding what counts as an important issue should also require young people to *reflect* not only on why it is important to them, but also on how it might affect other members of their communities. This is a crucial element of citizenship, and of developing emotional maturity, since it requires empathy and the capacity to appreciate the perspectives of others. It is not an automatic part of the process; it is perfectly possible for young people to decide on an issue which appeals or matters to them, and then rush into doing something about it without really thinking about how it matters to others. But most cases show young people thinking about how they can help other people, as well as pursuing something which interests and motivates them. It is also a component that teachers and other adults can assist with, prompting reflection about what a particular project will mean to others, and encouraging young people to take others' perspectives into account. Moral decision making and citizenship require that an individual can take into account the needs and perspectives of others. Organising and acting in the real world requires young people to confront these perspectives, to compare them with their own, and to examine the ways in which what they do alters or reinforces the perceptions of others. This combination, of practical action, direct experience and reflection, is the foundation of *responsibility*.

What are we aiming for?

Overall, the aim of this kind of activity should be to help young people to understand the public and moral spheres of their lives, to learn to be effective in them, and to help build *trust*. The role of trust in underpinning healthy civil society, as well as economic activity, has become the focus of intense scrutiny in recent years. Perhaps most important is the work of Robert Putnam, an American sociologist who carried out a seminal study of the effectiveness of government institutions in different regions of Italy (Putnam, 1993). His conclusion was that the level of social capital, the shared norms of trust, collaboration, mutual goals and expectations, was a crucial determinant both of the effectiveness of government institutions and of citizens' satisfaction with them. More recently, Francis Fukuyama, in his influential book *Trust* (1995), showed that levels of trust in different societies had a measurable effect on economic performance. In particular, high levels of trust helped facilitate the growth of large-scale economic organisation.

Fukuyama's criterion for success is what he calls the level of 'spontaneous sociability', the capacity to collaborate effectively with people who are relative strangers. Even in relatively prosperous, high-trust communities, the ability to engage with others, establish common goals and collaborate, is crucial to young people's prospects. In more depressed, disadvantaged communities, of which there are a disconcerting number in the UK, this need is even more urgent. Peter Hall's analysis, *Social Capital in Britain* (1997), shows that in comparison with other societies we have sustained relatively high levels of social capital, expressed in terms of membership of civic organisations, voter turn-out and political engagement. But the two major groups for whom this is not the case are young people and worse-off socio-economic groups.

In particular, people under 30 show markedly lower levels of *social trust*, the willingness in general to trust one's fellow citizens, than do older age groups. When combined with the loss of trust in institutions, this is a worrying trend. I would suggest that the opportunity to interact, to collaborate, and to present one's achievements to others in the communities beyond your school, family and immediate peer group is a crucial opportunity for building trust.

One of the deepest historical divides in educational thinking is between the idea that education systems should prepare young people for adult life by controlling them, teaching discipline through domination in order to transfer the knowledge, skills and values which society deems necessary, and the idea, which can be traced back as far as Rousseau, that education is the process by which each individual creates their own reality, flowering spontaneously into the world. This divide has seen some bitter conflicts. But the implication of this analysis is that the dichotomy is false. Without clear knowledge of the values, principles and institutions on which our moral and civic life is founded, young people will not develop the moral fluency they need in order to be responsible moral agents. Understanding authority, history and the value of the past is essential. Being familiar with the framework of rules is also vital. But culture, values and societies all change. Without the opportunity to help shape their own modes of action, to apply values in real-life situations, and to play an appropriate part in making decisions, the risk is that young people will grow up demotivated, disconnected and unable to make a full contribution to their social and political environment. Institutional authority has to compete with a constantly growing range of distractions and alternative pursuits. Young people need the opportunity to develop their own powers of moral reasoning, and their own forms of practical citizenship, in order to take their place in society.

Over time, the kinds of citizenship learning I have described – open-ended, project-based activity which requires young people to

- formulate their goals;
- work as a team to achieve them;
- approach and persuade others whose help or permission they might need; and
- review and present the results of their work

– can support young people in becoming both more sophisticated and more effective citizens. The constellation of contacts, both individual and institutional, which a young person will experience during her formative years would, on the whole, be far broader and richer than those she currently meets through family, friends and school.

As far as these outward-facing activities impact on the life of the school, young people should be able to draw confidence, insight and self-esteem from their activities as members of the school community. Wider citizenship projects help to establish and sustain a network of contacts which can bring significant benefits to educational institutions, giving them access to information and resources and helping to legitimise what they do by making it more transparent.

The practice of citizenship can be described as a connection between the particular and the universal. Through everyday activities such as voting, debating, consulting and working for others, people can connect their lives, their concerns and their abilities to the abstract concepts and beliefs which help to define our civic and political universe – concepts such as democracy and the rule of law, beliefs such as the inviolability of human rights or the importance of treating others with respect. David Perkins has articulated a new way of thinking about our spheres of thought and action which he calls *realm theory* (Perkins, 1995: ch. 5). Each realm, which can be as small as shoe-lace-tying or as large as citizenship, is made up of three major components: Actions, Beliefs and Concepts. The ways in which these three conjoin and interact for a given individual depend on many different factors, but Perkins argues that intelligence should be thought of as the ability to *find your way around* a realm. The challenge for citizenship education, as with any subject, is to find ways of integrating young people's actions, beliefs and conceptual understanding. Ideally, they should be able to grasp the core concepts of citizenship, to connect them to their everyday experience, to reconcile them with their beliefs, and to develop the strength of character and moral fluency to use them consistently. In this chapter I have argued that the most effective way to do this is to bestow sufficient trust on young people to allow them to take *responsibility* for what they do, and for defining their own goals in collaboration with those around them. This requires a leap of faith for adults. But if we want young citizens who are active, motivated and responsible, it is a leap which must be taken. Doing so can help to achieve the right balance between power and authority, between structure and creativity, and between self and other in the realm of citizenship. It can help young people to find ways of expressing themselves within communities, rather than by rejecting their values and norms. Perhaps most importantly, it can boost their readiness to help solve the social and political challenges of the future.

The twentieth century has seen a gradual extension of the democratic franchise to most of the adult population. The growing debate over children's rights reminds us that children and young people are the major group who, so far, have been excluded from this process. If, as is already beginning to happen, individual rights are to be extended to children, then surely an appropriate accompaniment to this process is to extend the opportunity to take responsibility as well. Rights without responsibility can be corrosive, and children can unfortunately be as adept as any adult at using their formal rights to make false claims, either maliciously or instrumentally, for their own gain. A sustainable balance between self and other, between right and responsibility, can only be achieved if young people are allowed a full part in defining agendas, in articulating their concerns, and in helping to find solutions.

An agenda for citizenship and moral education

A citizenship education agenda, based on this analysis, would include several strands of activity.

First, there is the job of specifying a common core of knowledge, concepts and understanding central to citizenship. This would include:

- historical knowledge of political and legal institutions;
- concepts such as democracy, the state, freedom, obligation and civil society;
- alternative theories of citizenship;
- practical understanding of the constitution and how it works, the processes of political decision-making, and the routes through which citizens (or subjects) can contribute to such processes, at both national and local levels.

Such a core would be defined through the design of the formal curriculum, and the use of subject-specific opportunities for teaching and learning and the specification of a series of learning outcomes. It is perhaps the most straightforward part of the task given to the Advisory Group on Citizenship Education established by David Blunkett, then Secretary of State for Education, in 1997.

It is very important to note, however, that such specification is only a starting point. By itself it would have very little impact on young people's capacity to become active, responsible, citizens, apart from those who manage to apply the formal knowledge gained from the curriculum in contexts other than the classroom.

Second, there must be opportunities for students to develop their understanding of moral rules and principles, and to develop their capacity for moral reasoning. These opportunities might come from dedicated lesson time, perhaps in Personal, Social and Health Education, from relevant National Curriculum subjects such as religious education, or from teachers using opportunities as and when they arise. Teachers are often concerned about taking this on as an explicit responsibility, for two reasons. Many feel it inappropriate for teachers to teach morality in a prescriptive way, because of an admirable wish not to impose their own moral perspectives on their students. Many others are concerned about the overcrowding of the curriculum. However, developing this kind of understanding and fluency is essential for developing the capacity to be a responsible, articulate, effective moral agent. If there is one lesson which emerges from Robert Coles's influential essay *The Moral Intelligence of Children* (1997), it is the fact that children and young people constantly pick up and absorb messages about morality from the behaviour of the adults around them. Formal or explicit teaching of morality does not take place in a vacuum, but in the complex moral and social context of people's everyday lives. One of the most important tools for developing young people's capacity for moral reasoning is the opportunity to discuss conflicts, issues and dilemmas which arise from day to day.

Again, this is difficult to timetable, but not impossible. Finding opportunities to plan learning about moral rules and principles helps to create a clearer foundation for discussing morality when the opportunity arises, and encouraging students to think and act morally. Opportunities for reflection and discussion can be maximised, using a range of techniques such as Jenny Mosley's 'Circle Time' and the resources provided by organisations mentioned earlier. Ivor Crewe's research for the Citizenship Foundation found that nearly 80 per cent of pupils aged 15–16 said they engage in very little discussion at all of public issues, including matters of public concern in their local communities. More than half reported that they never, or only rarely, had such discussions with their teachers. Eighty per cent said that they did not talk about these matters during after-school activities either. Discussion of what has been learned at the end of lessons emerges as one of the key opportunities for underpinning student understanding from Jean Rudduck's study of the role of pupils in school improvement (Rudduck *et al.*, 1996). Creating more opportunities for such discussion seems to be an urgent priority.

This kind of discussion and development also strengthens the potential for young people to take active responsibility for themselves and those around them within the school community. Tools for developing this kind of activity include pupil councils, behaviour policies, school newspapers, public hearings and debates. They also include trusting students with responsibility for peer education and for feedback on the ways in which schools try to deliver the curriculum. Wherever possible, pupils should have the opportunity to define the subject and format of such deliberation, and to follow it up with practical initiatives. Opportunities to hear from people beyond the school – parents, governors, employers, religious leaders and so on, and to discuss matters of interest and concern with them, play an important part in this process.

The third major part of the agenda focuses on opportunities for young people to pursue their understanding of morality and citizenship beyond the school gates. This is often more difficult and complex for schools, but in principle there is no reason why each child should not be able to enrol in a number of different learning organisations and projects, with the school acting as broker and monitor. Developing this kind of opportunity casts the school in a new role, that of the *neighbourhood learning centre*. While still playing a central role in the provision of learning opportunities, the school itself acts as a focus, or hub, for a range of activities and relationships spread across its local communities. In the later years of primary school, and certainly throughout the secondary years, young people should be able to take opportunities for self-organised learning, in small, project-based teams, negotiating, defining and refining their goals, allocating roles and responsibilities, identifying the people and institutions who can help to accomplish their objectives. This is challenging for schools, although every school has a set of relationships and connections with its local communities. Resources which can help include the management tools and framework developed by Pathways to Adult Life. Appointing a member of staff as school–community coordinator can also be an important step. This person takes on a role of brokerage and liaison, and of giving overall shape and clarity to the range of external relationships that a school has with the outside world.

Bringing these activities and opportunities together in coherent ways is very difficult. It implies a different kind of coordination and integration from those which many people in education are used to. Development strategies in schools are contained within curriculum guidance, programmes of study, individual departments and subjects. Learning morality and citizenship is a different kind of challenge. It requires some change to the curriculum, but just as important is the way in which opportunities for learning are distributed across the life of a school, and extended outwards into the community which surrounds it. Ethos and culture, the ideas, messages and norms which infuse the atmosphere of any organisation, are crucially important. The task is to make the messages and learning opportunities coherent across these diverse systems and practices, and to synthesise formal and abstract knowledge with the practical, immediate experience of each young person.

7

TACKLING UNDERACHIEVEMENT

Educational underachievement has become one of our dominant social concerns, deeply connected to debates over economic competitiveness, juvenile crime, family breakdown, the cost of welfare provision and social cohesion. Looking at the attainment statistics of the formal education sector, there is a clearly identifiable problem. But it runs deeper than mere levels of qualification. Educational failure is strongly linked to underachievement in wider spheres of life: the labour market, relationships and civic engagement. This is why it matters so much: not just for its economic costs, but because effective learning is the central route to a more enriched, fulfilling and integrated life for individuals, and a higher quality of life for all.

This chapter examines the main dimensions of underachievement. I argue that, while wider social and economic processes are fundamental to young people's chances – poverty and social exclusion do matter – these problems have often been exacerbated by the ways in which the education system works. I then examine the role that active learning can play in helping to raise achievement, by motivating and broadening the horizons of young people who could otherwise face lives of passivity, exclusion and bringing disruption to others. Many of the examples and lessons I present are based outside of mainstream schooling. For the young people involved, this is often part of their attraction. However, I argue that there are lessons for mainstream education to be learned from these examples. The final part of the chapter examines the problem of bringing together the wide-ranging resources and systems that can be used to draw out the potential of disaffected and underachieving young people.

Social exclusion inhibits young people's chances of achievement, not just because of their economic disadvantage, but because of the social and cultural isolation that it imposes on them. Informal social networks, which provide information, support, positive examples and role models, are often absent from the lives of young people who do not fulfil their educational potential. Schools often unintentionally entrench this isolation by failing to make themselves open to the wide range of support and influence which lie untapped in their local communities. Drawing on these resources, and using them to develop more flexible systems of provision for individual students, is one of the primary routes to raising achievement and equipping young people for the challenges and opportunities of adult life. As with citizenship, the argument implies that if we want to achieve a real shift in the chances of all young people, focusing only on what happens *inside* schools is misguided. Instead, we should be drawing in the fullest possible range of resources from outside the school gate, and creating delivery systems which can provide individualised packages of support to each young person.

The facts are clear. While attainment at the top end of the range has risen steadily, a large minority of young people at the other end of the scale are not managing to keep up. The Basic Skills Agency reported that up to 15 per cent of 21-year-olds had limited literacy skills, and 20 per cent had limited mathematical competence. Four out of ten 16-year-olds starting further education require extra help with basic skills. Almost one in ten 16-year-olds still leaves school without qualifications. There is a worrying gap between the performance of girls and boys. This is clearest at GCSE level but it is also increasingly the case for A levels, where attainment has risen for all young people since 1985, but where girls have improved faster than boys. Boys also outnumber girls by two to one in schools for children with learning difficulties, and there are six boys for every girl in special units for those with behavioural problems. Surveys have found that boys are also twice as likely to truant, ignore homework and misbehave in lessons. Qualitative research by Demos has found the attitudes of many young unemployed men towards education to be at best ambivalent, and often openly hostile (Bentley, 1996).

The consequences of such early failure can be disastrous. Educational failure is closely correlated with insecure labour market status and long-term unemployment, lower success rates in marital and family relationships, criminal behaviour and narrower participation in civil society through leisure, membership of associations and voluntary organisations, and social networks.

In recent years a worrying rise in permanent exclusions from school has also appeared. In 1990/1, 2,910 pupils in English schools were excluded. By 1994/5 this figure had risen to 12,458 (Parsons, 1996). Since then the problem has become a priority for government, investigated by the Social Exclusion Unit, and a new priority for the education service. Many factors are at work, not least the importance of guaranteeing teacher safety and ensuring that other students do not have their education disrupted. However, there is also concern that the rise in exclusions is part of a wider problem of 'dumping', where public agencies or service providers cease taking responsibility for a particular client group without responsibility for those clients being fully taken on by another agency. Currently, around two-thirds of pupils permanently excluded do not find their way back into full-time education. Concern that this situation may be exacerbated by the indicators used to measure the performance of schools is already high. Because the framework of league tables uses information based on attainment at the higher end of the scale – GCSEs achieved at grades A–C – there is an incentive for schools to boost their averages by excluding troublesome pupils who are unlikely to contribute positively to league-table performance. Tim Brighouse, Chief Education Officer of Birmingham, has estimated that for every pupil permanently excluded there at least three others of school age who are not in school, an estimate which implies that some 10 per cent of young people are not receiving a school education.

Schools do not bear sole responsibility for these problems. But the education system should treat the needs of all its pupils equally, and find ways of providing for those who cannot cope with the everyday demands of conventional schooling. Crucially, it must work to *prevent* such problems arising in the future. Schools will only be able to do this in partnership with a wide range of other players, including young people themselves.

The dimensions of underachievement

Emotional development: a foundation of achievement

The first dimension of underachievement is a failure of basic personal and social competence. Pupils who are able to thrive in a school environment and meet the expectations of their teachers and peers have a set of underlying personal characteristics which are a foundation of educational achievement. The most influential setting for the development of these characteristics is the family, the crucible of almost all effective learning in any society. Volumes of research have shown that parenting and family environment are the most significant factors affecting educational performance (for a summary, see Alexander, 1997). Family and informal social relationships, from an early age, are the basis of the social competence which allows us to interact, to communicate and to collaborate with others. Schools should, and often do, continue to develop these skills and capacities, which include self-awareness, self-esteem, empathy, persistence, the abilities to control and draw upon one's emotions, to follow rules and to defer gratification. They make up much of Gardner's interpersonal and intrapersonal intelligence (Gardner, 1983).

For young people whose emotional intelligence is underdeveloped, coping with the demands, expectations, conflicts and dilemmas of everyday school life is a major challenge. Their distress, boredom or confusion are often expressed as bad behaviour, disaffection and withdrawal. Without this kind of nascent personal capacity, it is simply unrealistic to expect that young people will accept or be able to cope with the demands that school inevitably places on them.

The results of this emotional underdevelopment are predictable and cumulative. They can be expressed through weaknesses of character: proneness to following others in bad behaviour, inability to cope with managing learning and personal organisation, excessive aggression and bullying, and anxiety and lack of self-confidence. They combine with weak literacy and numeracy to exacerbate the difficulties that many children face in coping with school, especially after the transition from primary to secondary. All of these are recognisable, especially for boys, among young people who fail at school, among those who leave with few qualifications and little appetite for further education, and among those who are involved in crime, persistent truancy and school exclusion.

Social exclusion and network poverty

The second major dimension of underachievement springs from forms of geographical, economic and social disadvantage. Over the last two decades, the social geography of the UK has become more polarised, with wealth and poverty increasingly concentrated in separate areas (Power, 1995). This is partly because of the changing employment structure of the UK economy and the fact that areas heavily dependent upon a relatively narrow industrial base, such as coal-mining villages, have suffered disproportionately from structural changes in the economy. It is also partly a result of general population change, and the gravitation of upwardly mobile groups towards areas such as the southeast of England. It is also partly due to the effects of government policies in fields such as social security and housing, which have helped to produce a 'residualisation' effect in many areas of council housing, leading to greater concentration of households with low incomes, dependent upon state benefits and less likely than most to include an adult earner. The wealthiest one-fifth of the population now live in wards where they are more than two-and-a-half times less likely to be out of work than the least fortunate (Dorling, 1996). One estimate puts the number of large, hard-to-let council housing estates at 2,000 (Taylor, 1995). Not surprisingly, secondary schools serving such estates perform far worse than the national average: one in four children gets no GCSEs, compared to one in twenty nationwide, and truanting in such schools is four times the national average. In many of these estates the majority of adults of working age are economically inactive. The support available to young people for learning and education are severely constrained by a lack of financial resources, of informal learning opportunities, and of role models and cultural support.

Data on changes in attainment by area since 1988 provide clear evidence of the overall effects that these factors help produce. Since the Education Reform Act and the introduction of the GCSE in 1988 there has been a rapid increase in the achievement of qualifications, and in staying-on rates. But there are clear differences between advantaged and disadvantaged areas. In the 25 per cent of local authorities with the highest proportion of families in lower socio-economic groups, the full-time participation rate for 17-year-olds has risen from 30 per cent in 1988 to 48 per cent in 1995, while in the 25 per cent of areas with most families in higher socio-economic groups, the rate rose from 39 per cent to 66 per cent. The pattern for GCSE passes is the same. In the most disadvantaged areas the number passing five GSCEs at A–C rose from just under 20 per cent in 1988 to 32 per cent in 1995. For more advantaged areas the change was from just under 30 per cent to 48 per cent (Smith *et al.*, 1997). The rate of improvement in better-off areas has been markedly higher. Social and economic disadvantage produce a potent set of barriers to educational success.

More traditional analyses of the effects of poverty have focused on material disadvantage, emphasising the crucial importance of low income, poor material conditions and lack of adequate physical resources, in inhibiting the life-chances and performance of individuals and families. The debate has shifted, however, in recent years towards a broader conception of social exclusion, one that emphasises the dynamic processes of exclusion which perpetuate and deepen conditions of multiple deprivation. While emphasising the importance of economic and material disadvantage, the social exclusion debate has also drawn attention to the processes of cultural, political and social marginalisation which accompany them (Demos, 1997a). The role of cultural norms and expectations, far harder to measure, analyse and interpret than economic conditions, is none the less taken increasingly seriously. Education is no exception: moves to increase parental involvement, emphasis on the ethos and values of schools and colleges, and efforts to involve employers and other groups more actively in education, all reflect a growing understanding that changing norms and expectations is crucial to helping transform the prospects of the truly disadvantaged. The romantic image, still strongly pervasive, of the changes in aspiration, awareness and attainment that can be brought about by an inspirational teacher is important. It reflects the ability of many teachers and schools to make a dramatic difference to their pupils' lives. But it is inadequate, because it does not address the systemic nature of the underachievement we see around us. It relies on the myth that individuals can buck the system and transform their destiny, but implicitly ignores the fact that these individuals are the exception. Their ability to catch the imagination relies on the fact that they leave many others, with similar potential for achievement, behind.

When we think about disadvantage, we are used to thinking about individuals and institutions, but not so used to thinking about what lies in between. We might, for example, think about the characteristics of a given person – her level of knowledge, motivation, access to information, family support and so on. Or we might think about her access to institutions: her ability to sustain a school career, to win a place at university or college, or on a training scheme. We would be concerned about her personal development, and about her access to formal, institutionally defined opportunities. This kind of thinking is important, but it misses one of the most influential factors influencing young people's access to information and opportunity: social networks.

It is a long-held maxim that it's not what you know but who you know that matters in achieving what you want. But, as Perri 6 (1997) has recently pointed out, it is not only who you know, but also *how you know them*, that matters. The type of social network that we have, the number of people that we know, and the ways in which we know them, help to define membership of the different socio-economic groups. The difference between the social networks of different socio-economic classes is well established in social science. As Peter A Hall puts it,

> The patterns of informal sociability of the working class are more likely than those of the middle class to revolve around close contacts with kin and a small set of friends all of whom are relatively connected to each other. On the whole, these are likely to be friends of long standing, often old school friends. By contrast, the social networks of the middle class tend to be much more extensive and diverse. They are likely to see twice as many colleagues from work fairly regularly outside the workplace; they draw their friends from a more diverse range of sources and those friends are often not closely connected to each other. Perhaps surprisingly, those in the middle class are also likely to know twice as many of their neighbours fairly well than do those in the working class; and much smaller numbers suffer from a complete absence of social support. Finally those in the middle class seem less likely to limit their interaction with friends to a particular sphere of activity in favour of engaging them in multiple kinds of endeavours.
>
> (Hall, 1997)

Twenty-five years ago American sociologist Mark Granovetter (1973) showed that people not only got their jobs by exercising their contacts, but that the contacts which are most valuable are not the close, strong ties of family and intimate friends, but those with whom an individual has relatively weak ties: former colleagues, acquaintances and friends of friends. These weak ties, which any middle-class child will grow up with, are a crucial determinant of life-chances. They are, I would suggest, a powerful factor contributing to the correlation between the level of parental education and the likelihood of a child reaching the same level (Ermisch and Francesconi, 1997). Successive studies have shown the importance of networks. Studies of unemployment, in particular, have found that the level of informal socialisation and contact with people beyond an individual's immediate circle of family and friends increases the likelihood of finding work. Professor Ronald Burt of Chicago University has shown that weak ties within and between business organisations enhance both the effectiveness of an individual worker and the capacity of an organisation to maximise the value of the knowledge that its employees and associates possess. Such ties are developed entrepreneurially and informally – through phone calls, lunches, chance meetings and social occasions – but their business value can be measured in hard cash terms. One of the best-known scholars of American urban ghetto poverty, Harvard professor William Julius

Wilson, argues forcefully that one of the principal determinants of prolonged disadvantage and worklessness in American ghetto neighbourhoods is the disappearance from such communities of thriving adults who helped connect those communities to the wider world. These adults acted as role models, but also as sources of information and opportunity: about employers, educational openings, civic and leisure-based activities (Wilson, 1996). Networks, even though they are fluid, informal, hard to map and constantly shifting, matter enormously.

The importance of this analysis for education should be obvious. Exposure to a range of positive examples, potential role models and sources of advice and information, is often essential for a young person to realise her full potential. Schools do provide some of these kinds of opportunities, but for many young people living in disadvantaged neighbourhoods and housing estates, teachers, social and youth workers and police officers are often the only working adult role models that they encounter on a regular basis. In such communities, these representatives of official authority are often profoundly distrusted. Educational success and effort, unfortunately, can also be discouraged and disparaged in communities where these are unfamiliar phenomena. In the 1950s, Peter Wilmott and Michael Young, in their seminal study *Family and Kinship in East London* (Young and Wilmott, 1962), reported the difficulties faced by working-class children who won a scholarship to Grammar School: the taunts that they faced from their peers for wearing school uniform, and the reluctance and hostility of parents towards their children entering an unfamiliar social and educational environment. Such discouragement still takes place today. Exposure to a wide range of positive role models, informal support and advice is a crucial component of the struggle to broaden the horizons and facilitate the success of disadvantaged children.

Motivation

Finally, and intimately connected to the first two dimensions of underachievement, is the problem of motivation. There is considerable evidence to show that many young people are often bored by school. Although the largest survey of pupils' attitudes shows that 90 per cent are happy with their school, at least 15 per cent of 14–15-year-olds in the same survey admitted to truanting 'sometimes' or 'often'. A similar proportion are disrupting their lessons and other pupils on a regular basis. It is easy to dismiss the complaints of pupils as being inconsistent, badly thought through, or an inevitable product of adolescence. But as Michael Barber has convincingly argued (1996), some of the criticisms are both consistent and penetrating. Among the most important are the complaints that teachers fail to treat pupils with proper respect, that lessons are too often boring, and that young people do not have sufficient influence over where, when or how they learn. The Keele University survey (Centre for Successful Schools, 1994) found 60 per cent of pupils agreeing that they 'count the minutes to the end of lessons', more than one-fifth believing that their work is boring, over 40 per cent saying that lessons are too long, and almost one-third contending that they would rather not go to school. A more recent survey by the Campaign for Learning found an alarmingly high proportion of 14-, 15- and 16-year-olds claiming that poor teaching was a significant barrier to doing well at school. Such lack of motivation is cause for concern in itself. But when combined with the remarkably consistent criticism that pupils are not respected or sufficiently involved in feedback and planning of their own learning, it becomes a powerful problem. Among the criticisms levelled by pupils in the Keele survey were:

> The teachers never explain anything, they're always on people's backs like that's wrong, that's pathetic, you're thick.

> Teachers favour the more intelligent students in our class and don't help us less intelligent students enough . . .

> Basically we are patronised and treated as though we are little kids.

> The teachers don't even try to understand us.

The criticisms that education fails to stimulate, that teachers do not earn their authority, and that pupils are rarely allowed to play a full part in contributing to and taking responsibility for learning in school, are telling. One can imagine the same complaints stretching back centuries, although perhaps never before have those in authority been so prepared to listen. What seems to have changed, however, is the wider context for these attitudes and criticisms. We have already examined some of the changes in social and institutional trust which have taken place in the UK over the last twenty years or so. Trust in institutions, and generalised social trust, are lowest among young people. The young are less prepared to follow rules unconditionally, to follow instructions blindly, and to accept received wisdom without questioning and testing it for themselves. For young people who are getting into trouble from an early age, who are easily distracted, and who suffer from a lack of family support, there is even less reason to trust and accept what those in authority say. For them in particular, there is a growing disjunction between the *power* of adults and institutions, and their *authority*.

Alongside these changes is the growth of *distractions*. Young people have a far wider range of distractions and alternative pursuits on offer than ever before. The growth of multi- and mass media, including computer games, pop music and the internet, as well as the proliferation of retail and consumer goods, and leisure activities and facilities, means that young people choose between an increasingly wide range of alternatives. While some freedoms, such as independent mobility, have reduced for children, they have inherited far more than previous generations, and this inevitably affects their evaluation of activities which are compulsory, especially the experience of school. Information is accessible in ways which older people are still struggling to get to grips with, while the young, more often than not, take to them like ducks to water. Educational institutions must compete with a dazzling array of alternative information, distractions, and sources of motivation and example. But the basic ways in which we deliver education have barely changed. David Hargreaves once compared the average school day to 'seven very dull television programmes which cannot be switched off'.

One of the most familiar responses to this change is to bemoan it. The growth in volume of available information, and the growing pace of innovation in products and services, does not necessarily mean that their quality is adequate. The rise of information services is constituted partly by the growth of 'infotainment', where knowledge and information are presented in easily digestible chunks with limited potential for deepening knowledge and understanding, and also by 'irritainment', whose value is at best marginal and at worst an irritating and worthless distraction. But whether we celebrate or bemoan it, this change is already happening, and will continue to engulf us.

Whether or not we think that teachers ought, in principle, to have to compete with such influences on their pupils' attention, they already do. Even though education to age 16 is compulsory, it is already all too easy to opt out, even while you are still going through the motions of attending lessons. We are beginning to recognise that being faced by such a barrage of information requires a new set of skills or competences. We are less good at recognising that children and young people are already developing them on their own, often alongside those they might gain from formal education. As consumers of goods, services and information, many young people are already highly sophisticated and sceptical agents. Cutting through marketing hype, choosing a magazine or a new pair of jeans, or finding relevant product information, all involve a capacity to sift through volumes of information, select what is appropriate, and match it to your needs or preferences. Such sensitivity to the material with which they are presented is often highly developed among young people, even if the material they select is not what adults would most like them to be absorbing. They are also likely to be applying this kind of sophisticated analysis to the messages and material with which they are presented at school, strengthening what Michael Barber (1996) has called their 'unerring eye for hypocrisy', and reducing their threshold of tolerance for materials and teaching which are dull or inconsistent.

These three dimensions of underachievement pose a great challenge. Finding ways to overcome structural and spatial disadvantage, develop the basic social and emotional competence of at-risk young people, and use the sources of effective motivation so that they contribute to effective learning, are huge tasks. How can 'active learning' contribute?

First, we must acknowledge that solutions to such complex problems will be as complex as the factors which cause them. There are no quick fixes. Second, a huge amount is already being done, and the following analysis does not seek to downplay or marginalise the work of dedicated teachers, parents, social and youth workers, probation officers and many others.

Places to learn

One of the most consistent responses from young people, when they are asked what they want, is the demand for safe, enjoyable places to go. Often this amounts to a place in which to pursue social and leisure activities – the traditionally conceived youth club setting, where young people can meet, talk, play games and take part in organised activities. For the most difficult young people, these are places from which they are often excluded, for the same reasons as they are likely to be excluded from school. But one tool used to increasing effect in tackling underachievement and low expectations among young people is to provide places and resources in which they can *learn* in their own time. It might seem like common sense, but for many the opportunity to use a quiet, relaxed, well-equipped centre to pursue learning which they themselves have chosen to undertake is a rare one. Home environments can be isolating, discouraging or distracting. Schools and colleges, which are there to support learning, are often open for limited times, and under quite stringent conditions – providing timetabled learning which is scheduled and largely controlled by teachers and administrators rather than by learners. The provision of a friendly, supportive environment in which to learn, either alone or in groups, with support available when requested but not forced on young people, can be especially valuable for those who have difficulty coping with the more demanding setting of the school day. This is a key assumption lying behind the Prince's Trust Study Support initiative; when learning is voluntary, but encouraged and supported, it can take on new meaning and significance, and help to enhance motivation, self-esteem and awareness, and educational attainment.

The Prince's Trust initiative involves collaboration between a wide range of different partners: schools, LEAs, TECs, Youth Services and other voluntary organisations. The results from the centres with which the Trust has worked since 1991 have already shown that they are an important investment – reducing juvenile crime and truancy rates, improving exam results and supporting the achievement of vocational and other qualifications. But the qualitative results – shared achievement, motivation, satisfaction, and the development of learning skills – which will stay with young people beyond their years in formal education, are just as important. Many other agencies also provide this kind of support. Opening up spaces for learning, in which the atmosphere bridges a gap between formal, structured learning and informal, unorganised, unsupervised and unsupported activity is a crucial foundation for attracting those at risk of underachieving towards purposeful, self-motivated learning, and towards realising the full benefits of participation in formal education.

Learning off-site

For some young people, even crossing the threshold of a 'learning centre' can be too much. For a range of reasons, they are not ready to meet the conditions of participation. But because effective learning can take place in many and varied contexts, it is possible for them to engage in positive learning activities and relationships almost wherever they are. Again, the starting point is trusting relationships. Many committed and imaginative practitioners are succeeding in engaging young people who, from an institutional perspective, might well be thought of as beyond reach. Very often this comes under the banner of detached youth work. Successful projects are run by a wide range of agencies, and involve less formalised activities, with lower threshold conditions, more flexibility, and an even greater recognition of the need to begin from where young people *are*, rather than where others would want or expect them to be. The aim of such projects is to engage young people in dialogue and positive activities, to reduce behaviours which increase risks of unemployment, problem drug use and crime, and to assist young people in moving towards greater independence and integration into the common life of their communities.

One focus of such activities, rather than being the content of learning and its relationship to formal educational curricula (although content is crucial as well), is to develop the qualities and capacities which underpin effective self-direction and participation in society: self-awareness, self-esteem, communication skills, motivation, personal discipline and relationships. They seek to match the capacities, potential and real interests of their participants with challenges and activities which are realistic, fulfilling and developmental. Matching the two requires a careful process of negotiation and a degree of openness and accessibility which is not always found in educational institutions.

Examples include the Youth Works Programme, developed collaboratively by Crime Concern and the Groundwork Trust, which offers activities and support aimed at crime prevention for young people on depressed housing estates. The presence of a skilled youth worker, whose task is to establish contact and trust with young people on the estates, to provide purposeful and enjoyable activities, to encourage them to use initiative and imagination in responding to problems of crime and vandalism, has helped to produce positive outcomes for individual young people and for the estates as a whole. The success depends crucially on establishing networks of collaboration and trust among those on the estate, and acting as an agent of connection between the young people's aspirations, interests and experience, and opportunities for extending them through activities which are not harmful.

Such activities include partnerships against vandalism and car crime, visits to places of interest to young people, a range of estate-based activities. Workers who have established trusting day-to-day relationships with young people are also able to act as an important source of information and reference, enabling young people to access facilities and entitlements which they may not have the personal resources to find and make use of by themselves. As such, they act as a bridge between the immediate context in which young people operate, and the services, rules and agencies which shape their wider environment.

The use of detached and site-based youth work as a horizontally organised, multi-disciplinary approach to reaching disaffected young people has also been developed through the Youth Works NE strategy. Though it shares the same name, it is a separate initiative from the Youth Works estate projects mentioned above. Comprising fourteen separate agencies, its aim is to develop understanding of best practice in working with disaffected young people, and a holistic framework for developing and managing such practice. Once again, the approach involves establishing trusting relationships with young people in their own local environment, encouraging them to take responsibility for their lives and their actions and to explore issues affecting their lives. The project has produced a body of research and practice which goes a long way towards the kind of preventive, multi-disciplinary management framework needed effectively to serve marginalised young people, a series of resource packs which give young people a structure through which to explore such issues as drugs and crime, and the Key Fund, a grant-making fund to which groups of young people can apply to pursue projects which they have planned with the support of youth workers. Young people are involved in making grant decisions, and the fund has won several awards for its innovative and responsible role in extending opportunities to and encouraging successful collaboration among young people.

Other examples abound, including work by Save the Children Fund, Fairbridge, the Weston Spirit, Youth at Risk and NACRO. Their focus on contact, trust and relationship-building is a basis on which meaningful connections can be established between young people at risk and wider society. Using these relationships to support effective learning depends on a range of other factors.

Expanding horizons

As well as creating attractive, accessible places to learn, taking young people away from their normal environment can be an important means of confronting risky behaviour, sparking energy and enthusiasm, and encouraging achievement. Residential courses are consistently reported as one of the most popular activities by young people. For those from deprived backgrounds, they are often opportunities to travel further than they have ever done before, and to find out about the world beyond their immediate neighbourhood. Outward Bound or adventure activities also challenge young people to draw fully on their resources of knowledge, motivation and physical strength, and work closely with others to achieve. Just as important, being away from your normal circumstances, in a new environment where there is a focus on reflection, personal development and self-awareness, can encourage young people to think more deeply about themselves, their goals in life, and the barriers to achieving them. One of the leading providers of such activities is Brathay Hall, an adventure centre which has been active in the youth development field for more than fifty years, and which works with a wide range of partners including local authorities and young offenders agencies. Many other providers of learning opportunities also make use of residentials, including the Dalston Youth Project, Prince's Trust Volunteers, Duke of Edinburgh Award, Youth Clubs UK and the Weston Spirit.

One particularly powerful example is Youth at Risk, an organisation founded in 1992 with the aim of giving young people with chronic problems an opportunity to begin a new, more positive life-course. Youth at Risk works closely with Brathay Hall, and near the beginning of its nine-month programme it takes participants on an intensive, week-long, adventure-based residential course, which involves the young participants, professional workers and community volunteers in long days of outdoor team exercises and group sessions which aim to build trust, overcome some of the barriers to achievement, and develop self-awareness and self-esteem. As an illustration of what can be achieved, Youth at Risk is powerful because it works with some of the rawest and most difficult young people – repeat offenders, drug addicts, those in local authority care – who often have huge problems to overcome. The residential courses are the beginning of a much longer period of follow-up support and activity, which include matching young people with individual mentors, or Committed Partners.

The results are often positive, as the comments of those involved testify:

> What I have learned from Youth at Risk is control . . . keep your chin up – and like If before, if the shit hits the fan – keep on! Don't give up or you'll be letting yourself down!

> My advice to me is that I can do better!

> You have given me back a son that I am very proud of.

> If you want to change your future only you can do it.

Other projects take young people even further afield, often through international exchange schemes which can help to lift the sights of young people and show them how much there is to learn, and also what they can offer to others, both abroad and in their home lives. Children's Express has recently begun exchanges with its sister bureaux in America, sending young editors to

Washington DC for summer placements and receiving young American volunteers in London. Youth Charter for Sport has organised exchanges between young people in Manchester and those in Los Angeles and Johannesburg, to meet, discuss the problems of gang culture, crime and violence, and bring their experiences back to the challenges that they face at home.

A striking example from the United States is Project HIP-HOP (Highways into the Past: History, Organising and Power), which seeks to create ties between young people of different ethnicity, life experience and educational background by taking them on a journey through the US Southern states to investigate the history of the Civil Rights movement. By visiting the sites of conflict, museums and political centres, meeting people who have been involved in the Civil Rights struggle and sharing their experiences, young people from American cities are encouraged to connect their different identities and cultures to the past, and to find new ways of understanding the present. While on the journey, the students are also responsible for deciding and enforcing their own collective norms of behaviour, as well as for helping to plan their activities and learning. The journey is followed by peer outreach programmes, presentations, and community-based projects which encourage other young people to become involved in understanding their history and in taking active responsibility for combating racism and helping to create 'a society in which all are considered of equal worth and have genuine equal opportunity'. Veterans of the project have also travelled to South Africa to witness the birth of the new democratic constitution, and to learn about the mass social movements which helped to bring about change.

Immersion

New practice from around the country also shows that it is possible to accelerate learning by applying new techniques for teaching and learning in circumstances different from the average school day. One pioneer of such practice is the University of the First Age (UFA) in Birmingham, which works to extend and enrich young people's learning in partnership with their schools and local communities. It offers vacation courses in a range of subjects, and takes a broad, interest-led approach to learning based in part on Howard Gardner's (1993) theory of multiple intelligences. The combination of enthusiasm, immersion for long periods of time, and multi-sensory learning – for example using music and dance to teach maths – has already helped to boost the achievement of the young people who took part in its pilot stages. As well as its focus on widening the range of ways in which school subjects can effectively be learned, the UFA emphasises individual reflection and recording of learning, encouraging pupils to take personal responsibility for their progress. The project also builds active use of information technology into the process, providing software and internet connections as resources for tutors and pupils, and supporting them to use them fully in the quest for learning.

Summer courses are followed up by distance learning programmes, where pupils communicate with their tutors by fax and email and work on material brought together in distance learning packs. The UFA shows that learning can be made more enjoyable and effective by bringing a wider range of resources and approaches to the process, and emphasising the active involvement of the individual learner, rather than their place in the routines and methods of institutions. In this sense it is helping to lift education from its place inside institutions, and bring the resources of multiple institutions and many different people into the service of individual, self-directed learners.

The UFA, which has only been running for two years, has already created strong ripple effects. Individual schools in Birmingham are beginning to set up accelerated learning programmes. The Tower Hamlets Summer University worked with UFA in 1997 to establish accelerated language programmes for students with English as a second language.

Comments from UFA tutors and students help to illuminate some of its differences from conventional schooling.

> At school we are told what to study. I like this class because it is my choice, and if I didn't like it, it would be my mistake.

> When I go back to school I might find that these new ways of learning and remembering help me, so I'll use them when I'm doing my homework and in class.

> In school we suppress the energy of the students, here we use it – this makes all the difference.
>
> (tutor)

> I realise now that building in early opportunities for success can make all the difference to the levels of motivation and therefore the quality of learning.
>
> (tutor)

> I have seen the other side of maths.

Making the most of culture

We understand culture in different ways, and identify ourselves in relation to cultural norms and beliefs with varying degrees of self-awareness. The world of public services and policy-making has had a fairly unsophisticated view of culture, understanding it in terms of the fixed and constant, or the rapidly changing and unpredictable. Only recently has a new view emerged of any coherence: that it should be a specific aim of government policy to induce and encourage cultural change which reduces risks and enhances opportunities for healthy, fulfilling, productive lives (6, 1997a). With this view comes a recognition that the tools of cultural change are often subtle and complex, depending upon the beliefs and norms not just of the population in question, but also of those at the front line of service delivery – individual practitioners – alongside those of policy-makers, senior administrators and strategists.

This resistance to accepting the role of culture in government services is less strong in education than in other policy areas, because the importance of culture is more self-evident. Part of the basic function of education is to pass on a body of inherited cultural values, beliefs and practices to the younger generation, even if the appropriate values and beliefs are disputed. Equally, the importance of culture to the success of education, the extent to which it is actively supported by parents and others in the community, the esteem in which education and educators are held by the wider society, are self-evidently important to the effectiveness of education and the quality of learning.

None the less, the extent to which culture is used as a source of strength, motivation and reinforcement of educational achievement, at individual school level, is still insufficient.

The reasons for this are complex, but possible to analyse. First, there is the problem of generations – teachers are often much older than their pupils, and often feel out of touch with the strongest cultural forces acting on the younger generation. Second, an emphasis on creating an appropriate, self-contained, institutional culture, and strong belief in a set of educational values, often leads to a deep implicit assumption that many cultural influences are erroneous and distract young people from what they should really be learning. This belief leads educators to try and block out culture from the task in hand, or at least to filter it in highly selective ways. In some cases this has been successful: one thinks of the English public school tradition, which blocked out other influences to the extent that it removed pupils from home in order to shape and control them more effectively. This is reinforced by the fact that the vehicles by which popular culture is carried into the classroom by young people – personal stereos, music and teen magazines, football results and so on – are very often rightly seen as immediate distractions from the task in hand – the teaching and learning of the curriculum.

As a result, educators can often feel that cultural influences should be held at bay, blocked from the formal routines of education, and as far as possible from the consciousness of pupils, at least while they are in school. Focus on 'culture' as it is often more traditionally meant – on classical music, great literature, teaching of the classics and ancient history – is sometimes encouraged, although not always.

But culture – the systems of norms, beliefs and practices upheld within social groups, institutions and communities – will always be at the heart of the educational process. Even if they are not outwardly articulated by pupils in lessons, such systems will influence the way in which education is received and treated by young people. If there is a clash of beliefs, this will be expressed in conflict somewhere, however openly it is articulated, in the private reflection or subconscious of individuals, in break-time discussions in the playground; and these conflicts and competing influences will also be expressed in young people's behaviour and attitudes to education. Since this will always be the case, culture in its widest sense should rightly be seen as a powerful force which can often be harnessed to motivate, excite and encourage young people to learn. Fighting against it, especially in an age when global media are ever more accessible and influential, is fruitless. Rather than blocking it out, effective educators allow it to penetrate to the core of the learning process, and encourage the development of young people who are equipped to understand, judge and shape it, rather than being passive receptors of whatever happens to come their way.

Using cultural resources can also be an especially effective means of motivating underachieving and disaffected young people. In particular, the cultural influences of sport and popular music hold great potential, which often lies untapped. Both enjoy greater media exposure than in the past, and dominate the consumer markets which young people are most active in. Both produce icons and role models, both positive and negative. And both hold unprecedented sway over the interests and imaginations of even the most hard-bitten or damaged young people.

The most striking example of the use of sport to help young people to learn is the Youth Charter for Sport (YCS), based in Manchester. Founded by Geoff Thompson, a former world karate champion, its mission is simple: to use the cultural capital and influence of sports stars to bring together the interest and motivation of at-risk young people, and the resources of private companies to create opportunities which will help to divert young people from 'anti-social youth culture', violence, crime and unemployment. YCS has provided sports courses and youth facilities in Manchester and beyond, organising visits from sporting personalities to schools and youth centres, endorsing the investment of resources by private companies with scrolls of signatures from leading sportsmen and women, and striving to create a virtuous circle of mutual comprehension, collaboration and shared achievement between sections of the community which otherwise have remained separate and suspicious of each other. YCS does not necessarily aim to be a direct provider of education and training opportunities, but rather a catalyst and agent of connection. It also promotes a strong ethic of fair play, discipline and mutual respect which many of its young beneficiaries have embraced, emphasising the importance of sporting values for personal development and achievement. The benefits are clear - the cultural value of sports stars, the prospect for young people of vouchers for sporting goods, and the positive effects of being taken seriously, these are matched by the marketing value to companies of association with sports stars and community investment, and the prospect of reduction in their security, insurance and retail theft bills. YCS has also emphasised the creative and positive aspects of youth culture, arranging for spectacular displays of graffiti art on hoardings around its headquarters in one of Manchester's regeneration districts, and developing entrepreneurial employment projects such as car washing and stewardship, which give young people responsibility, income and work experience while helping to reduce the risk of car crime.

Another sporting example is the Somerstown United football club, started in response to the rising incidence of racial violence in an area of north London. The team is ethnically mixed and is helping to promote mutual understanding and respect between different groups of young people, to provide a focus for purposeful and positive activity, and it has helped to achieve a reduction in racial violence and a qualitative change in the atmosphere around Somerstown. The team has already competed in international tournaments, established a junior squad, and become a growing focus of interest, approval and support for young people in the area.

Other examples include the football and literacy schemes established by the National Literacy Trust, in which clubs and players participate in reading days and the distribution of free books to children, and other schemes involving premier league clubs in study support, which have been embraced and developed by the government.

For some young people, arts – and especially the performing arts – can also be a powerful resource for lifting motivation and encouraging learning and shared achievement. Many organisations committed to reaching disaffected or marginalised youngsters use drama, music and creative writing, through which they can express their views and present issues which concern them. One example is the London International Festival of Theatre, which puts on a series of productions across the capital, involving young people in working with professional artists, actors, technicians and theatre managers, and creating collaborative performances which present the results of their work to a wider audience. Recent projects have included a pyrotechnic display in Stockwell Park, south London, which saw local young people working with world-renowned designers and pyrotechnicians to produce a professional display watched by several hundred people. Such projects take young people seriously, involve them in collaboration with adults who have professional skills to be learned and shared, and require them to work seriously towards a goal of performance which is public and publicly celebrated. They are also accessible to those who, for whatever reason, are unable or unwilling to participate in school education. Learning to collaborate in a less institutionalised setting can also encourage young people to reappraise their relationships with professionals. As one young man said of his educational psychologist: 'When I saw him in his tracksuit I realised he was alright.'

Another example of the use of culture for shared learning is the Columbia School mosaic. Columbia, a primary school in east London, is located in an area of extraordinary cultural and ethnic diversity. Looking for a focus for a whole-school local history project, the school decided to design and create a mosaic for its outside wall. Working with a local artists' centre, the children and teachers interviewed local residents, including the elderly, about the area's history and produced a series of mosaic designs reflecting different aspects of the neighbourhood's cultural heritage and composition. The result was a mosaic created by the whole school – every pupil and member of staff – sponsored by local businesses, stretching seventy feet along the school's external wall. In the five years since the mosaic was completed, it has not been vandalised once.

Information and communications technologies also make it increasingly possible for young people to access cultural resources in publishing and music, film and television, and to produce and present their own creations, even to publish them electronically. A 17-year-old recently won a prestigious Website of the Year award, ahead of several commercial companies, for a Spice Girls site which he designed as a birthday present for his little sister. While the influence and penetration of popular culture can be seen as a threat and disruption to the processes of formal education, their force can also be harnessed to help motivate and learn, in the process helping young people to become more discriminating consumers of what the global media culture throws at them.

Taking culture seriously can open up a powerful set of resources for attracting and motivating young people whose negative attitudes to education often seem fixed and impossible to shift. When such projects are open and accessible, when they require young people to take responsibility for shaping the processes and content of learning, and for their own role in achieving the desired outcomes, and when they are based on relationships of trust and mutual commitment, they become crucibles of learning and achievement.

Bringing other resources to life: making the most of people

So far we have considered the importance of places, cultural resources and new techniques. What brings these resources to life? The answer, fairly obviously, is people. The stuff which binds resources together and shapes them into cultures of learning and achievement is the web of human relationships created by people who contribute their time, effort, care and expertise. These relationships cross between places and institutions, as well as developing within them. Effective efforts to tackle underachievement and reduce the risks of failure rest, therefore, on the creation of new, positive learning relationships.

We have already seen the importance of social network structure for understanding the context of underachievement. The range and quality of a young person's ties to her peers, family, teachers, and other community members have a crucial bearing on her prospects. Improving the motivation and achievement of young people at risk, and helping them connect what they learn to their understanding of the world and the way they shape their lives, depends on widening their range of social experience, and on deepening the strength and quality of their relationships with others.

This process of widening and deepening learning relationships is already taking place in many different ways. It is evident in the success of successful study support initiatives, which complement and enhance their focus on exam revision, coursework and homework by developing looser partnerships and forms of collaboration involving a wide range of partners. Thousands of schools already make enthusiastic use of any adult who is in the building to assist in the learning process, encouraging police, clergy, parents, employers and former pupils to make a positive contribution. Parents in disadvantaged areas are often encouraged to learn with their children, developing literacy and other skills while becoming more actively involved in partnerships aimed at developing their children's potential. Youth projects like Youth Works, Somerstown United or Youth Charter for Sport aim to establish new relationships between young people and a range of others, creating partnerships for the sake of shared goals. As such initiatives begin to bear fruit, they become a focus of interest and activity, drawing in further support and expertise in a virtuous cycle of development and growth. Further development comes both from injections of money and demonstration of positive results: crime reduction, better exam results, work and performances which can be displayed in public; and from less formal, more haphazard offshoots: word of mouth, chance ideas which lead people in unexpected directions, new activities based on the success of what has gone before. All such development depends on a continuous process of relationship-building, strengthening the effective ties between those involved, and extending the network of human resources.

Some examples of this involve bringing together unlikely partners in learning. The image of a corporate financier from the City of London sitting down to read once a week with an impoverished Bangladeshi child is both counterintuitive and appealing. It is already happening many times over in east London. The outcomes, alongside the explicit aim of helping to improve reading levels, include surprising amounts of satisfaction and fulfilment for the corporate volunteers, and growing mutual comprehension of the separate worlds which the different partners inhabit. Work experience, which will be examined in the next chapter, also allows young people to find out about and learn from an organisational context beyond their school, and often from people in roles that they would never otherwise have come across. The evidence seems to suggest that when relationships are established without too many preconceptions, without young people being required to fit into previously defined categories, they have more chance of success.

For some young people it is extremely difficult to establish and maintain relationships because of damage to or underdevelopment of their emotional capacities. For them the challenge is more difficult and complex, but it remains essentially the same. Through trust, time and careful support, they can begin to develop their emotional intelligence, understanding themselves, empathising with others, managing relationships and beginning to harness and strengthen their motivation, creating a foundation for more purposeful and ambitious learning. The task of establishing bonds of trust and communication requires more skill, and perhaps more patience and sensitivity, but in the end is basically the same as for all learners – to enable individuals to understand the relevance of learning to the world around them, and to give them the capacities and techniques for shaping their lives, rather than being controlled by forces which remain alien and beyond their reach. The challenge is to provide such support in time to prevent chronic, entrenched problems, and to ensure that it is connected appropriately with longer-term paths of progression which allow young people continually to develop their understanding of themselves and the world, making use of all the resources in their learning environment.

Mentoring

One tool used to increasing effect in supporting educational achievement is mentoring. Here the focus is on creating trusting relationships between a young person and an older one. Mentoring relationships run back into ancient history, taking their name from the bond between Telemachus and Mentor in ancient Greek legend. In the past they have been largely informal, and structured or facilitated programmes of mentoring carry special risks and conditions for success. But such a relationship, free from the baggage of family or institutional relationships, but aware of and sensitive to them, can be a powerful source of confidence, information and support. Several projects aimed at diverting young people at risk from harmful and damaging life-courses use mentoring to great effect.

A leading example is the Dalston Youth Project. It works with young people already involved in or on the fringes of the criminal justice system, whose education has either broken down because of exclusion or chronic truancy, or who are at risk of such. It provides a flexible and intensive package of support, including informal learning, residential courses, short 'taster' courses in colleges and workplaces, and guidance on personal development. Part of the programme is the matching of young people with individual mentors, drawn from a pool of volunteers in the local community. This relationship, because it is one-to-one and confidential, is able to encompass more than the specific transfer of knowledge and skills which formal educational curricula specify. It is a voluntary association between individuals which, when successful, helps to synthesise and make sense of the opportunities, threats and influences in a young person's life. The combination of seniority, confidence and commitment which a mentor provides can be an important resource for young people – not in isolation, but through interaction with the other learning experiences and resources which they encounter.

As the project's first director, Sarah Benioff, says, the project 'has been able to give support, advice and challenge, allowing each young person on it not only to address their needs and achieve their goals but also to see how they can become responsible members of their community'.

At the end of the project's first year, 73 per cent of participants were in full-time education, training or paid employment, and were committing 60 per cent fewer criminal offences.

Mentoring schemes have rapidly taken hold in the UK, partly driven by the establishment of 'Compact' agreements between schools and businesses. Such schemes usually target pupils in the later stages of secondary education, facing the crucial transition to post-compulsory education or employment. Mentoring plays an increasing role in study support, often facilitated by Education Business Partnerships. There are risks involved – not all mentoring relationships work out, and there needs to be clear understanding of the goals and expectations of the relationship. The temptation to think that 'super-mentors' can single-handedly transform a young person's prospects must be overcome. But establishing such relationships is clearly an important part of helping young people to overcome their barriers to achievement. One-to-one mentoring relationships can also be developed into a wider sharing of goals and communication. One particularly interesting example is the Society Innovators project in Sweden. Aimed at tackling youth unemployment in sparsely populated areas, the project involves young people in creating and managing their own projects, and connects each participant with a slightly older peer mentor, who guides and supports their efforts, but also with an adult mentor, who is partly responsible for supporting the older peer. The result is a three-way relationship based around the learning needs of one individual. Training of mentors is also crucial – techniques for communicating and listening, ways of overcoming obstacles and avoiding false expectations can all be provided by effective training and support.

Learning relationships are at the heart of any successful learning endeavour. Their core characteristic is not a professional or institutional property, a relation of power or authority or accordance to a set of rules, but a shared commitment to a set of goals. These goals are not functionally defined, nor contained by the rules or methods of any one organisation. Their focus is the hopes, fears, needs and talents of learners themselves. Learning relationships connect the widest possible range of resources to the goals of individual learners. They help to sharpen young people's focus on what they want and need to do, and on how to accomplish it. In the process, they create hugely valuable by-products which can last long after a specific task is accomplished. These include trust, mutual respect and understanding, and networks through which knowledge and information can flow far more efficiently than between formal institutions. In short, they contribute to the formation of social capital.

The projects I have described in this chapter have reconfigured the resources available to support learning, and often added some new ones, around the *learner* rather than around the institutional and administrative structures of schools. Their use of resources is often highly flexible and imaginative, and as a result they are able to succeed in engaging the interest and ability of young people who are less able to cope with formal institutional processes. They require young people to take responsibility for their learning, but also give them opportunities to shape and influence what they do and how they do it. As such, they can often succeed where larger organisations with more rigid procedures and larger numbers of students fail. But to succeed in the longer run, to integrate the motivation and achievement that they help to kindle with wider opportunities to learn, they must also be able to integrate what they do with other sources of education and support for young people.

Bringing systems together

Perhaps the greatest and most complex challenge, one which recurs throughout the different themes of this book, is that of creating systems which function effectively as a whole, and make up more than the sum of their parts. For the full benefits of active learning to be realised in tackling underachievement, this must have high priority for those who plan and manage wider educational provision.

Many of the initiatives described here are relatively small in scale. They involve localised, custom-delivered work with individuals and small groups of people. Their approaches are often intensive, and they necessarily develop in creative, spontaneous, haphazard ways. Yet their aim is to help young people to make sense of the world; to compare, synthesise and simultaneously manage different challenges and opportunities, and to develop understanding and techniques which help them to function effectively in a wide range of situations and organisational settings. To achieve this fully, different projects and learning resources must be able to work together, to act in concert, and to make sure as far as possible that the messages and opportunities that they deliver work well together. Many of the problems faced by young people are exacerbated by the inability of different providers to integrate their services properly. Once a pupil has been excluded, or begun to truant regularly, it becomes progressively more difficult for him to keep up with his peers. Once outside an institution, it becomes progressively more difficult to get back in. Intensive and often highly beneficial courses lose much of their value over time, because when they finish there is insufficient support to ensure positive long-term progression. Confronted with the reappearance of familiar problems – confusing messages, inflexible institutional rules, lack of information and informal support – fatalism, rebellion and insecurity can quickly reappear.

Rather than being seen as exclusive alternatives to more conventional educational approaches, many of these initiatives must be able to work alongside them. This requires a fundamental reappraisal of the ways in which information and management systems operate, and a restructuring of the incentives for different organisations to share information and to collaborate. Again, there are examples of good practice from which there is much to learn.

The first fundamental lesson is that there is no substitute for trusting, long-standing relationships. The Youth Works NE strategy has shown that trust is a precondition of positive work with young people, and that it is possible to establish such trust even with those who have totally rejected education. But developing and implementing the strategy revealed a staggering amount of duplication, short-termism and lack of communication, even in a county known for its support of youth work and community education. Trust is difficult to gain and easy to lose. Effective communication between those whom a young person does trust and other professionals with an interest in their education is crucial for maximising their opportunities to learn. For this kind of outreach work, a neighbourhood approach, where a team of professionals in a particular area act as sources of information, reference and liaison between young people and other agencies, is an effective and efficient way of coordinating resources, and also therefore of saving public money.

Teachers, youth workers, educational psychologists and volunteers often work in almost total isolation from each other, directing effort towards the same goals with limited, fragmented resources, and often at cross purposes. When a young person's problems become too much for one set of professionals to contain, either because they opt out or because their conduct is too disruptive, they are passed on to another set, either deliberately or by default. Whatever the value of an individual programme, it can be amplified by making sure that it works in concert with the other agencies which a young person will deal with. Systems which improve the coordination of activity and resources often *prevent* those problems which can be diagnosed early from becoming serious.

This approach is exemplified by INCLUDE. Its strategy uses a model of 'progressive redeployment of resources' aimed at preventing school exclusion, reintegrating those who have begun to fall through the cracks in the system, and offering those who have already experienced multiple exclusions bridges back into education or training. Emphasising prevention, INCLUDE provides peer counselling projects in schools aimed at encouraging young people facing low self-esteem and behavioural problems to communicate with others, seek out help, overcome problems with teachers and other pupils, to reduce the risk of fighting, bullying and disruptive behaviour. To reintegrate excluded pupils, INCLUDE employs intensive one-to-one methods to assess, train and prepare pupils for the return to school, while also negotiating a package of support with the school which facilitates the return and supports the young person in making a positive transition back into the educational mainstream. Such an approach helps to cut the amount of time excluded pupils spend out of education, and reduces both the long-term individual risks and the cost of providing services.

Rather than attempting to develop separate provision for young people at risk of exclusion, INCLUDE works to redeploy resources to overcome the barriers to a young person's flourishing within mainstream education. This kind of model requires more than skilled intervention with the young person. It also involves finding ways of bringing the professionals and others concerned – parents, relatives, sometimes peers – together to formulate common goals and the ways in which they will work together to find an appropriate solution. INCLUDE thus acts as an *agent of connection*, helping to ensure that all those involved in a young person's learning can act in concert to help achieve a set of common goals.

INCLUDE most often works at an individual level, responding to problems and trying to arrest a vicious cycle of exclusion, failure and disaffection. But its success depends on its ability to bring institutions and professionals into harmony, and ensure that the systems by which they work do not counteract each other. Another good example of this is the Youth Link network developed by Surrey Education Services. Its core objective is to develop the links between schools and other agencies working for young people, and to provide support for young people at risk of disaffection and failure. The pivotal role is played by a locality team comprised of teachers, educational psychologists, educational welfare officers and youth workers, who respond to referrals or requests for help which can come from schools, parents, other agencies, or from young people themselves. Once an assessment has been carried out and a relationship established, an individual programme of support is developed from resources including psychological support, individual action planning and personal timetables of both school-based and out-of-school learning, participation in after-school activities, residential opportunities, classroom learning support, pre-employment training, and young-person-led self-help groups examining such issues as bullying and HIV. Evaluations have shown that the model contributes to more confidence and enjoyment of school, increased exam performance, greater understanding among professionals of the reasons for young people's behaviour, and better communication between the agencies involved. This depends upon securing the consent and willing involvement of young people, and also on professionals being prepared to develop a common language and a flexible approach to prevention. The core of each package of provision is the negotiation of a combination of resources and opportunities which is individual and customised to the needs, interests and abilities of each young person. Many of the activities are open to pupils who are not enrolled with Youth Link, providing benefits to a wider group of young people and preventing segregation and misunderstanding among peers. A similar partnership is being developed in Oxfordshire, building on the work of several smaller projects.

At an even broader institutional level, several Further Education colleges are using informal learning and youth work services to help young people make the most of their formal further education courses. Wirral Metropolitan

College, for example, which has thousands of students pursuing GCSE, A level and vocational qualifications, also works to include its wider community in the use of its resources, and works actively to develop youth service provision. The college is a base for Prince's Trust Volunteers, and has youth workers and facilities on site, available to assist young people in dealing with problems or barriers which may affect their formal attainment. The mix of provision helps young people to focus on their learning needs and goals, and to use a range of resources to help them achieve, as well as to enjoy the different kinds of learning available.

Effective learning projects for young people at risk are constantly extending their networks and relationships with other agencies and social groups which can play a part in supporting young people's education. Dalston Youth Project, for example, is constantly seeking to develop the web of relationships surrounding its tightly focused programme, through teacher liaison, parental involvement, and support from employers and the wider community. This focus on developing networks which can add value to existing activity is vital, and reflects a drive to find the best possible combination of resources – physical, cultural, professional and human – with which to help young people achieve their goals. Of course, new partnerships and relationships do not always work, and a focus on quality and relevance is also vital. But these examples show that successful strategies cross the boundaries of service provision, of professional competences, and between formal and informal learning. Tackling underachievement, which begins with a focus on the individual learner, their motivation and strengths, as well as their weaknesses and barriers to success, depends on expanding outwards to include the whole learning environment, and the full richness of resources which it has to offer.

8

THE CHALLENGE OF
EMPLOYABILITY

Preparation for the world of work has become a growing preoccupation for educationalists over the last fifteen years. As the structure of the labour market has changed, as schools and colleges have looked around for extra resources, and as governments have pondered on how to develop the skills for a thriving economy, the role of education in developing employability has gradually come into focus, and educationalists and employers have moved towards each other, building closer partnerships, developing a common language, and seeking ways to achieve shared goals. A 1995 survey found that 92 per cent of secondary schools and 58 per cent of primary schools had links with business (DfEE, 1996). There have been hundreds of initiatives, their growth sparked by the launch of the Technical and Vocational Education Initiative (TVEI) in 1982 and fuelled by the introduction of the National Vocational Qualification (NVQ), the establishment of 120 Education Business Partnerships (EBPs), 'Compact' schemes, where local employers promise resources in return for pupils meeting attendance and achievement targets, reading partnerships, work experience, mentoring programmes, the Teacher Placement Service, Enterprise Education and many others.

A lot of time, energy and money is spent on efforts to improve employability. But there are still significant problems. The value of NVQs has been questioned, and their reputation is still patchy among employers. Forty per cent of employers recently stated that there was a significant gap between the skills of their younger recruits and their current business needs, with personal and communication skills among the most deficient. There is growing recognition that effective employees need strong *personal qualities*, as well as good qualifications. Youth unemployment, while lower than in many other European countries, is still around twice the national average. Previous government training schemes have on the whole had a poor reputation with the young people who take part in them. Poor employability in the UK was recently estimated to cost an annual £8 billion, without taking into account the social costs of crime and unemployment. There is also evidence that parents, while concerned about the need for their children to be employable, are not confident about their ability to guide them in the fast-changing world of work.

99

This chapter argues that, while many of the changes which have taken place in education for employability are valuable, and some schemes are highly effective, there is much more to be done. Active learning has an important part to play in ensuring that young people are fully prepared for the rigours and challenges of work in the twenty-first century.

The new world of work

What are the key changes that will affect the working lives of today's school students? The labour market has undergone huge changes, driven by a revolution in productivity, structural change in the economy, the impact of information and communications technologies (ICTs) and intense global competition. The first, well documented shift is that away from the primary and heavy industrial work that formed the basis of Britain's industrial prowess in the past. Since 1950 the UK has lost 5 million jobs in the producing industries and gained some 8 million in services. We now earn more revenue from Indian restaurants than from coal, steel and shipbuilding combined. While manufacturing still plays an important part in our output, it is no longer the primary source of employment that it once was. On a broad definition, services now account for 90 per cent of net job growth (Cambridge Econometrics, 1994). Since 1950 we have gained 2.3 million jobs in finance, insurance and property, and 1.7 million in distribution, restaurants and hotels. Community, social and personal service jobs have grown by 3.5 million over the same period, including a million in health and 1.2 million in education. New entrants to the labour market at more likely to find work in service occupations, from the knowledge-intensive, highly-paid professions, financial or creative services, through to lower-paid, insecure work in retail, leisure or catering.

Productivity

The pressures on employment are partly accounted for by a revolution in productivity which has been especially rapid since the mid-1970s. An hour's work is on average twenty-five times more productive now than at the beginning of the century. This is the primary driver of the restructuring of large employer organisations, which in many cases has hit new entrants to the labour market especially hard. It has been aided by the introduction of new technologies – the mechanisation of production lines and the application of new forms of information processing and communications technologies, and driven by the intensification of competition, especially from the economies of the Pacific Rim, which is why restructuring has so often been justified by employers in terms of cost-savings and employability.

A service economy?

While it is true that services account for a growing proportion of output and employment, the UK is not exclusively a service economy. Manufacturing is still important, and services vary so much in content and nature that it is difficult to give an accurate impression of the nature of employment by focusing solely on service occupations; in many ways, they defy a common definition. It is probably more useful to see the new economy as a knowledge economy.

A knowledge economy

We are entering an era in which the most important productive resource is knowledge. This is true in two ways. The first is that economic activity increasingly involves the processing and communication of digital information. In the past, exchanges of information were physical – face-to-face meetings, analogue phone calls, TV and radio, reports, cheques, cash, invoices. In the new economy all these interactions are digitally produced – email, video-conferencing, digital phones, and smart production using microprocessors to control everything from agricultural machinery to answering machines, billing systems to shipping and transport. Information technologies make it possible to exchange information faster and more effectively than ever before, and reduce the need for joint working to take place in the same physical location. In themselves the computing, communication and content industries are among the fastest-growing sectors of the economy, and the greatest generators of jobs, especially in content: software, broadcasting, and so on.

The second, and possibly more important, key point about the knowledge economy is that it is based not just on flows of information, but on the creation and application of human knowledge – applying know-how to our activities and production, and adding value in the process. Knowledge industries – not just the high-tech ones that we are used to hearing about, but core industries like health and education – are increasingly sources of employment over the last forty years. This is a fundamental shift. In the past, the key resources of wealth generation have been land, labour and physical materials. In the future they will be ideas, creativity and knowledge.

Knowledge and information are increasingly built into the products that we use: smart clothes, smart cards, smart tyres, smart roads. Our tools to find and synthesise information are also increasingly smart. Many of the fastest-growing occupations are knowledge jobs – the professions, technical and managerial jobs, software designers, computing and systems analysts. Increasingly, manual or production-line work involves technical knowledge and the use of mental and analytical skills – programming machines, monitoring quality standards, managing the interface between information systems and material things. Alongside the growth of 'pure' knowledge work, where people never get their hands dirty, traditional blue-collar jobs increasingly demand that employees have sophisticated and complex mental skills, and can apply their abstract knowledge to very concrete problems (Barley, 1996).

All this has profound implications for employability. Workers need good education to start with, but they must also be able continuously to update their knowledge and understanding. By the end of a four-year engineering degree, half the knowledge learned in the first year of study will already be obsolete. Growth in the volume of information requires new skills of synthesis and communication – being able to sort information into appropriate categories, synthesise it from disparate sources into one coherent body of knowledge, and communicate it effectively to co-workers.

From vertical to horizontal

There is another basic shift which is transforming the skills and qualities needed to be a successful worker. That is the shift from a vertical to a horizontal division of labour. For most of the industrial age we have divided labour vertically: power and authority are arranged hierarchically, based on the assumption that knowledge and expertise can be nested cumulatively at the top of an organisation, and cascaded downwards in the classic pyramid model. Vertical divisions of labour encode expertise in rules, procedures and hierarchical positions. Those further up the hierarchy are assumed to possess greater knowledge and expertise than those lower down. In the typical twentieth-century enterprise, the Fordist manufacturing organisation, those at the bottom were given a highly specialised function to perform over and over again, with little use of judgement or discretion, and their work performance was governed by rules, procedures and standards set from above.

In a horizontal division of labour people, rather than positions, are assumed to be the vessels of knowledge and expertise. This logic assumes that knowledge is too complex, and too specific to a particular domain of work, to be nested at the top of a hierarchy. Knowledge is transmitted and preserved through training and learning, rather than by procedures and rules, and individuals retain authority over their own work, with reference to other people, shared goals and quality standards.

The organisational paradigm for this new division of labour is not the hierarchy, but the network. In many areas of life, networks are becoming ubiquitous – we have already seen the importance of social network structures for extending opportunity and life-chances. The successful firms of the 1990s are also based on a network logic, organising production not through a single organisational enterprise, but through webs of collaboration, where each unit is focused around a core task and people work in teams. Coordination of work takes place not through command and control, but through collaboration. The crucial test of a worker's employability and productivity is no longer the ability to master a task and perform it reliably and repeatedly according to the rules of an organisation, but the ability to bring a particular kind of knowledge to a task, and to be able to collaborate effectively with others to achieve a common task. The function of managers and directors is not to control, but to orchestrate, helping to clarify and communicate goals, to motivate workers and to encourage innovation and experimentation for the sake of productivity. This fundamental change in the division of labour is the driving force behind the restructuring of large employer organisations, despite the fact that it is so often explained in terms of cost-cutting. The 'de-layering' of middle management is about removing layers of hierarchy, devolving authority downwards and depending on technology to ensure effective communication within and between teams of workers.

Network structures are looser than hierarchies. They allow greater room for manoeuvre and they make more space for creativity and innovation. But they are more demanding of individual workers, precisely because they give them greater responsibility and discretion. Employers increasingly look to workers for suggestions and ideas about how to improve productivity and product quality. People are often more responsible for managing their own time, for assembling the resources and knowledge required to complete a task, and for directing themselves in pursuit of excellence. Their value depends greatly on the extent to which their skills and knowledge are *transferable* across different worksites. Enterprises are linked into a system by their interactions, their common goals, rather than by the rules and hierarchy of a single organisation. For individual workers, communication and relationships with other workers become the keys to success. Constant feedback and learning are indispensable, for both organisations and individuals, to surviving and thriving in this new environment. Companies are beginning to shift their focus away from decentralisation and de-layering towards 'multi-skilling', creating a 'learning organisation', and 'organisational empowerment', shifting from the structure of organisations to the quality of interaction and learning among their members and associates (Henley Centre, 1994).

There are many striking examples of the move towards horizontal organisation. The restructuring of large corporations around 'work teams' is one. The growth of technical and professional occupations is another – pure knowledge work, such as law or accountancy, has traditionally been organised horizontally, through partnership structures. The steady rise of the 'contract culture' is another – the appearance of what Charles Handy (1995) has called the 'portfolio worker', who manages a portfolio of individual contracts with different employers, and retains responsibility for organising and managing their own workload. The growth of self-employment, of part-time work, and the growing importance of small firms for creating new employment opportunities, all depend on the same logic – networks of horizontal collaboration which cross the conventional boundaries of employer organisations.

In a knowledge economy, power lies not so much with those at the top of an organisation as with those who possess its key intellectual assets, the people who create and apply knowledge using their creative or technical skills to master the challenges in front of them. Andrew Grove, president of microchip manufacturer Intel, was recently asked why he did not have his own office, but just a workstation with no door at Intel's headquarters. His answer was that the power in his organisation rested with those who have the knowledge, and that he wanted to be as close to them as possible. Similarly Archie Norman, head of the ASDA supermarket group, occupies a desk no different from those of hundreds of his staff.

A *network economy*

As we have seen, the functioning of this new economy depends greatly upon networks. These networks are not just digital, though organisations and workers are increasingly linked by electronic flows of information. They are also human. Studies of the economic prowess of certain regions, such as Silicon Valley in California, or the creative and cultural industries in London, are increasingly focusing on the role of informal social networks in supporting innovation and success. The clustering of relatively small companies around a particular geographical area facilitates the growth of informal relationships and information exchange, which are not limited by organisations or by contracts.

Such networks, founded on norms of trust and collaboration and sparked by common interests and goals, are being recognised as an essential underpinning of economic development (Fukuyama, 1995, 1997; Leadbeater, 1997). Research on the sociology of business has also shown that an individual's network connections are a vital part of their value to an employer, and of their chances of career success. In particular, 'weak ties', connections which extend beyond a person's immediate circle of colleagues or collaborators, are valuable because they facilitate access to knowledge and resources which would otherwise be beyond the formal reach of an organisation or a team of workers. Friends of friends, acquaintances, people met at conferences, seminars or social gatherings, are all potentially valuable conduits of information and knowledge, and the skills of networking – conversation, informal exchange, sociability – are important for self-development and for increasing the value of one's work. Overall, what Fukuyama (1995) has called 'spontaneous sociability' – the capacity to form bonds of trust and sustain relationships with those outside our immediate circle of family, friends and colleagues – is a capacity which forms an important part of employability. Helping to develop this capacity, I will argue, is the major contribution which active learning can make to developing a workforce that can thrive amid the economic challenges of the next century.

Workstyles of the future

First, we need to set out the key characteristics of work from the perspective of the individual. What will people need to be able to do to make the most of opportunities in the labour market?

Formal educational attainment

The first thing to establish is that qualifications are still important. The growing differential between the incomes of those with degree-level education and those without shows that formal education, and knowledge of specialist subjects, is still crucial for success in work. The growing importance of other types of ability does not remove the need for academic or technical prowess, although there are fundamental changes in the ways that such knowledge is communicated and applied in the new world of work.

There are a number of softer, less tangible abilities that are increasingly important for workers.

Orientation to change The ability to adapt to changing circumstances, to learn new skills quickly, to anticipate change, and to be self-reliant in determining one's response to the changing environment.

Interpersonal skills The importance of inter- and intrapersonal intelligence in employment is growing steadily, because occupying a particular position in an organisation is becoming less important. Not only will fewer workers have a fixed hierarchical position, but those that do will find their roles more fluid and variable than before, and that their success depends on their ability to influence, communicate with and learn from others.

Analytical skills Numeracy, computer skills, financial literacy, risk assessment and decision-making all become more important as people use more technology in their work and are given greater responsibility for assessing the longer-term implications of what they do. These abilities will not be used in isolation, but rather will be applied to the content of what they are doing. They require an ability to see the 'big picture', to take a broad perspective, and to understand the implications of broad changes in the environment for the specific content of their work and for the development of their goals. Analytical skills are also important because of the growing volume of information which is incorporated into people's work. The capacity to sort, synthesise and then share relevant information from widely varying sources is crucial because, without it, workers will either miss information which could be valuable to their work, or be buried in a mass of information whose sheer volume they are unable to cope with (Mulgan, 1996).

Problem-solving Increasingly, work is not structured around the repetition of a set of functionally defined tasks, but around *solving problems*. Rather than systems of production being designed in advance and implemented from the

105

top down, employees are responsible for finding ways to achieve common goals, to analyse the barriers to achieving them, and to find ways of overcoming those barriers. Problem-solving involves the enterprising application of all the skills discussed above, and requires people to combine the resources necessary in a way which is structured around the task in hand, rather than in the way things have been done in the past, or the way that an organisation is structured.

In general, what we are describing is a shift towards a much more fluid working environment, where the limits are not set by job titles, organisational membership or formal contracts. As Geoff Mulgan has written (1997), it is a 'more intensively social model of labour', in which productivity is determined by the quality of relationships rather than the rules of organisations. The range of opportunities and resources is massively broadened by connection to people and information across the world, but making good use of such resources is a more complex task which depends on the personal capacities of individuals, and the quality of team working. As such, the new environment offers great opportunities for creativity, productivity and job satisfaction, but also poses significant risks – of disappointment, insecurity, confusion, and inability to translate short-term opportunities into longer-term career progression.

The costs of low employability

We have already seen that the financial cost of low employability has been estimated at £8 billion annually, in lost economic activity, savings to employers and greater productivity. Alongside the money, there are important social and psychological costs which result from insecurity over and misunderstanding of the new world of work. Surveys have shown that those in work are already probably more concerned about the loss of long-term job security than they actually should be. The fall in average job tenure, which has often been exaggerated but is none the less a clear labour market trend, has caused a growth of concern over the possibility of redundancy. An Industry in Education survey of school pupils found that parents exerted a strong influence over their children's perceptions, but in general 'there was a widespread feeling among pupils interviewed that their parents were at a loss to give them any positive advice about what to do with their lives' (Industry in Education, 1996: 14). Psychological insecurity increases stress and diverts people's energy away from more positive activity. It represents a significant opportunity cost because, although people need to be aware of the challenges that may face them, if they do not have the means to convert their awareness into positive preparation they will not be any better equipped to face the future.

One of the major obstacles to be overcome is the separation of different perspectives on the same problem, and the lack of communication and mutual understanding between schools, parents, employers and pupils over a set of goals which are common to all. Industry in Education found that there was little appreciation of the importance of personal qualities for employability among pupils, and that qualifications were thought to be the main route to a worthwhile job. When asked about personal qualities, most said that they could be developed informally – with peers, at clubs, and through social activities. School was not seen as a place where such qualities could be developed. Many employers have relatively clear expectations of successful young recruits, but obviously have not been effective in communicating these to parents, young people or schools, despite many initiatives. Schools, similarly, pay attention to work preparation, but all too often only in the specific timetable areas where it is perceived to be appropriate, such as careers education, work experience, and Personal, Social and Health Education. It is a frequent complaint of pupils that subject teaching does not do enough to draw out the implications of what is learned for everyday life, or for the future. The question is how these differing perspectives can best be harmonised.

Are the new work skills transferable?

The Dearing review of qualifications for 16–19-year-olds has already emphasised the importance of the kinds of skills that we have discussed here, and identified them as a priority for education providers:

> . . . skills in working effectively with other people; presentational skills; a problem solving approach; and the ability to manage one's own learning as a necessity in a society that needs to be committed to life-long learning.
>
> (Dearing, 1996)

The review did not recommend how such skills should be taught or learned, however A strong, still prevalent assumption about the development of 'key skills' is that they are generic, and can be transferred to other contexts with a minimum of further learning. Much of the development of the NVQ framework rests on this assumption – that the performance of certain actions is evidence of competence in a range of contexts, and that participation in a school- or college-based course is enough to ensure these abilities can be transferred to the workplace. However, this assumption is increasingly questioned (King, 1997). This is partly because the focus on the 'action' components diverts attention away from the underlying conceptual and situational aspects of knowledge, which are essential for it to be applied effectively in a new context. Many aspects of skill development in a specific situation are developed intuitively and experientially, with little conscious attempt to transfer that understanding into more formal, propositional knowledge. This argument echoes Howard Gardner's criticism, set out in *Frames of Mind* (Gardner, 1983) and reviewed here in Chapter 3, of the 'correct answer compromise', where a focus on getting the right answers in the highly specific context of school-based tests inhibits a pupil's ability to apply her knowledge in different situations, where the knowledge might actually be of practical value. It also chimes with the growing emphasis in management thinking on releasing the 'tacit knowledge' of workers – the assumptions, experience and understanding which is never formalised or converted into rules and procedures, and is communicated informally through shared experience and storytelling. One study, for example, of Rank Xerox photocopier engineers (cited in Tapscott, 1996) found that they relied less on the official manual for diagnosing and repairing copier breakdowns, and more on stories of past encounters with troublesome machines. The criticism is also one possible reason for the growing perception that NVQs do not provide the economic return to employers that was originally claimed for them, and for the fact that their quality is perceived to vary so widely across the different subjects.

There is still significant disagreement about the extent to which supposedly generic skills are transferable from one context to another. But there are two important lessons which we can draw from the problems encountered with vocational education and the transfer of skills. The first is that learning for work is often most effective when it takes place in a context as close as possible to the situations which students are preparing for: that is, the workplace. Second, that paying attention to a student's reflection on the nature and relevance of her learning, and its connection to other knowledge and experience she may possess and other situations she may encounter, is crucially important.

By now it should be clear that active learning can play a major part in developing employability. It can contribute in a number of ways. First, it can extend the range of contexts in which a young person learns, and involve people from the world of work in that learning. Second, it can make a strong contribution to the development of team and communication skills. Third, it can act as a vehicle for developing norms of collaboration between schools, colleges and employers. Fourth, it is potentially a strong tool of motivation.

Taking learning out into the world

As with our discussion of citizenship, one of the most important aspects of active learning is that it can connect the learning that young people undertake in institutions to the world outside. The evidence, both quantitative and qualitative, is that young people value this kind of learning activity – real situations, real problems to solve, real people with whom to work. Direct experience of work-related challenges and tasks, and the examples of adults who function in a work environment, are a rich and powerful resource with which to encourage and develop learning, compelling learners to apply their growing knowledge and understanding in real-life contexts, and helping to connect learning to life beyond the school.

This is recognised by many teachers and parents, and already has a limited place in the curriculum – one of the achievements of the TVEI has been to ensure that almost every pupil has a work-experience placement of one or two weeks in the final year of compulsory education. But the potential of this kind of learning experience is still hugely under-used. Work experience has become the norm in secondary schools, but in a highly limited form: a brief placement which gives pupils a taste of one work setting, but is often largely ignored by subject teachers who, by then, are concentrating on GCSE preparation. The general assumption is that such placements are valuable for prompting young people to think about what kind of work they want to do, and what kind of organisation they might find themselves in once they leave formal education, but there are few lessons to be learned for the process of education itself, and few connections between a student's experience and what they come back to school to do.

Cases of good practice in active learning show that there is a more important place for out-of-school experience in developing pupils' understanding of the world of work, and also in making their school learning more effective.

For example, the focus on self-directed, project-based, team activity exemplified by many active learning projects can help to develop exactly the kinds of qualities which employers increasingly demand. Changemakers projects require young people to establish a working group, develop and refine a project idea, and then establish the stages of action and the different roles of group members in achieving the group's objectives. While the projects are based on the idea of creating positive change in young people's wider communities, the activities often involve employers or corporate volunteers directly, and the tasks which young people take on for the sake of their overall objectives are often ones that they will encounter in working life, from presenting and explaining their goals and methods to raising resources, setting performance targets, reviewing successes and failures, and collaborating effectively. Above all, completing a Changemakers project involves taking responsibility, both individual and shared, for achieving one's goals. Employers become involved in such projects in various ways: by giving advice, money, or resources in kind, or by making facilities available to young people, giving feedback on their achievements and helping to celebrate and publicise project outcomes.

> I was really pleased to be able to talk to our community helpers or one of the extra teachers we had working with us. It was great being able to make telephone calls to people helping us with our project and being able to visit people if we needed to.
>
> (Changemakers participant, Colne Community School)

Developing a project in the community beyond school and immediate peer group also confronts young people with the values, forms of communication, and expectations of other institutions and social groups, including employers. In so doing, they begin a process of *integration*, which helps to harmonise the perspectives of key figures who will help to determine a pupil's transition into the labour market. When the learning involved is intensively evaluated, it can also help to connect its content to the wider perceptions, aspirations and external experience of the young people concerned. Exploring the reasons for different people being involved in such projects, and for valuing the outcomes, is also an important way of learning about the priorities and expectations of other people on whom young people will depend for their future. It can show how the pursuit of altruistic goals also contributes to enlightened self-interest — personal development, self-awareness, visibility and contacts for the future.

Changemakers is an example of young people organising themselves horizontally around a shared objective, or what David Clark (1996) calls a 'focal task'. As we have seen, this division of labour is increasingly relevant to the world of work which young people will enter, even when the focal task itself is not explicitly related to employment. But there are other ways in which direct experience can be used to help young people to develop their work-readiness. Pathways to Adult Life. Conceived as a project which should aid the development of broader personal qualities for employment and adult life, but also contribute to raising academic achievement, Pathways schools have consistently made use of direct experience through workplace visits, work-based extra-curricular activities, and involving employee volunteers in school. In the evaluation of its pilot phase, Pathways teachers and pupils unanimously agreed that direct experience was valuable. Pathways activities were usually not organised on the team-based, self-directed model, and tended to follow more familiar organisational principles which reflected their location in the mainstream curriculum — either within Careers Education and Guidance (CEG) or Personal, Social and Health Education (PSHE), or less often within specific subject areas such as geography or business studies.

The Trident Trust, primarily a large-scale organiser of work experience in the UK, has also integrated its placement activities into a framework called Skills for Life, which brings together programmes of 'personal challenge', 'community involvement' and 'work experience' to encourage the development of a cluster of skills relating to teamwork, self-reliance, communication and problem-solving. Again, the guiding aim of the framework is to enhance the value of learning through experience by connecting it with the goals and challenges of other parts of a student's education.

The success of these projects points the way towards a development of learning for work which goes beyond work experience and limited careers guidance towards a more structured form of workplace learning, in which students learn through direct experience, but relate that experience to a set of explicit learning outcomes which are directly connected to their goals for personal development and to their accredited school-based learning. The best example of such learning comes from Australia, where a recent study has shown the potential of extended work placements for improving employability and raising the status of vocational education (Cumming and Carbine, 1997). In the schools studied, workplace learning was factored into the curriculum as part of a range of course options, so that it was pursued over time alongside more academic subjects. Placements are seen as part of a student's long-term educational development, rather than a short burst of context-specific experience. Often the development of these programmes took place as part of a wider reform and restructuring of the individual school, so that workplace learning was part of a wider strategy to improve overall performance.

The effect of introducing structured workplace learning and relating it explicitly to generic skills and learning outcomes, in all the schools studied, was that 'program participants – employers and teachers as well as students – became more highly focused and motivated. All were clear about what they were doing, why they were doing it, and how the achievements of all parties could be measured' (Cumming and Carbine, 1997).

Integrating the learning into the rest of the school

This kind of development requires significant reorganisation of school timeta-bles, assessment systems and record-keeping, but every school in the Australian study saw it as well worth the effort, because of its effectiveness. Students saw the experience as contributing to valuable skills, and increasing their access to employment; employers said that it had increased their under-standing of education and their appreciation of young people, and also created a possible mechanism for recruitment. Teachers involved in the programmes found that their participation had a significant impact on their approach to teaching and learning, and that contributions from students on the knowl-edge and expertise they had acquired during their placements was highly valued in the classroom. The general shift is described as 'teachers' emerging self-perception as facilitators of learning, rather than directors'. Students were frequently encouraged to take on a more proactive role in teaching and learning in order to share and develop their knowledge and experience.

This kind of shift, and its potential benefits, point to the importance of facing a further challenge, more complex than simply extending opportuni-ties for learning through direct experience and self direction: ensuring that such experience is integrated with, and deeply connected to, the other forms of teaching and learning which schools practise. The Dearing report on quali-fications at ages 16–19 (Dearing, 1996), like other reviews before it, firmly stated the need to tackle the historical assumption that vocational education is in some way inferior to academic learning. This assumption is extraordi-narily deep-rooted, and often expressed in the view that some kinds of school are more suited to certain kinds of pupils, an assumption that comprehensive education was supposed to undermine, but which remains alive and well. In the end the only way to prevent some kinds of institution and educational practice from being seen as inherently inferior is effectively to integrate resources and learning experiences around the needs and abilities of the individual learner, rather than around the institution. To do this effectively, forms of learning outside the conventional classroom and subject framework must be connected fully to the pursuit of conventional qualifications. What happens outside the classroom must impact positively on what happens inside it.

Again, there are cases of good practice which help show the way forward. Schools using Pathways to Adult Life, for example, have often made explicit connections between the generic learner outcomes of the framework – such as being able to identify one's learning needs, seek resources and plan learning opportunities, or understanding the implications of living in a diverse society – and the outcomes of specific subjects, expressed through attainment in Standard Assessment tests, GCSEs or coursework. One of Pathways' principal sources of value is that it assumes the co-dependence of the two kinds of outcome. It recognises that schools will often be unwilling or unable to put resources into initiatives which distract or detract from formal educational achievement, since exam results are still the main indicators of a school's success. Its outcomes are both specific enough to be connected explicitly to curriculum subjects and individual learning projects or activities, and broad enough not to exclude the full range of learning resources and out-of-school experiences which will influence or aid a young person's development. The Pathways framework helps to stimulate not only new activities and the development of relationships with Education Business Partnerships, employers, and outside relationships, but also to place such relationships and activities within the context of the whole school's development, and to relate them to other kinds of learning activity.

Recognising that there are connections to be made, however, is not enough. To ensure that the full potential for adding value is realised, teachers and learners must be able to make and strengthen the connections at the level of individual teaching and learning. The Pathways evaluation found that the framework was most effectively implemented at departmental level, where individuals had written policies concerning the relationship between subject learning outcomes and Pathways outcomes, and where they had schemes of work to translate these policies into classroom practice.

Another example of an institution forging these connections is found in the way that Wirral Metropolitan College seeks to integrate its vocational courses with real-life projects in its local area. This is slightly easier to do with explicitly vocational courses, such as engineering, design or construction. But it still requires the college actively to develop partnerships with companies, voluntary organisations and local government, and to build active participation into the delivery of its courses. Students at the college have been involved in local building projects, for example, taking part in design, planning and construction.

As with any kind of organisational reform, these cases show that change is most effective when its impact on the structure and ethos of the whole institution considered, planned and rigorously implemented. Rather than bolting additional components on to the existing structure, most value is added when the change is integrated into the whole, and when practitioners find ways of synthesising the innovation with what already happens, changing both in the process. Doing this successfully demands a lot. It requires teachers to be alive to new possibilities, resources and opportunities for learning, and to be able to incorporate them into their objectives and strategies for delivering their courses. It requires senior managers to develop structures of planning, curriculum delivery and feedback which allow sufficient flexibility, without losing a rigorous focus on outcomes, quality of learning, and depth of understanding. And it often imposes new responsibilities on students: to think hard about how to apply what they have learned in other contexts, to communicate it appropriately to others, and to recognise what is most relevant and important. But the signs are that all those involved can achieve this, and that doing so can motivate them to excel in their respective roles.

New learning relationships

Once again, at the heart of active learning for employability are relationships. Working with adults with whom young people would not otherwise come into contact also aids the development of weak ties – relationships with people who can provide information, advice, example and sometimes opportunity. Even if employers or outside organisations turn down a specific request for help, Changemakers facilitators have often found that they ask if there is anything else they can do, and take a growing interest in the progress of young people's projects. Employers involved in successful educational partnerships often find that they have opened up new recruitment channels which give them knowledge of possible candidates and greater understanding of how to recognise the potential and talents of individual students. A culture of voluntary collaboration is based on the informal communication of individuals, channelled and clarified by organisational procedures, leaders and ambassadors. There is a wide range of benefits for institutions when such partnerships work well: improved reputation, staff development, high-quality recruitment for companies, improved attainment, extra resources, wider understanding and approval for schools. But all these effects are dependent on the motivation, personal learning and satisfaction which flow from individual involvement in shared achievement.

Creating such relationships, and basing them on the principle of reciprocity which all effective partnerships involve, is a difficult challenge, especially for people who are used to operating in cultures and working environments which often seem alien to each other. The role of those who coordinate and broker new partnerships is central to progress. The challenge here is to construct *interfaces* between organisations through which new forms of collaboration can be developed. If you take a look at the activities of a flourishing study support partnership, or a school which takes its community partnerships seriously, or a sporting or cultural project which draws young people into collaboration with community partners, the picture is complex, dynamic and at first glance often chaotic. The activities and achievements are based on any number of individual learning relationships – between students, teachers, adult volunteers, employers, artists and parents. Such relationships are the foundation of whatever valuable learning is taking place, but they are stimulated and made possible by a number of factors.

The first, and perhaps the most important, of these is the social or civic entrepreneur. Social entrepreneurs are people who use entrepreneurial talents to help create social value (Leadbeater, 1997a; Leadbeater and Goss, 1998). They use their own networks of relationships, which typically span different fields of activity and types of organisation, to stimulate new connections and relationships, to unlock resources and to help focus people's energy around common goals. They work flexibly and are highly pragmatic, but they typically have a clear vision which they excel at communicating to others. The role of the social entrepreneur in helping to shape new educational partnerships can hardly be overstated. Of course, the lasting value of the relationships they help to create will only develop over time, but their function as agents of connection is vital. This task, of linkage, is one which Education Business Partnerships are charged with performing, and many have done it well. But their success lies not in the administrative systems or the formal structures which they create, but in their ability to bring people together, and they need to be rooted not in a specific kind of organisation, but in, or rather between, the different values and knowledge of those they are trying to bring together. Often this is aided by a degree of independence from wider administrative structures. Tower Hamlets Education Business Partnership, for example, which has been one of the highest achievers over the last ten years, was founded as a company limited by guarantee, rather than as a division of the Local Education Authority, giving operational independence and the freedom to circumvent the politics or procedures of its parent body and focus on forging relationships between individual schools and businesses. As an intermediary organisation, it also has the independence and authority to decide whether the conditions for a successful partnership are being met – judging, for example, whether a school has committed sufficient thought and effort to be ready, or whether the motives of an employer are right. Granting this kind of freedom, of course, raises risks of accountability and loss of control, but these can be offset by a focus on transparency, communication and the underlying goals of a project. As David Warwick has written, it is these 'end-questions' that really matter: not so much "What are you doing?" but "Why does it matter?"' (Warwick, 1995).

The second major form of interface is the *shared facility*. The idea of schools being resources for a wider group of users than just their staff and pupils is not new; it is a basic part of the philosophy of community education. Many new schools built in the 1960s and 1970s were designed as integrated community learning centres, offering adult learning, spaces for community groups to use, and open access. Shared facilities are important because they encourage their various users to understand their learning in a wider context, and to reflect on their roles as part of a community of learners which extends beyond their immediate membership of an organisation or narrow group. They are also important because they can make investment in infrastructure more productive, making more intensive and multi-faceted use of the capital sunk into a sports facility, science laboratory or computer centre.

Contemporary examples bring together different groups of learners. Impington Village College, for example, combines adult education facilities with its function as a school, and also uses its facilities for international language schools and conferences during vacations. The Garibaldi School in Nottinghamshire has used business investment to build company showrooms at the school: a modern languages centre, a science laboratory and a home economics room, which are used by the school for learning and by the companies involved as working demonstrations of their products. Wirral Metropolitan College makes its IT centre available to people from its wider community.

Using such facilities for multiple purposes carries risks, of course. Many are still suspicious of investment in education being used for commercial gain, and different groups of users may not understand or show due respect for the needs of others. It is also possible for resources to be used by different groups without them ever really communicating with each other. But such sharing can turn educational infrastructure into a crucible for forging new relationships and strengthening collaboration. Impington Village College is organised so that users of adult education facilities have physically to pass through other centres of learning, such as the Early Years unit. Many teachers might see this as a disruption, but when approached sensitively it aids transparency, mutual understanding and appreciation of different people's roles in contributing to educational achievement. Again, the foundation of success is not so much the nature of the activity, or the way in which it is organised, but a set of shared norms, a shared understanding of the underlying goals of the various activities, and a readiness to grasp opportunities for learning between the different groups of users rather than just within them.

The third way in which interfaces between organisations and groups of learners can be developed is by working to break down the different systems of concepts, beliefs and language which practitioners in different organisations employ. As Peter Senge has shown, the failure of many of the best ideas to be implemented successfully is often due to the strength of our 'mental models' – 'deeply held internal images of how the world works, images that limit us to familiar ways of thinking and acting' (Senge, 1990). These models, of which we are often not that conscious, can act as barriers to the development of successful collaboration, because even if we agree in principle with a new way of doing things, in practice our behaviour follows a different set of beliefs. When people from completely different organisational settings come together, the need to uncover and examine mental models is particularly acute. Processes of reflection and dialogue which help people do this are essential to maximising the value of collaboration between schools and employer organisations. One way of doing this is to stimulate shared experience, especially for organisational leaders. Structured learning resources aimed at breaking down the boundaries between the different assumptions and methods of business and education seem relatively hard to find, and the most I can do here is to point to the work of David Warwick, who has developed such resources for teacher training (Pathways to Partnership, Industry and Teacher Education Liaison), and for those involved in business–education liaison (Warwick, 1994). In practical terms, shared experience and reflection on mental models are facilitated by groups such as Common Purpose, a national charity which brings together emerging leaders from different sectors and organisations in local areas, to consider common concerns, problems and challenges and reflect together on ways of tackling them. These opportunities to bring people together to consider generic, rather than operational or sector-specific, questions and problems, and to strengthen networks of trust and information exchange, are extremely valuable.

Strengthening economic activity

The implication of this chapter, and its emphasis on bringing the worlds of education and work together, is that there is a closer relationship between education and economic vitality than we are used to thinking of. Most discussions of the economic value of education take place either at the macro level, where the relationship between the skill levels and the quality of the workforce contributes to the growth rates and power of a whole economy, or at the personal level, where better education improves the job prospects and earning power of individuals. The lesson we can draw from successful innovation is that there is a connection between economic health and education which lies between the two levels, at the level of local economic organisation. In a number of ways, the projects and collaborations that I have described involve direct, instantaneous connections between the productivity of organisations and their involvement in education. The Garibaldi School markets the products and services of a number of companies, in return for the use of their resources and the involvement of their staff in learning activities. Ideas generated by young people are increasingly picked up by corporate volunteers and taken back to their organisations. Especially in creative industries, young people are increasingly seen as a source of innovation: in 1996 a local education authority entered a legal dispute with a computer company over ownership of a computer game programme which a teenager had written using school computers, and subsequently sold for commercial development. As we saw in Chapter 7, a 17-year-old beat several leading companies to win a Website of the Year award in 1997 for a Spice Girls site which he had designed in his bedroom as a birthday present for his young sister. Involvement in educational projects is recognised by many employers as an important source of staff development. Sharing facilities makes more intensive use of capital investment. Contributing to a culture of learning and achievement among young people helps to reduce crime and vandalism, reduce pressure on employees who are also parents, and stimulate the optimism and confidence that buoyant consumer markets require. The processes that we have examined involve the development of a symbiotic, co-dependent relationship between learning and economic prosperity, expressed through active collaboration and exchange, rather than a long-term investment by taxpayers in an educational process which is isolated from the productive activities which pay for it.

The idea of such a direct relationship may alarm some people. The historical separation of education and commerce stretches back a long way, and originates in the mentality which says that the pursuit of learning and knowledge should not be contaminated by the pressures and morals of wealth creation. There is also the strong belief that anything which involves young people in economic activity must be exploitation; it took decades of struggle to banish the systematic use of child labour from the UK, and we should guard against its reintroduction by the back door. Of course this is true, and young people must be carefully nurtured and protected against the pressures and dangers of adult workplace responsibility. But sticking to this view too rigidly robs us of rich opportunities, and ignores reality. Many school pupils, and a rapidly growing number of university students, are involved in part-time work, and many enjoy the challenges and responsibilities that it involves. Rather than seeing it as a necessary evil which should effectively be minimised, the challenge is to use young people's involvement in the economy as an opportunity to enhance their education, and to reinforce their ability to apply what they know to real life.

This view sees educational institutions as important agents in local economies, making a real-time contribution rather than simply churning out people who can contribute later on. In other countries, universities already manage the relationship between learning and work more effectively. The Co-operative education movement in Canada, for example, originated by Waterloo University in the late 1950s, places students in work settings as an integral part of their degree courses, and markets its services to business as a way of involving talented, highly qualified young people who can make a direct contribution to short-term or special projects. Waterloo has an established reputation for producing some of the highest-quality graduates in Canada, who are often snapped up by major employers, especially those whose business success depends on creativity and innovation.

This use of a matching and placement service to improve the quality of education, and to win resources for the institution, should be emulated in the UK, not just by universities, but also by schools and colleges. The concept of employee mutuals – jointly owned organisations whose function is to match their members with employment opportunities, and to provide guidance, training opportunities and occupational benefits – is an idea already circulating in business and trade union circles (Mulgan and Bentley, 1996). A similar principle could be applied to young people's part-time work, with the matching and quality control services organised through schools and colleges. Running such services could be a valuable source of work experience in itself for some young people, and, in broader terms, locating such a service within education would encourage connections between the learning experiences of school and work. Rather than using blanket bans and formal rules and controlling young people's use of their own time, their interests would be protected by paying close attention to the quality and relevance of their experiences, and by organising opportunities around an individual's own priorities and goals, which will have been actively developed in partnership with parents, teachers, advisers, counsellors and so on.

An agenda for employability

There are several paths of development for increasing employability further through education, some more ambitious than others.

1 Opportunities to experience the workplace should begin earlier in a school career, and ideally should involve extended part-time involvement rather than short bursts of full-time placement.
2 Young people's own part-time economic activity should be advised, guided and supported by matching services based in schools and colleges, and at least partly run by young people themselves.
3 Experimentation and research on the most effective ways of integrating context-based learning into curriculum subjects should be supported and disseminated by the Teacher Training Agency, the Department for Education and Employment, the Economic and Social Research Council, and other relevant organisations.
4 The good practice of some Careers services in developing beyond the provision of information and the organisation of short work-experience placements should be disseminated and developed.
5 Mechanisms for joint investment in facilities for learning, and for the right kinds of shared use, should be developed as part of the government's review of the Private Finance Initiative. Schools, colleges, local education authorities and library services should review the opportunities for developing the use of facilities beyond their current scope.
6 Resources for appointing people as brokers and coordinators of collaboration between education and employer organisations should be made a priority. In the Netherlands, pupils often have access to teachers respon-

sible for guidance and counselling who spend half their time working in industry and half in schools (Jarvis, 1995).

7   Students should be more intensively involved in choosing and planning their own paths of development, and for assessing and reviewing their experience.

8   The exposure of teachers and trainee teachers to other forms of work and organisation should be greatly increased, perhaps by requiring that every teacher should spend at least six months on an external placement for every five years of their teaching career.

Developing employability in education enables us to focus on breaking down a series of barriers: between formal learning and informal experience, between the mindsets of teachers and of employers and employees, between abstract knowledge and its concrete application, and between the operating systems of different kinds of organisation. The relationships and activities that I have described involve fluid and uneven development, building on prior achievements and tailoring joint projects to specific circumstances and opportunities. They cannot be driven solely from above, but must instead be nurtured and encouraged, rewarded and celebrated. Their primary tools of development are not schematic blueprints, rules, or even curriculum requirements, but rather the development of shared goals, the strengthening of relationships and the willingness to innovate and communicate in the service of common objectives. As such, they are inherently demanding; often they require additional resources, but more often they require us to rethink the way we do things, to understand the perspectives and abilities of others, and to work hard to ensure that the means we employ are the best ones available to serve the ends we desire.

9

PERSONAL CAPACITIES

What is it that we want young people to have as they enter the adult world? The argument so far is that conventional education does not do enough to prepare them for the wide range of roles, responsibilities and challenges that they will face. Too much talent and potential is wasted by blunt methods, limited resources, institutional inertia. Too much motivation is stifled by the presumed need for control, deep-rooted assumptions about the purpose of education, and the inflexibility of the ways in which learning is organised. Certain kinds of ability and talent are neglected, because schooling focuses on too narrow a range of intelligences.

If this is right, it has important implications for the way we think about ability. Our conceptions of skills and knowledge are both outdated and confused. One reason for this is that definitions of educational qualification, by and large, are still set by universities. Through their roles in determining professional qualification, in training teachers and, through the examination boards, in defining the syllabus and assessing competence, universities occupy a powerful position in defining educational achievement. The expertise and wisdom of universities in some fields should be valued and respected, but we must also recognise that, at least for the time being, universities excel in a relatively narrow field of human achievement. Universities, by definition, are staffed by people who never left school. Many universities still struggle with the distinction between the subject knowledge required for a particular degree course, and the learning skills, techniques, and dispositions needed to thrive in higher education. Unfortunately most still concentrate on the former at the expense of the latter.

Another illustration is the confusing debate about 'core skills' and 'key skills' in vocational education. The Dearing review of qualifications for 16–19-year-olds (Dearing, 1996) attempted to clarify the debate over which skills were foundational to all vocational education, and which should be tied to specific subjects. The response to Dearing's efforts was sustained criticism that the ones he chose were too narrow. There is still considerable confusion, even among researchers and practitioners, about what the 'key skills' are actually supposed to entail.

120

This confusion is not just in education. Employers have come under growing pressure to redefine the packages of skills, knowledge and understanding that they want workers to have. As knowledge has become more important to organisational success, and organisations have been restructured, new emphasis has been put on the 'softer', less tangible abilities such as interpersonal skills, motivation and adaptability. Practical definitions of such abilities are still in short supply; in most workplaces managers still rely on relatively informal instruments such as reputation, informal feedback and unstructured observation, to assess people's strengths and weaknesses. Employers are struggling with the distinction between specialised, technical or occupational knowledge and the more general personal qualities and dispositions necessary for a worker to collaborate effectively, maintain appropriate relationships, adapt to changing circumstances, solve problems and exploit opportunities.

It is still often assumed that passing certain defined tests of ability implies that a candidate possesses the other capacities needed to thrive; someone who has had a successful school career and come out with a clutch of 'qualifications' must, in some way, have developed discipline, social abilities, self-awareness and so on. But this is a poor guide. Many academically successful students are unable to apply their knowledge in contexts where it might be useful. Many others lack the reflectiveness to change their learning strategies in response to new challenges. Even more find themselves unable to cope with emotional challenges, or the task of forming their own personal goals once the structures and certainties of conventional education are removed. Anyway, such assumptions turn out to be unfair. If formal educational 'qualifications' are used to sort candidates, then those without them will be systematically excluded on the basis of qualifications which are not necessarily relevant. The most graphic illustration of this is the bias of employers towards candidates with academic qualifications for jobs which do not necessarily require them, and the even more prejudiced bias of some employers and professions towards candidates from certain types of school.

As David Hargreaves has pointed out, examination passes are rarely 'qualifications' as such. They do not actually qualify students for anything more than further study (Hargreaves, 1994). The argument so far implies that the list of abilities which young people need is longer than the list by which the education system currently sets its goals. While emotional intelligence, character development, collaborative skills, reflectiveness and the ability to apply knowledge in novel situations are all embedded in education to some extent, they are half-hidden, often poorly developed and left too much to chance.

But simply adding to the list is not enough. Many of the important abilities can be expressed and developed while pursuing knowledge already specified in formal curriculum subjects. It is impossible to develop or demonstrate emotional intelligence in the absence of some other question or issue. One cannot work in a team for its own sake. Also, it is unreasonable simply to add to the list of things which schools are charged with developing in their pupils. Instead, we must rethink what we mean by ability, skills and knowledge. We must change our framework for understanding and assessing ability, to reflect the qualities and capacities which we have rediscovered as important, rather than trying to bolt them on to the existing structure.

How should we organise this new framework?

The first, basic criterion of ability should be *understanding*. In *The Unschooled Mind*, Howard Gardner defines understanding as:

> a sufficient grasp of concepts, principles, or skills so that one can bring them to bear on new problems and situations, deciding in which ways one's present competences can suffice and in which ways one may require new skills or knowledge.
>
> (Gardner, 1991: 18)

Note that this definition applies not just to conventional educational settings, but to any sphere of action. It applies equally to understanding personal relationships as it does to understanding physics or French grammar. Two things are indispensable to genuine understanding. The first is that it entails being aware not just of what you know, but also of what you *do not* know. When presented with a novel situation or problem, understanding requires a learner to be able to judge the resources she already possesses, and what she still needs to find in order to solve the problem. The second is that it requires the ability to represent the problem from a number of different perspectives, and to recognise that there will be more than one route to solving it. David Perkins has described this ability as the ability to *go beyond* current knowledge (Perkins, 1992). Clinging to one particular representation of a problem, or one strategy for solving it, is a sign that a learner does not understand the place of the problem in its broader context, or its relevance to other things they may know. Very few educators would claim not to teach for understanding. It seems an obvious goal. But if we remember the signs of distress and misunderstanding examined in Chapter 2, we should be wary of the idea that schooling automatically promotes understanding.

If understanding is the core general criterion, how can we organise our framework of abilities around it?

Mental characteristics

One way to do so might be to describe each individual in terms of her inherent ability, or potential. Each of us has a broad portfolio of intelligences, rooted in our genetic and neural endowments, which we could try to analyse in each and every individual. With time, close observation and expertise, it might be possible to assess them, to produce a picture of each person's mind which tells us what she is able to do. We might be able to measure each intelligence and give it a score based on some scientifically derived scale. It would be a profile based on a kind of educational brain scan.

At first glance such a profile looks ideal, because it would accurately reflect the unique mix of intelligences each person possesses. But it is wrong, for two reasons. First, it would be impractical. The minutiae of personal experience are impossible to record or to document comprehensively. Even if it were possible to connect individual events in the brain and body with the performances that they produce, it would be impossibly time-consuming and expensive to do it as a routine part of the educational process. Second, and more important, such a process would be founded on a spurious assumption: that ability is something that is contained inside a person's head, locked up as part of some kind of mental 'power'. The work we examined in Chapter 3, which contributes to a new view of intelligence, refutes this assumption. Ability is founded on interaction between people and their environment. Even if people's intelligence is 'biopsychological potential', including the 'genetic and neurological substrates' of their behaviour and their 'cognitive powers, traits, and temperamental disposition' (Gardner, 1993: 50), it can only be assessed in relation to domains of action which are valued in the world beyond the brain. Any action involves intention, or purpose. Actions have to have a goal, and the goals, or the purposes to which we put our minds and bodies are given value by their relevance to what we, as individuals, communities and societies, see as being important, useful or beautiful.

So, in order to understand and classify abilities, the employment of intelligence to do useful things, we need an external frame of reference with which to work. To say that somebody is exercising intelligence, or is able to perform a particular task, we must refer not only to that person's internal characteristics, but also to how these characteristics fit the challenges of the outside world.

Where could we look for such a framework? To be useful in education, it would have to be accurate, in the sense that it reflected things that are genuinely valued in society. It would also have to be rigorous, because we would want to analyse it carefully, referring to its different components and comparing a learner's performance against them. Finally, it would have to be practical, because such a framework would be a tool for everyday assessment.

Institutional positions

One place to look might be inside institutions. Institutions, governed by a set of aims, rules and principles, are organised around a division of labour based on expertise and authority. Each member's role and responsibilities reflect the knowledge, skills and personal characteristics required to get their bit of the job done, or to fulfil their responsibilities. Whether a family member, a public service manager, a university professor, a technician or a bishop, institutional roles offer a set of definitions.

If we followed this route, ability could be defined by a person's capacity to thrive inside an institution. This would mean possessing the knowledge and experience to perform a particular role, understanding and accepting the division of power and authority, meeting the threshold conditions of overall membership in terms of behaviour, etiquette and relationships with others. To some extent this is what conventional education does; pupils must meet the threshold conditions of school, and their abilities are measured, at least in part, according to definitions of what a learner should have achieved by a certain stage of their school career. The National Curriculum defines ability at a series of Key Stages, which are designed to be generic but, in practice, are quite closely correlated with the years of schooling and a standardised progression through them.

But there is a problem. We have already seen that, in the world of work, organisations are being radically restructured. Institutions change all the time, and they are changing faster at the moment than they have done for a long time. Hierarchical position is a poor guide to real ability. More and more people live and work outside large institutions; trust in national institutions has fallen, self-employment is rising, and the changing values of the younger generation place a higher premium on individualism, self-invention and authenticity. Organisations should *reflect* appropriate definitions of achievement rather than containing them. They are a means, not an end in themselves. In the business world there is a growing recognition that rigid organisational forms are a brake on performance. If the institution is too strong, too inflexible, then people come to define themselves by it, rather than recognising the deeper value of what they do, inside or outside institutions. We already know that the current organisation of schooling fails to maximise the transfer of useful knowledge, between subjects, between learners, and between different contexts. Trying to frame abilities through institutions would aggravate, rather than alleviate, these problems.

Academic subjects

Faced with this problem, some people might ask what is wrong with the traditional academic organisation of subjects and disciplines. The point of the curriculum is to classify subjects according to a rigorous and coherent framework, drawn mainly from the intellectual division of labour used in universities. This divides subjects into meaningful, internally coherent groups which define the domain in which a learner's ability is developed. In one sense, this is surely right. Promoting active learning of the kind I have described runs the risk of emphasising excitement, diversity and concrete experience at the risk of losing rigour, clarity and depth. Students may have skated the surface of many different experiences and disciplines, but they will not have the depth of knowledge or understanding to pursue any one seriously.

The problem with this view is that scholasticism is a relatively narrow field of human achievement. It implies, rather than explicitly addresses, kinds of intelligence and ability which are vital for people to thrive. It is true that academic disciplines have a core of knowledge, concepts, principles and ways of thinking which any emerging expert needs to master. But academic disciplines are not as tightly bounded as many people are used to thinking. Schools of thought are porous and have blurred boundaries. Scientific breakthroughs depend as much on the interface between disciplines as on mastery of a single one. For example, artificial intelligence theory depends as much upon philosophy as it does on physics, computer science and mathematics. Howard Gardner, one of the most influential academics of the 1980s and 1990s, occupies two professorial chairs, one at the Harvard Graduate School of Education and one at the Boston Medical School. In all areas of life, creativity is increasingly sought after and often depends on the ability to bring together insights from different fields in order to shape new ways of doing and thinking. The traditional scholastic division is important, but on its own it is inadequate as a way of organising learning.

Tasks and competences

What about coming at the problem from a different perspective? Throughout this book we have emphasised the importance of context and practice. Perhaps we should focus on practical tasks, assessed by experts, including but not restricted to traditional scholastic tasks. Such a framework has obvious advantages. It connects ability to practical, real-life situations, which do not have to be assessed inside educational institutions. This approach has influenced recent developments in vocational education, where NVQs and GNVQs have been assessed through evidence that a student has performed tasks, such as using a photocopier, in workplace settings. But this is not enough, on its own, to show evidence of understanding. Of course, performing specific individual tasks is an integral part of the demonstration of understanding. But genuine understanding entails being able to integrate the knowledge and actions required for a task into a broader whole, linking them to other possible courses of action and ways of tackling a problem. A loose collection of tasks performed does not constitute a mature understanding. What happens if the photocopier jams? Does the student have an idea of what strategies she might use to solve the problem? Just like remembering pieces of factual knowledge and abstract concepts, performing isolated strings of tasks is not enough to demonstrate ability and understanding. It is telling that, in moving away from job specifications based on an organisational hierarchy, task specification has been tried by many businesses but quickly abandoned as employers increasingly expect workers to take on new tasks and solve new problems, and want to assess performance in broader, more fluid ways (Strebler, 1997).

Realms and roles

So we have rejected institutions, scholastic divisions and task-based competences as the basis for a framework. What do we have left? The first part of the answer is to take a closer look at *realms* and *domains* – the arenas within which understanding is developed. A domain is 'the discipline or craft by which intelligence is practiced in society' (Gardner, 1993: 37; see also Csikszentmihalyi, 1988: 325–39). The quality or value of an action is determined by the *field*, the set of people and institutions which are skilled or expert in a particular domain, and therefore qualified to judge. Domains come in all shapes and sizes, from the routine and relatively mundane to the abstract and highly specialised. Domains overlap, in the same way that intelligences overlap. It is important to recognise that domains are not fixed, but are continually developed by new practice, new ideas, new scientific discoveries. The domain of basketball playing is developed by new applications of athletic ability, such as the invention of new ways of shooting at the basket, by new technologies, such as shoes which enable players to jump higher, and by ways of thinking which create new strategies, such as the zone-based defence. In this case the field would include players, coaches, officials, and perhaps experienced spectators. All such developments are constrained by the rules of the game, and to some extent by physical laws, such as gravity and the speed of human reflexes. A more academic example of a domain is quantum physics. This domain requires understanding of the basic laws and concepts of the physical world. It also contains more specialised concepts, such as the time–space continuum, black holes and, a more recent addition, wormholes. It requires certain ways of thinking and framing problems associated with experimental method, analysing results, and communicating findings. Understanding the constraints of a particular domain is the key to overcoming them; only by delving deep into the rules and structures which govern our actions can we make those actions more valuable.

This view of domains is immensely helpful in developing a view of how education should assist understanding. It shows how the intelligence of individuals and groups is mapped on to the contours of the outside world. It indicates that education as a process should encourage students to develop abilities which reflect the constraints, rigours and unsolved challenges of different domains. Domains are universal. They include parenting, cooking, citizenship and personal relationships. The boundaries between domains constantly shift, as we discover new connections and apply the skills and knowledge learned in one to others. They are hugely practical, because they give us a framework for understanding actions and abilities which is rooted in the real world. They also show how different intelligences can be combined in the performance of domain-specific tasks. Playing the violin, for example, requires musical intelligence, but will also probably require bodily–kinaesthetic intelligence, mathematical intelligence and interpersonal intelligence in different degrees. The intelligences are not employed in isolation from each other, but combined in a performance which has value within the domain. But there is one major question unanswered by domains as we have described them. Where does the distinction lie between intelligence as 'underlying biopsychological potential' and domains as the arenas within which intelligence is displayed? Domains are shaped by thoughts and concepts as much as by external characteristics. We are used to seeing thoughts and concepts as purely internal, as properties of the brain. Surely they are inside our heads? But internal characteristics are expressed and shaped by the interaction between our selves and the outside world. Self and world are not easily separated. Take strategic thinking as an example. We know that being able to think well is a constituent part of intelligent behaviour, in almost any domain. The capacity to reflect, to stand back from the immediate problem and draw comparisons with it, is valuable and often highly prized. But surely this kind of thinking is itself a domain? It has a field of experts, the people who best understand, analyse and practise good thinking. It has a wide range of applications, expressed in the performance of specific tasks. But if thinking is a mental property, part of our underlying potential, a personal characteristic which is internal, how can it also be a domain in the outside world?

This problem mirrors a deep historical question in the philosophy of mind. What is the difference between brain and mind? Do they have distinct identities, or are they the same thing? If they are the same thing, why do we not refer to mind as brain, and equate thoughts with individual brain events? Why do we have a language of thought and action? If they are not the same thing, how can they both be located in the same place? A novel answer to this problem has been proposed by Oxford philosopher William Child. Roughly, it goes like this. It may well be that thoughts, expressed in language and behaviour, are 'micro-physical events' in the brain. We would use a particular framework of language and concepts to describe them as such, based on our understanding of the physical and chemical processes by which the brain functions. But the framework of concepts that we use to understand and describe thoughts as they relate to action in the world is different. It involves intentionality, or purpose, and is based on the role of thinking in our lives, as opposed to scientific analysis of brain events. A thought and a brain event might be one and the same thing in terms of physical–chemical events. But the language of physics and chemistry could never capture the full meaning of a thought, because that meaning is grounded in a conceptual framework inherently connected to the world of people and things.

This argument is very similar to the move made by David Perkins in *Outsmarting IQ* (1995) in answering the question of what the mind is made of. He daringly declares an 'open-immigration policy' in order to answer it, asking whether things that we do not usually associate with the mind are in fact part of the mental landscape. His answer is based on a theory of *realms*. A realm is very similar to a domain, but includes things that happen within the mind.

> Any topic or activity people can come to know their way around constitutes a realm. Ballroom dancing is a realm. Carburetor repair is

a realm. So are quantum mechanics, kite flying, weight lifting, reading classical mystery whodunits, English literature of the nineteenth century, arbitration, public speaking, collecting butterflies, and . . . getting around Harvard Square.

(Perkins, 1995: 249)

As well as these primarily experiential kinds of knowing your way around, for Perkins there are realms of reflective intelligence, such as decision-making, remembering and memorising, reasoning, argument and everyday problem-solving. A realm is made of three groups of components: actions, beliefs and concepts. To take one of Perkins's illustrations, the realm of memorising comprises:

1   An Action System, including:

- rehearsing
- organising ideas into categories
- finding links to something you already know
- inventing visual associations
- testing yourself, and concentrating on what you miss

2   A Belief System, including such beliefs and values as:

- rehearsal aids memory
- my memory is good or not so good
- when I organise something for myself, that helps me remember it
- visual associations help me remember things

3   A Conceptual System, including the concepts of:

- memory
- rehearsal
- association
- image
- organisation
- forgetting

The concept of realms gives us a framework which can stretch from the immediacy and familiarity of everyday activities such as dining and tying shoelaces, to general and highly specialised realms such as computer systems analysis and astrophysics. It includes realms of thinking and, importantly, feeling and disposition. It acknowledges the complexity of many disciplines, and the rigour and depth required to understand them, but it is rooted in the formation of realms through repeated everyday activities. As a concept it can travel from a child's earliest experiences and activities to the furthest edges of human knowledge and achievement. Realms connect and combine in complex, fluid ways, depending on what we are trying to achieve and what resources we have at our disposal. Without a lot of experience in a particular realm, we may resort to more generalised realms of thinking, or to a related experiential realm which we do know, in order to find solutions.

It also provides us, as Perkins (1995) explains, with a powerful new metaphor for understanding what happens when we get smarter – we *learn our way around*. Knowing our way around involves more than facts and knowledge. It includes feelings, values, beliefs and concepts. It is not just a question of being able to traverse routes that we have been over before, but to find new ones through the landscape according to the specific context and goal of our activity. It enables us to make 'flexible compositions of new patterns of activity', drawing on the full riches of our environment, past experience and reflective capacities, to find the best way of doing something new.

Together, these ideas offer us a way of organising the challenges and spheres of action which require understanding and intelligent behaviour. Knowing your way around a realm will include propositional, theoretical and practical knowledge. It will also include insights gained from direct experience, values, beliefs and feelings. It connects the individual perspective of the learner with the wider systems of knowledge, practice and understanding with which they will have to grapple in order to thrive. It is important to notice that realms are not bounded by any of our traditional frameworks or institutions for organising knowledge, whether they be schools, universities, businesses, libraries or anything else. Such institutions operate within realms and often specialise in particular ones. But being inside them is no guarantee that you will learn your way around the realms in which they operate.

Any parent or educator who has read this far might justifiably be feeling depressed by now. The message is that our conventional ways of categorising and organising ability leave too much out and are rigid and inflexible when compared with the complexity, richness and diversity of the realms into which our understanding and actions are organised. When time is short, resources limited and priorities need to be set, how can we possibly hope to organise learning so that realms are fully explored and genuine understanding nurtured? How do we synthesise and integrate learning about different realms so that it matches the intelligences and learning needs of our young people? It is all very well to muse philosophically about the nature of mind and the staggering complexity of the human universe, but how, practically, do we organise it? The answer, of course, is right in front of us, but we are not used to looking at it clearly. How do people integrate and organise their realm knowledge into manageable packages which are useful and practical, but leave space for more learning, not just in education but in all walks of life? The answer is that they do it through *roles*.

Role-playing is found in every kind of human activity. Roles range from parent, citizen, peer, class member, to coach, teacher, manager, mentor, steward, exemplar, administrator, governor and critic. Some, such as 'Queen of England' or 'Archbishop of Canterbury', are ancient and highly formalised. Others are fluid and informal. Roles are the means by which we organise our understanding and abilities, translating what we are capable of doing into meaningful performances in a particular realm. Whenever we perform an act, it is in one role or another.

Roles are typically performed in organisations, but they do not have to be. They are not ultimately fixed, but reflect responsibilities, goals, priorities, values and the environment in which they function. Any individual manages a portfolio of roles at any point in their life. Often, roles can clash. For example, the conflict between being a parent and being a worker is one that has come under growing scrutiny in the last few years, as women have entered the workforce and working hours have risen. Roles do not define us comprehensively, but they are a means to express different parts of our identity and ability. Finding the right ones and the right balance between them is one of the fundamental challenges of adult life. Roles reflect the shape and size of the realms in which they operate. The role of centre-forward in a soccer team is highly specific and context-bound. The role of match steward at a soccer ground is a bit more general, requiring different kinds of knowledge and judgement, attention to a wide range of factors, and conferring a different kind of authority. The role of teacher will be familiar to many readers, though its content and scope are subject to vigorous debate. Should teaching involve the amount of paperwork that British teachers currently labour under? Is it primarily about the transmission of knowledge and information to pupils, or about the facilitation of discovery and self-directed learning? People have different views, and teachers will shape their own role according to their abilities, beliefs and the resources available to them.

Roles mirror realms, in the sense that they can travel from the relatively narrow and context-specific to the broad and highly general. Using the two together, we can create a practical, rigorous and flexible framework for understanding what we want young people to have as they leave their first period of full-time education. In general, we should want them to have an emergent understanding of the most important realms of thought and action, and to be able to relate these realms meaningfully to the fulfilment of valued roles in society. The specific realms and roles will depend partly on a student's talents, abilities and aspirations, and partly on what society counts as valuable. There are a number of generic roles which we should be able to agree as being essential. A tentative initial list of these generic roles, and the capacities they imply, would include:

Learner The capacity to understand what it is to identify one's goals and learning needs, to identify and gain access to the resources which enable one to achieve those goals, to set appropriate criteria for assessing the achievement of those goals, and to evaluate reflectively how one's learning impacts on one's understanding of other realms, and how one defines one's future goals.

Worker The capacity to understand how one's abilities and energy can be employed in productive activity, including forming and sustaining working relationships, developing motivation and discipline, understanding the relationship between inputs and productive output, and applying oneself creatively to finding more appropriate, productive ways of working.

Teacher The capacity to pass on appropriate knowledge and understanding in a particular realm, and to facilitate the development of genuine understanding. The capacity to motivate and encourage the habits and disciplines of effective learning and to assess and evaluate progress in learning.

Citizen The capacity to understand and enact the responsibilities and opportunities entailed by membership of a civic and political community, to recognise and fulfil obligations, understand and realise rights of entitlement, and be committed to appropriate forms of collective action, including debate and dispute resolution.

Parent The capacity to understand and fulfil the obligations and responsibilities of parenthood, the range of skills, knowledge and commitment required to fulfil them, and the forms of satisfaction and fulfilment which flow from successful parenting.

Expert The capacity to understand and develop the key components of expertise in a given realm, including the range and types of knowledge, the contexts in which they can be applied, the people and institutions which constitute the field, the conceptual frameworks and ways of thinking which govern the realm, and the unanswered questions and puzzles which are still to be solved.

Peer The capacity to understand and perform the function of co-member of a particular occupational, educational or social group, including understanding the common aspects which co-membership entails, the obligations and responsibilities towards other members, and appropriate rules of conduct, including the place of competition and mutual assistance, within a particular group.

Mentor The capacity to understand and perform the role of mentoring, entailing the establishment of a one-to-one relationship based on authority in and experience of a realm in which the mentee is developing, including the establishment of trust and confidentiality, recognising the limits of the realm in which one is mentoring, and the processes of communication and exchange by which one can assist a mentee's development.

Leader The capacity to recognise and formulate goals and challenges, to motivate people to meet them in appropriate ways and to reward and celebrate achievement, both individual and collective.

Problem solver The capacity to recognise, frame and analyse problems, to investigate possible ways of representing and approaching them, and to employ a range of techniques, resources and abilities in order to solve them.

These specifications are deliberately generic. None of them could be exercised in the absence of specific contexts, realms and relationships. But each of them shows how roles which are valued in society are framed, and hopefully how the different dimensions of understanding and ability are integrated and synthesised within them. People can hold multiple roles at the same time, and might shift between them almost from moment to moment, just as they might simultaneously employ knowledge of different realms such as dining and conversation.

Implications for education

What are the main implications for education? The first, obvious one is that exposure to and exploration of a number of different roles is an integral part of high-quality education. Schools require many different roles in order to work as they are, including teachers, learners, leaders, administrators, cleaners, technicians, peers and parents. But if students are learning their way around different realms, surely they should observe and experience a wider range of roles associated with them? This confirms my earlier argument that part of the effectiveness of active learning programmes stems from their ability to involve a wide range of adults and young people in their execution. The teacher of a specific subject is definitely part of the field of experts in that subject, as well as (we hope) something of an expert in ways of learning. But the realm that students are learning their way around is not restricted to the classroom, and the field is not restricted to the school's departmental staff. People use, for example, physics in many different kinds of activity, which can be explored and analysed in a vast range of settings. Citizenship includes concepts, such as democracy and pluralism, which may be best introduced through reading and discussion within school, but which are applied by every member of a political community, from national political leaders to individual voters.

Good education should involve learners in observing and rehearsing a wide number of roles which relate to those that they may fulfil in later life. The material for such roles should be drawn as much from the roles which young people are learning to perform in their own lives as from controlled simulations or prepared material. It should involve, as often as possible, rotation of roles, so that learners have the opportunity to examine situations from different perspectives, and to observe others performing roles which they have also experienced.

Four kinds of capacity

Having set out a framework for understanding the contours of knowledge and action through realms, and the organisation and synthesis of different forms of knowing and acting through roles, I now propose four fundamentally important types of personal capacity which education for young people should help to provide. They are set out in general terms, but would be channelled through specific activities, realms and roles. I am suggesting an underlying set of capacities which should serve as basic foundations of educational effectiveness.

Dispositions

Dispositions are 'the proclivities that lead us in one direction rather than another within the freedom of action that we have' (Perkins, 1995: 275). We are all used to recognising dispositions and attributing people's behaviour to them. But we are also used to thinking that dispositions are fixed and unchangeable. If we are at a loss to explain the specific reasons for somebody behaving in a particular way, we often ascribe to it to disposition or temperament. Dispositions are difficult to describe with precision because they are general and diffuse. They underlie specific actions but do not explain them entirely. Dispositions can be moral or emotional, related to specific ways of approaching problems or of reacting to events. We also have thinking dispositions: tendencies to think in particular ways. If there are weaknesses in the way we think, and for all of us there are some, we might tend towards fuzzy thinking, hasty thinking, sprawling thinking which wanders back and forth without clarity or apparent purpose, or narrow thinking, which fails to recognise things that go against the grain of what we want to believe.

Dispositions partly reflect our genetic endowments and our combination of intelligences. But they also reflect the environment in which we have developed our beliefs, attachments and values, and the sensitivity with which we respond to what we encounter. In *Emotional Intelligence*, Daniel Goleman (1996) describes the work of Jerome Kagan, a Harvard psychologist who has studied the temperamental qualities of young children. He distinguished at least four kinds of emotional disposition: bold, timid, upbeat and melancholy. Any parent will recognise the differences between children's temperaments at birth, and there is often a strong correlation between the innate dispositions with which we are born and the kind of adult we develop into. However, because of the remarkable plasticity of the brain in the first two decades of life, Goleman argues that these years represent a crucial window of opportunity for emotional development. Dispositions are shaped and nurtured as much as they are fixed by our genetic endowments. Some children, by a trick of nature, are born with happy, outgoing dispositions, although these often change dramatically during different phases of childhood, triggered by new situations such as starting school, or by events like the birth of a sibling or the break-up of a family. But there is sufficient evidence to show that emotional dispositions can be developed through the subtle interplay of our mental circuitry, the stimuli and direction we receive from others, the dominant features of our experience and our emerging capacity for reflection. The same can be said of moral dispositions, our capacity to distinguish right from wrong and to guide our behaviour according to that judgement. As David Perkins argues, dispositions towards certain kinds of thinking are also crucially important and can be developed through practice, reflection, encouragement and direction (Perkins, 1995).

Dispositions are fuzzy and fluid. They soak our specific thoughts and actions, and help to guide our reactions to events: successes, failures, setbacks and surprises. Their overall value must be assessed from more than one perspective – in relation to a person's individual talents and strongest abilities, but also to their goals and values, the beliefs and aspirations which guide their progress through life. They must also be evaluated in relation to the challenges, risks, opportunities and responsibilities which we all face and the needs and judgements of others. The goal of education in respect of dispositions should be to encourage students to recognise and understand their dispositions and how they are shaped, and to evaluate them for themselves. During childhood, while young people are dependent on others for their wellbeing, the judgement of their protectors is all-important. But, almost from the earliest age, the dawn of self-awareness and communication through language, children can begin to recognise and take responsibility for themselves.

As they grow older, that responsibility grows, and psychologist Mihaly Csikszentmihalyi has shown that people who can set their own goals are most likely to achieve long-term psychological wellbeing (Csikszentmihalyi, 1997: ch. 8). But the ideal is not for students to leave education completely self-sufficient, sealed off from others and defining themselves and their goals in isolation. We are all interdependent, relying on others for fulfilment and achievement as much as they depend on us. The goal is therefore to support young people in gradually mastering their own destinies, by shaping and refining their abilities and goals, recognising the influence that others have over them, and understanding how they can gain the trust and support of others in order to achieve.

Deep disciplinary understanding

All forms of personal development, including personal and social development, dispositional and emotional development and moral fluency, involve disciplinary understanding. However, the more familiar curriculum subjects are also indispensable. There is no way in which this book argues that understanding of such subjects is of secondary importance. It is partly through disciplinary understanding of domains such as modern languages, sciences, mathematics or literature that we can develop the softer, less tangible qualities which we have emphasised. In any case, good understanding of a number of domains is essential to economic self-sufficiency and self-fulfilment. Such domains are not irrelevant to life, as many schoolchildren and some adults complain, although it may be that the way they are learned is not relevant enough. An emergent understanding of a number of mainstream curricular disciplines is therefore a crucial foundation of personal effectiveness. On the surface, such disciplines or domains can be described in the way that we are used to thinking of academic or school subjects. But to constitute genuine understanding, they must represent far more than is usually tested by public examinations or some traditional teaching methods. Following Howard Gardner (1991), such understanding would include:

- possession of the key facts, laws and principles of a specific domain;
- mastery of the conceptual frameworks, ways of thinking, dominant methods and constraints of a discipline;
- ability to represent and describe problems in or features of a domain in a number of different ways;
- ability to apply the knowledge and techniques of a discipline in a number of contexts, primarily those in which the discipline is most often used or useful;
- evolving awareness of the linkages between different domains, their similarities and differences;
- appreciation of the deep underlying questions and assumptions of a specific discipline, its unanswered puzzles, its purpose, relevance and contribution to society;
- ability to discuss and analyse them in both domain-specific and more general terms.

This approach to subject-based understanding is more ambitious than our conventional conception of what it is to 'know' a subject. Serious and practical work has already been done to start turning it into a set of tools for learning and teaching which can be used in everyday settings (Stone Wiske, 1998). If it is to be achieved in schools, it implies that the current priority of 'coverage' must be relaxed. There is a simple trade-off here, between the range of subjects which can be covered in the course of a school career, and the depth of understanding of each subject. While developing understanding in a relatively broad range of disciplines is essential, we should not assume that the broadest possible range is the most desirable. One way of justifying this implication is by placing it in the new context of 'lifelong' learning. If we want people to be able and motivated to learn throughout their lives, and if the educational resources are going to be available for them to do so, we should be confident that knowledge of a wide number of subjects is not as essential for a 16- or 18-year old it might once have been when their opportunities for further learning were more severely constrained. Developing the motivation, the depth of understanding and the personal discipline required to understand in depth is surely the more important priority for education during childhood and adolescence. Deep disciplinary understanding also implies the ability to make connections between subjects, and to make reflective and general observations, helping to lay the foundations for understanding new disciplines later in life.

Reflective and metacognitive capacities

An often-mentioned property of human beings is our capacity to think in abstract terms. We can generalise, and develop principles which apply to a wider range of contexts than the one we are in at a given moment. We can think about our own thinking, to observe, in some sense, our own cognitive acts. Reflection is a key to value. We can only learn to value something specific if we can draw back from it, consider its importance in the wider scheme of things, and analyse its relationship to other parts of our experience. We use this capacity, more or less, to guide our specific thoughts and actions. Often we are not immediately aware of the fact that we are doing it, which is where reflection becomes integrally linked to our dispositions. Reflection has all sorts of different techniques and components. Much of the time we reflect in ways that are largely unstructured and spontaneous. But there is, as David Perkins (1995) and many others have shown, a coherent and systematic core to mental management and reflective capacity.

It is important not to overstate the ability or importance of reflective, or metacognitive, ability. Mental strategies are valuable in all sorts of situations, but they cannot ultimately substitute for understanding derived from experience. If we focus too hard on the strength of general principles and strategies, we soon fall down in the face of problems which demand context-specific, experiential knowledge. But, as Perkins (1995) explains, reflective intelligence can help us to face novel or complex problems with confidence. Faced with a problem which we have not come across before, or which seems particularly difficult or important, we can stand back from it, analyse its different components, think about past experiences which might be helpful, and consider the different angles from which we might approach a solution. Reflective ability is a 'control system' for our other kinds of intelligence. It can compensate for the limitations of experiential intelligence, which is formed from repeated patterns of experience. It is particularly valuable in situations where patterns from the past are not quite right for the task in hand.

A slightly different kind of reflection is also at the heart of our ability to motivate and value ourselves. Self-esteem and motivation always depend on secure, loving attachments formed in childhood and on the respect and encouragement of other people. But they also depend on our capacity to work out, as individuals, what we value and why we care about it. Understanding ourselves, an integral part of emotional intelligence, depends on reflection.

Reflective capacity is something that we are all born with, and some people are better at it than others. But it can also be cultivated. Many different methods have been developed to support the development of thinking abilities. Michael Barber quotes one, CASE, where a controlled experiment showed that pupils who learned to think and reflect while learning science produced markedly better results than the control group, not just in science but also in mathematics and English (Barber, 1996: 180). Schemes such as Matthew Lipman's Philosophy for Children, Edward de Bono's CoRT, and High Scope, a method which emphasises the importance of a learner developing and executing her own plan of action to achieve learning goals, have all shown that a greater reflective capacity can boost educational attainment and creativity (Lipman et al., 1980; de Bono, 1983, 1986). Such abilities have often been taught as a separate part of the curriculum, devoted specifically to reflectiveness and metacognition. But the challenge is to infuse them into the subject matter of school and everyday life, to ease the transfer of knowledge between different kinds of situation, and to nurture understanding of the connections and relationships between different kinds of knowledge. To do this, our ways of thinking about education and instruction have to change, to recognise that it is not just *what* a student knows that matters, but also *how* they know it. As Perkins puts it, the difference is comparable to that between a heap of bricks and a building. 'Conventional instruction in the subject matters comes close to providing a heap of facts and skills . . . with the main hope that the learner will magically transform the heap into a building' (Perkins, 1995). Developing disciplinary understanding requires a learner to be able to integrate her heap of knowledge, skills and experience into a coherent structure, and reflective capacity has a crucial part to play. Leaving such integration to students to work out for themselves, or to other educators such as parents and mentors, is a basic neglect.

Once again, this analysis has strong implications for the way that learning is structured. First, it will take more time. Second, it points to the importance of seeing education, not as a one-way transmission of knowledge and attitudes, but as a series of cycles or loops. Building reflection into the educational process means finding time and space to do it, and being able to respond appropriately to what that reflection might produce – responses, questions and insights which neither teachers nor curriculum designers are able to predict. This might seem impossibly hard to do, but in fact it is already being done in many places. Matthew Lipman's Philosophy for Children is used successfully with children as young as six and seven. Anecdotal evidence from the use of High Scope with three- and four-year-olds suggests that when they reach Key Stage One of the National Curriculum, which necessitates more teacher-directed learning to ensure that it meets the various criteria, their ability to plan their own learning can already be so well developed that they resist the imposition of pre-planned pathways. Programmes such as Jenny Mosley's Circle Time, a schema for group discussion and conflict resolution in schools, also show the valuable role of shared reflection and how it can impact on the ethos within which learning takes place.

Collaborative capacities

Establishing, maintaining and developing social relationships is one of the most important challenges of growing up. Sociability is in our genes; the impulse to cooperate is as deeply embedded as any other human instinct. But making relationships work is not easy. Relationships are vital from a number of different perspectives. They are at the heart of emotional intelligence. They are increasingly important to employability. They are integral to personal identity, self-awareness and self-esteem. Even those who lock themselves away from the outside world are shaped and influenced by the thoughts and actions of others. Active citizenship is deeply connected to our ability to establish relationships with other people, not just with ideas and institutions.

The analysis presented in previous chapters points to the importance of informal networks of relationships in determining our access to formal opportunities and our effectiveness in formal institutions. More often than not, achievements in life are shared. Not only do we depend on other people to support us while we try to achieve, but most things of value are created by the shared effort of more than one person. Sociability is, therefore, a foundation of personal effectiveness. But conventional education often constrains the development of this capacity, for two main reasons. The first is that relationships are too often defined by institutional structures rather than on the basis of trust, authority and mutual respect. Second, we are still used to thinking of education's unit of output as being a self-contained individual, and that what education has given to her is contained inside her head. This automatically cuts out much of the quality and value of the relationships she will have developed during a school career. We implicitly assume, partly because of an admirable desire that education should match the needs of individual students, that the outputs we want to see are all individual. We couch our requirements for sociability in general terms, such as behaviour policies in which people treat each other as equals, or with consideration and respect. But we often start with a vision of the institution and its perceived needs rather than by looking at learners and how they learn together.

Chapter 11 will be devoted to learning relationships, so I will not devote too much space to sociability here. However, there are some core features of collaborative ability which should be mentioned. The crucial point is that people working together in the right ways can achieve more than they would be able to achieve on their own. The whole of a good team is far more than the sum of its parts, as any football fan will tell you. When the knowledge, goals and energy of a group of learners are aligned in the right way, their capacity to learn as a unit is heightened beyond their ability to learn on their own. As the economy returns to a more horizontal division of labour, and opportunities to communicate and to combine resources are heightened by technological connections, the importance of learning in teams also grows.

There are two fundamental aspects of team learning on which efforts at reform should be based. They are both brought out by Peter Senge in his book *The Fifth Discipline* (1990). The first is the distinction between discussion and dialogue, the two basic forms of discourse. Discussion has the same root as percussion and concussion, and is fundamentally about presentation and response. It is conflictual, and its emphasis is on the view of one participant, or one side, prevailing over the others. In dialogue, the emphasis is not on which perspective comes out on top, but on the 'flow of meaning' between participants. Dialogue is the process by which intelligence is pooled, so that individual learners become a part of a wider meaning, achieving more than they ever could on their own. It requires three basic conditions: that all participants suspend their assumptions, not in the sense of burying or abandoning them, but in that of making them clear to others and subjecting them to critical examination; that all participants must regard one another as colleagues, sharing in a common endeavour from which all will gain if it succeeds; and that there is a facilitator who 'holds the context' of a dialogue. The aim, as Senge explains, is not to achieve some abstract ideal of ultimate coherence and order, but to be sensitive to any possible forms of incoherence. In this way, the process becomes one which detects and overcomes faults, problems or weaknesses in order to do something better. The parallel with Howard Gardner's argument (Gardner, 1991), that education should primarily be about extending students' understanding by supporting them to assimilate new ways of knowing the world with their existing beliefs and understandings, is very strong. The emphasis is not on creating a perfect, objective and totally coherent model which is then injected into the learner. It is about enlarging the limits of understanding by facilitating encounters which require reappraisal of past assumptions, encouraging a learner to integrate new insights into their overall understanding.

The second basic aspect which supports the development of team learning is the creation of environments in which teams can practice. These environments are constructed representations of reality which allow experimentation – trying out different techniques and combinations of resources, assessing the impact of different strategies, and so on. Senge refers to 'microworlds', technology-based simulations of real-life situations (1990: 232). But, for young people in education, you can practise in real-life situations. If the overall goal of education is to prepare for the responsibilities and challenges of adult life, then any experience or situation in which young people encounter the kinds of challenges that they may meet counts as a simulation.

The capacity to collaborate is essential in a world where intelligent action depends upon combining the appropriate resources at the right times. It should be a basic criterion of effective education systems that they support the development of such capacities: the ability to define common goals and tasks, to establish and maintain appropriate norms of behaviour, to identify the strengths, weaknesses and interests of others and to allocate roles and responsibilities accordingly. The kinds of team learning that we have seen in active learning projects make possible a far wider range of roles, responsibilities and collaborative groups than the structure of our schools and colleges currently allows. Organising education around teams of learners does not mean surrendering the content of the curriculum to the whims of young people, but it does require us to be more imaginative in the ways that we deliver learning environments and opportunities, and to recognise that the responsibility for generating understanding must be shared *between* students and educators far more richly than it currently is.

These four kinds of capacity – dispositional, reflective, disciplinary understanding, and collaborative – are foundational characteristics on which individuals can live lives which are fulfilling, responsible, wealth-creating and problem-solving. They require us to rethink what we mean by ability in young people, recognising that it is as much about creating the potential for further learning as it is about demonstrating current ability. They recast the definition of educational achievement to reflect the fact that learning is not contained within schools and colleges, but can take place in any situation. They demand that education takes on a more ambitious set of challenges, but at the same time they acknowledge that formal education can only develop them in active partnership with the rest of society. The nature of these partnerships, of learning relationships, is the subject of Chapter 11. But first we must consider a more practical question: how should systems of assessment change to reflect the contours of the new educational landscape?

10

SYSTEMS OF ASSESSMENT

How should the achievements of active learning be assessed? The kinds of project that we have examined pose a problem for people who want to assess their quality. The problem is that much of what gives them value militates against their being tested in conventional ways. This chapter sets out the purposes which the assessment of active learning needs to serve, examines some of the approaches used by different projects, and outlines some principles for developing systems of assessment.

Despite our steady progress towards a society which strongly values education, we still live in a culture which assumes that the primary outcome measure of educational achievement is public examination results. Exams, taken at key points in an educational career, are seen as the true test of ability. But such examinations are only part of the story. Standardised individual testing, usually based on written examination papers, is the 'ultimate scholastic invention'. Its dominant assumption is that, in order to lay bare the real knowledge of an individual candidate, it must be tested under controlled conditions, as in a scientific experiment. Such assessment, if it is undertaken according to a standardised framework, has the added advantage that the results can be compared within and between cohorts of students. Examination grades are therefore taken as accurate proxies for knowledge and understanding, a decontextualised measure derived from decontextualised surroundings. Sustaining such a view relies on some supporting assumptions: that what people know is buried inside their heads, that if they are able to reproduce it under controlled conditions then they must be able to use it elsewhere, and that what they can do under such conditions relates both to their general underlying ability and to subject-specific knowledge.

But the value of active learning programmes – of a children's journalism project which develops literacy, editing and interpersonal skills by investigating and reporting on real issues affecting young people; of a citizenship project which sets out to find ways of reducing neighbourhood crime levels; or of a live arts project culminating in a pyrotechnics display in a local park – seems to lie somewhere else: not in their contribution to a general, abstract, test score, but much closer to the contexts in which they are executed.

For their participants, their goals are direct and close to home. They can see the point of doing them, they are enjoyable and satisfying. This is a primary source of their motivational power. But the point is not just about enjoyment and stimulation, valuable though they are. The point is that ability, as we saw in Chapter 9, is most often defined in relation to the realms or domains in which it is employed. It does not necessarily make sense to ask whether somebody 'knows' something in isolation from such realms. They may be able to produce competent or skilled performances under the right circumstances, if they recognise the kind of situation they are faced with, the availability of certain kinds of resources, or the presence of people with whom they are used to working. Without these elements, no amount of investigation will necessarily reveal the existence of the ability. Standard IQ tests, despite their lingering influence, are limited in their power to predict future performance beyond a candidate's subsequent year of education. Examination results, as David Hargreaves has argued (1994), are not really qualifications for anything other than progression to another stage of education.

Testing students' knowledge and understanding 'under controlled conditions' still means testing them in a specific context. We just tend to assume that conventional exam conditions are neutral. But no assessment conditions are neutral, because different learners have different aptitudes and profiles of intelligences. Conventional testing through written exams, therefore, tends to favour candidates who are strong in logical–mathematical and linguistic intelligences, while penalising those who may have a highly developed understanding of the subject in question, but be less able to express it through written argument and deductive reasoning. A graphic illustration of this inbuilt bias is provided by the problems faced by people who are dyslexic. Failure to diagnose dyslexia has destroyed the confidence and self-esteem of many young people who struggled in vain with conventional teaching methods. However, once identified, it becomes clear that dyslexia can be overcome by developing unconventional strategies for learning and using written language and by recognising that there are other ways of nurturing understanding. Some of the most talented and influential figures in modern history and contemporary society are dyslexic. But, all too often, the difficulties with notational systems that dyslexia implies are taken to indicate a general lack of ability. A young British woman recently won damages in the High Court from her Local Education Authority for failing to spot her dyslexia, and for the failures and frustration she subsequently experienced.

Two poles of assessment

Assessment of ability takes place at some point along a continuum of validity. At one extreme is the completely subjective assessment of the expert whose authority is widely recognised, but demonstrated through practice rather than codified evidence. In the past, apprentices were assessed on this basis.

Their proficiency would be judged by the person they aimed to imitate, their performance tightly bound up in the context in which their craft or art was practised. When guilds and professions governed the rules of entry to their ranks, their authority to judge when and whether an apprentice had attained the knowledge, skill and understanding required to join was unchallenged, and the bases on which such judgements were made were largely closed to the outside world. Authority is embedded in the purpose, practices and lifestyles of the craft in question. The introduction of twentieth-century methods of factory organisation often met with bitter resistance from the traditional guilds which objected, not just to the imposition of authority by larger employer organisations, but also to the external analysis of their work which it implied. Refusing to make the elements of one's own skill transparent to outsiders is a way of protecting it, and went hand-in-hand with the practice of recruiting apprentices from the families of existing guild members. From an outsider's perspective, the authority of such experts is based on our willingness to trust in the validity of their judgements, and on their ability to create products which meet our wider requirements.

At the other extreme is the standard, decontextualised test mentioned above. Apart from the spurious assumption that such tests are scientific and neutral between candidates, there are important reasons for trying to standardise. The first is that education is supposed to be relatively general; if it is a preparation for adult life, we would not want the development of understanding and competence to be bound *too* tightly to context. In earlier times apprentices were preparing for a way of life, and their development of productive skills and knowledge were inseparably connected to the norms, cultures and social standing of their particular vocation. Most contemporary societies do not function in this way. People are much more mobile, occupationally, socially and geographically, than in the past. The form of preparation, the mode of educational delivery, is not supposed to fix our opportunities in advance. We surely want to maximise the possible routes that a student might take in later life, to ensure that her access to opportunity is as great as possible. This means that evidence of achievement and ability must be recorded in ways which can be used more generally, so that the information is available to a wider range of people. Aside from this, we no longer trust people so easily. The massive growth of professional and organisational audits is testament to the fact that we expect their effectiveness to be documented and transparent for non-experts.

Both of these extreme approaches, therefore, have costs. Subjective, context-bound assessment is not demonstrably valid beyond a relatively narrow range of contexts and situations. It is most appropriate when the range of situations for which a student is preparing is bounded. The problem is that the range of situations and contexts in which someone might need to behave intelligently is very wide, and these days we are constantly reminded of the need to prepare for a future which is uncertain. So there is a natural tendency to look for measures of ability which can act as general proxies, which can be combined, aggregated and subdivided. But the process of standardisation can cut out much of the value of a performance, so much so that many standardised testing instruments barely scratch the surface of the understanding they are supposed to assess.

Our aim should be to look for forms of subjective, context-based assessment which are transparent and rigorous, combining the fine-grained judgement of on-the-spot evaluation with the transparency and portability of standardised assessment frameworks.

Assessment in context

In most cases the only way to test genuine understanding is to observe performances in contexts as close as possible to those in which such abilities are actually practised. In organisations where understanding and ability are demonstrated and continuously improved, assessment is deeply embedded in the organisational culture. Formative assessment, the evaluation of achievement in order to plan the next phase of action, is an integral part of high-quality learning. But such assessment always takes place in context. Assessment cannot be formative unless the judgement of ability is made in relation to opportunities and resources for further learning, and to the goals and ambitions of the learner herself. In fact, the ability to assess and evaluate is an indispensable component of understanding, since demonstrating understanding involves making a judgement about what skills, knowledge and resources one has at one's disposal, and what one needs to acquire in order to solve a new problem or meet an unfamiliar challenge.

Responsibility for such assessment lies with a range of people involved in supporting the learner's progress; the teacher has an especially authoritative role, while the learner has a basic responsibility to evaluate her own actions and progress. This evaluation may well be guided and informed by the assessment of others, but it should not be defined exclusively by it. Unless the learner herself is involved in deciding what goals she is pursuing in her learning, and what criteria she might use to assess whether she has reached them, she is unlikely to learn much that she can use productively in later life.

Assessment in context requires us to create environments and challenges which mirror those of the real world. The context should reflect the domain in which understanding is being developed. The resources and methods used should be domain-specific, rather than reflecting the conventional restrictions of school. This point intuitively makes sense, but it can be difficult to follow through the implications. It was brought home to me quite early in my school career by a classmate who, following our teacher's instructions, chose a 'project' to pursue individually during a particular free period that came up every week. The choice was completely open, and for that reason was potentially quite exciting. My classmate decided that his project was going to be

144

about 'art'. For the next six or seven weeks, every time the free period came up, he proceeded to copy pictures of sports cars from a glossy book of photographs into a lined exercise book. I can remember being struck at the time by the sense that there was something amiss, but it took me a very long time to work out what it was. There was nothing wrong with wanting to do a project about art, or one which involved drawing pictures of sports cars. But the activities and methods that my classmate used, quite unreflectively, were drawn from his conception of what ought to happen at school, and were completely inappropriate to the domain in which he was trying to learn.

This presents a problem for those of us who would like to assess, evaluate and celebrate the achievements of active learning. Many of the projects I have described are unpredictable, and take place in contexts and situations which cannot be replicated under 'controlled' conditions. As we saw, for young people this is one of the keys to understanding their value. But pursuing these kinds of learning helps to nurture capacities which we know to be important: the capacity to motivate and organise oneself, the capacity to collaborate with others and work in teams, the capacity to explain and present oneself to adult strangers, and so on. They can also, if done well, contribute to a deeper understanding of individual subject areas, by presenting opportunities for applying knowledge learned in classrooms to problems and challenges from the real world.

The challenge is therefore to create frameworks for assessment which genuinely reflect progress towards valued goals, which are sensitive to the contexts in which the genuine understanding is displayed, but which also provide clear, hard evidence which can be communicated to others. We can begin to meet this challenge successfully, for two main reasons. First, we are beginning to recognise that judgement of performance is not done best from a single perspective, but is a synthesis of different perspectives relevant to the domain of achievement. Second, we increasingly have technology which allows us to record, synthesise and present clear information about learning achievements in a number of ways.

In the field of community-based learning, one way to develop tools for assessment and accreditation is to create an award structure focusing on aspects of personal development which are not *content-specific*. By focusing on generic personal qualities, such awards free themselves from the constraints of more conventional assessment systems. They take the content of activities seriously, but do not tie learners to specific pieces of factual knowledge or to an artificially narrow range of contexts.

For example, the Youth Award Scheme, developed by the Award Scheme Development and Accreditation Network (ASDAN), is now used by more than 1,800 educational establishments as a way of developing personal qualities and skills which are foundational to effective learning. Organised around the specification of core skills in the national framework of vocational qualifications, and the capacities required for effective learning in employment,

145

further and higher education, the framework offers a way of structuring and recording achievement which is centred around the choices and goals of individual students, but relates them to specific kinds of learning outcome. The ASDAN award is probably the most widely recognised of its kind in the UK, being accredited alongside the NVQ as a way of developing core skills, and increasingly recognised by universities as a valuable accompaniment to academic qualifications. The framework is modular, allowing students to build up credits from a number of different activities over time and to choose the specific focus of their activity.

The challenges which a student may take up are broadly structured into five areas: community action, work-related activities, leisure activities, international relations and a free option. For each module, the award structure sets out the kinds of activity or challenge which might be appropriate, including aims, objectives and examples of what they might entail. There is a strong emphasis on self-assessment and on the need to present evidence, both of final achievements and of the stages of progress through which a student has passed. While ASDAN is one of the most developed and widely accredited, there are many other award schemes which follow similar principles. The Trident Skills for Life programme, for example, offers a strikingly similar structure based on 'personal challenge', community involvement and work experience. The recently established Youth Achievement Award offers a framework for assessing and accrediting community-based learning in relation to graded levels of progression, from initial contact and participation through to leadership and self-organisation. The Prince's Trust Volunteers programme also assesses the development of core skills, self-awareness, progress towards identified goals and different kinds of achievement. Many other award structures, such as the Duke of Edinburgh's Award, those offered by the Scout and Guide associations, the City and Guilds Skills Profile and the RSA, profile work along similar principles.

Such frameworks offer significant value. They support the development and recognition of personal characteristics and disciplines which are important for success in a number of different realms, including within formal education. They also offer a way of collecting and presenting evidence of ability which often falls outside the range of more conventional, subject-specific assessment tools. They are being developed and used by a number of different organisations, and they offer the prospect of validated learning achievement to many young people who find it harder to meet the demands of formal educational institutions. But they also carry a number of risks. First, if they continue to proliferate it will be difficult for others to recognise their quality. Employers, parents, universities and so on need to be able to know that an award is rigorous and consistent, but if there are many competing frameworks which are not subject to common criteria it is difficult to do this, and the awards will be devalued as a result. Second, they run the risk of compartmentalising generic personal qualities and disciplines, accidentally building barriers between them and the demands of, for example, individual National Curriculum subjects. This does not have to be the case if explicit attention is paid to their relevance to other areas of learning. But it is a clear risk, because creating an organisational framework around an activity can always have the implicit effect of screening out other connections which may be of value.

We can look at ways of countering such risks by examining the principles of assessment which we should try to follow in creating systems which reflect, accurately and rigorously, the ability and understanding which they seek to frame.

Starting with the learner

The first principle is that, if the goal of the activity being assessed is to develop the capacities of the learner to thrive independently, the assessment must partly focus on the assessment of the learner herself. Our dependence on public examinations, and the idea that competence can only really be assessed from afar by 'experts', encourage the view that the subjective perceptions are of marginal validity. In fact, they are central to the quality of the learning, and the extent to which what has been learned will be retained and applied in other contexts. Many active learning projects, such as the University of the First Age, use journals for learners to record their experiences and progress, and encourage them to form reflective judgements about what they have achieved and where else it might be applied. The practice of self-assessment, crucial to mastery in any realm of activity, is still not sufficiently used in mainstream education. Often it can be developed simply by cultivating a reflective attitude towards the organisation and execution of projects. Children's Express, for example, encourages its journalists and teenage editors to ask themselves a series of questions, the answers to which will help create a good news story. All start with Who? What? When? Where? Why? How?, and encourage responses which are not simply Yes or No. Children's Express also makes extensive use of the 'story mountain', a simple general framework describing the stages of researching, writing, editing and publishing a news story, which provides the overall contours for structuring a project. Neither of these tools constrains the content of a project, but they encourage learners to take responsibility for identifying and recording accurate, relevant information – central to the requirements of professional journalism – and for using that information to assess the results of their work. The Prince's Trust Study Support Programme has developed a piece of computer software for students to carry out self-assessment of personal objectives and motivation, which can be returned to in order to build up a picture of progress over time. Such tools will become increasingly important.

147

Recognising multiple perspectives

While the learner's perspective is crucial, the value of learning achievements must also be *validated*. This is often the stage at which we leap from an idea of the subjective assessment as relative and individualised to the objective assessment as scientific, decontextualised and carrying total validity. But such a leap is unjustified and inappropriate. To demonstrate understanding we must carry out a performance which embodies it. That performance does not *constitute* the understanding, but provides evidence for it, bearing in mind the specific context, purpose and audience. Actions are given value by those who are competent to judge, but value is always judged in relation to the realm or domain in which they are performed.

To illustrate this point, take the example of a group of young people raising money to build a wheelchair ramp at a local church so as to ease the access of a disabled chorister to rehearsals and services. Achieving this objective involves a series of actions which have value for a number of different people. For the young people themselves, the value includes doing something useful for somebody else, showing others what they are capable of doing, using knowledge gained from other situations and experiences, making contact with people beyond their normal circle of acquaintance, and working with friends and peers. From the perspective of an educator, the project has value for a number of reasons. It makes use of knowledge and skills learned in school, such as written and oral literacy, numeracy required for fundraising, the spatial awareness involved in thinking through how the ramp might be designed and exactly where it should be located, and the interpersonal skills required to secure support from others, to convince people to part with their money, and to work together coherently to achieve the goals they have set themselves. From the perspective of the disabled person, there is a concrete value attached to the project: it will make his life easier in practical, day-to-day terms. But there is a social value as well, arising from the contribution the project makes to raising awareness of the needs of people who are wheelchair-bound, and from the opportunities the project creates for establishing new relationships. There are also risks which might detract from the other kinds of value. For example, if the group go about fundraising in the wrong way, they might create an image of disabled people which the chorister found patronising or offensive. The motivation to 'do good' and the ways in which it is expressed must be sensitive to the self-perception and concerns of those to whom the good is being done. The project might be perceived to have spiritual value if it helped to focus people's attention on what happened at the church. It might have musical value, for similar reasons. Finally, raising money and employing somebody to build the ramp has an obvious economic value.

For each of these kinds of value, a slightly different field of people could be called upon to validate the achievement. But how we describe the project, and how we assess it, depends upon the primary criteria by which we measure its success. These criteria, and the objectives which they are designed to reflect, depend upon what we value. There is no magic framework which automatically defines value and validity, guarded by experts who possess some kind of mysterious access to the secrets of the universe. Different people have different kinds of authority, relevant to certain realms and developed through experience, reflection, communication and the trust and esteem of others.

Finding your way around a realm, as we saw in Chapter 9, involves being able to approach it from different perspectives. The value of a performance, similarly, depends on the perspective from which it is being assessed. For the kinds of learning that we have been looking at, some perspectives are particularly important.

This has important implications. For learning projects which are executed in the wider community, there is a wide range of potential assessors who are currently under-used in validating and encouraging young people's progress. It is no accident that many of the projects with the strongest external reputations, such as Children's Express and the Dalston Youth Project, see independent evaluation as a priority. Such evaluations incorporate a wide range of data-representing perspectives, including young people, parents, teachers, employers and so on. Transparency, twinned with a rigorous focus on the young people themselves, can produce results that few would argue with.

Who should be involved in assessing active learning? Teachers, of course, have important ongoing authority, and their judgements should be called for and respected. But they should not be accepted without qualification. Teachers are often not as skilled as they might be at evaluating progress and assessing understanding. Their powers of observation are limited by their need to pay attention to large groups of students, and by the fact that they generally only observe in the context of the classroom. Staff at the University of the First Age have found themselves being invited to lead training in schools on 'how children learn'. Developing teachers' capacity for rigorous, sophisticated assessment should be a priority for reform in teacher training. But there is a much wider pool of authority to be drawn upon – that of adults from the outside world. In particular, direct feedback and assessment on the relevance of active learning projects to the world of work could play a much greater part in the assessment of learning. Presenting projects to 'gatekeepers' – local business volunteers from a range of employer organisations – could be brought much more closely into the processes of evaluation. Adults from the wider community are equipped to assess on the basis of their specific expertise, but also on the relevance of different kinds of learning for the demands of adult and working life. Such assessment should not be totally informal and haphazard – assessors would need some training and understanding of the goals of education – but they could bring a wider range of valuable perspectives into the evaluation of ability and achievement.

Another tool which could be more intensively used is peer review. Both for individuals and organisations, peer review can be immensely valuable as a source of formative assessment. It is used extensively by the ASDAN network, partly as a way of spreading good practice. Using peer review effectively depends on two things: the degree of trust between individual projects, and between projects and those who manage the whole network, and the extent to which different partners share objectives. If trust is lacking, as between central government and some groups of teachers, it is very difficult to create cultures of assessment which optimise the flow of high-quality information.

Ongoing assessment

If we think of learning as a generative, ongoing process, it seems problematic to assess it primarily through isolated snapshots. Rather than a single, isolated performance, the most reliable evidence of achievement comes from accurate information about the stages of development a learner has gone through. For the more general capacities which sit on top of specific actions and thoughts, such as strategic planning, decision-making or working in teams, different rehearsals and performances can provide evidence over time of emerging understanding and ability. Often such capacities can only be refined, deepened and brought under the control of the learner herself when their manifestations are examined reflectively. Understanding the stages through which we go on the way to achieving an overall goal is crucial to the ability to define the stages in advance for ourselves in the course of approaching a new challenge or task.

So performances, as end-states, are evidence of understanding, although the further they are from the context in which such understanding is usually practised the less likely they are genuinely to reflect it. But the stages leading towards a performance or presentation are just as crucial to the development of understanding, and monitoring them can therefore yield information that makes accurate assessment possible.

The framework for evidence which this insight most obviously suggests is the *portfolio*. Portfolios are used primarily by people whose understanding and ability are expressed through visual creations, such as artists, sculptors and photographers. The range and quality of the work which they contain is a way of presenting to others different aspects of their ability, understanding and achievement. The element usually missing from standard portfolios is evidence of the stages through which a candidate has gone on the way to the end-states presented. Collecting together evidence of this progression is therefore essential to the demonstration of understanding, not just the capacity to produce a particular kind of performance on one occasion, but the stages of development, integration, rehearsal and reflection that have produced the underlying capacity which enables successful performance. This kind of framework for progression, recording and assessment, which Howard Gardner has called the *process-folio* (Gardner, 1993: ch. 9), is beginning to show up more and more in educational settings. It offers a method which learners can use to support their own development, and a means of collecting evidence which can be presented to others. As a way of organising one's own skills for learning, it seems to offer the best possible way forward. Its principle actually underlies the development of the National Record of Achievement (NRA), which was created as a portfolio framework to collect evidence of all kinds of learning achievement, not just a repository for examination certificates. However, the first phase of the NRA was limited by the excessive emphasis on exam results and by an inability to place it highly enough on the list of priorities for school-based assessment. The revision and reforming of the NRA, now called Progress File, with a greater emphasis on providing evidence of self-directed learning and study skills, is an important development, and should be taken seriously in the context of wider reform in assessment.

Putting performance data in the right context

The overwhelming advantage of standardised test scores, which we still have not dealt with properly, is the ease with which they can be aggregated and compared, divorced from time, place and context. Such quantitative aggregations seem to take on an objectivity which context-based assessment will struggle to match. To make decisions about who to employ, or who to admit to a university course, we need to be able to compare performances without spending excessive time observing candidates at close quarters.

But raw data, in any sphere, are of limited value in telling us about the kind of achievement that they represent. There are so many different factors involved in determining educational attainment that it can be mind-bogglingly hard to know where to begin. Early versions of school performance tables were of limited value in assessing school effectiveness because they did not tell us how much of a difference the school has made. This problem is being addressed by the goverment's work on 'value-added'. But devising flexible, rigorous methods for recording and combining data to produce value-added indicators has proved incredibly difficult. Indicators of performance only make sense if we are able to place them in some kind of context, in relation to the performance of others, past or present, in relation to the goals of the activity in question, or in relation to some predetermined standard or norm. Taking individual measures of performance in isolation can produce perverse results: for example, the apparent link between judging schools by academic attainment and the rise in permanent exclusions, or judging the quality of policing by the arrest rate without looking at underlying crime rates or the relation between arrest and conviction.

This a problem that all public services struggle with, especially since the massive growth of performance indicators in the 1980s. There are no simple solutions, but there is one important reason to be hopeful – the growing power of information technology to support the aggregation and synthesis of information relating to students' progress and abilities. The growth of formal assessment and standardised performance criteria for teaching and learning have imposed a burden on teachers, whose leaders increasingly point to the amount of time they spend doing paperwork rather than teaching. Recording progress is an essential part of a good teacher's work, and it is misleading to argue that the essence of a teacher's job is direct contact with students; one supports the other. But the use of integrated IT systems for recording student performance and other relevant information should be developed as an urgent priority. Progress is already being made. The Qualifications and Curriculum Authority (formerly the Schools Curriculum and Assessment Authority) already holds a large database of useful information on school and student performance. The Prince's Trust Study Support Programme is also creating a sophisticated national database. Integrated IT systems make it possible to collect and use information on a scale previously unimaginable. It depends on the willingness and ability of educators to use them, and on the creation of common standards and formats with which to present information. Being able to call up a student's record of achievement on screen whenever it might be required is a powerful, attractive ideal. But it is already possible in some schools, and developing the capacity more widely is a vital strand in creating a new culture of rigorous, transparent assessment.

The other significant benefit that IT now offers is that it can be used to present *direct* evidence of achievement to employers and universities. One of the criticisms of context-based assessment is that its results cannot easily be transported to others; outside institutions need standardised, number-based frameworks so that they can judge fairly between candidates. Project presentations must be converted into evidence that can be transported beyond the immediate context in which they take place. But digital recording technology increasingly makes it possible to do this. The Key School in Indianapolis, for example, makes video recordings of all project presentations so that they can be used later on, both for formative assessment and as hard evidence of achievement. The introduction of CDROM and digital recording technology means that such video evidence could soon be collected on a central database, transferred to a disk-based portfolio, and sent to an employer or a university department. Rather than filtering students' abilities through the highly imperfect medium of standard test scores, evidence can be sent direct on disk, in a bespoke portfolio put together to show evidence of particular kinds of ability.

Bringing it all together

The implication of this chapter is that assessment, while at the core of effective learning and education, should be far more diverse in its scope and methods. In some ways it already is more diverse than our conventional assumptions allow. All the approaches I have described above are already used in practice. But if the forms and uses of assessment simply proliferate willy-nilly, there is a danger of overload and confusion. Different systems of assessment must be able to mesh with each other, to be used in conjunction, if we are to avoid a cacophony of different assessment languages and criteria, forms of evidence and approaches to recording.

Just as different intelligences and expressions of understanding sit on top of each other, parcelled up in integrated performances and roles, so different systems of assessment must correspond to a coherent whole.

I can offer two insights into how this might be done: one, an example from the field of active learning; the other, a principle borrowed from another sphere of society. The first is the code of practice developed by John MacBeath and others for Study Support. In order to bring order, rigour and clarity to a burgeoning movement, the Study Support code of practice has been designed to give practitioners a series of criteria and principles by which to assess and develop their activities. This represents a near-unique challenge, because study support varies so widely according to local resources and circumstances and incorporates so many strands of learning activity. The code establishes three categories of good practice: 'emerging', 'established' and 'advanced'; and sets out sixteen components which it deems essential to achieving excellence. However, the code also recognises that the different strands of activity are unlikely to fit neatly into one of the three basic categories. What it does is to set out definitions, examples and profiles of good practice in each of the sixteen components, and suggest ways in which each can be assessed and developed. Practitioners will assess their own centres according to the structure laid out in the code, and they are then visited by an external assessor who investigates and moderates that assessment.

The result is a series of awards, or hallmarks of good practice, which are clearly understood and accepted by practitioners and validated by expert external assessors. Crucially, they also provide the basis for clear dissemination of good practice and for planning the next phase of development, meeting the demand that assessment should always be formative. This kind of framework offers an important way to integrate evidence and practice of different kinds, stemming from different strands of activity. It does so not by imposing an external framework on to an existing body of activity, but by helping to lay the underlying principles which support good practice, and encouraging collection of evidence that progress is being made. The resulting structure is the product of engagement between external demands and internal reality, focusing on clarity, rigour, purpose and evidence. The framework serves to integrate and synthesise, rather than to contain and define from without. It marries rigour with flexibility, general with particular, internal with external, without losing the discipline and transparency which are essential to attaining continuing excellence.

The second, more general insight comes from the problem of common standards faced by the computing and software industries. In fiercely competitive markets the urge to differentiate products, so that they exclude the possibility of use with machines or programmes produced by competitors, can be very strong. But during the 1980s many manufacturers realised quickly that the ability to combine different products easily was key to their value for consumers, and that developing software applications which could operate on a number of different computer platforms was a key to success. As Apple has found to its cost, superior quality is not enough if your machines and programmes cannot speak to and work with others. The opportunity to define a common standard underlies Microsoft's current dominance of the world software market. But beyond these two extreme examples, a complex process of collaboration between competitors has been going on. Interoperability – the capacity of different machines, programmes and systems to work with other ones – is one of the big challenges facing the information revolution. For computers to become permanently embedded in our lives they need to be able to adapt to our specific requirements and changing needs, and they will do this best by working to certain common principles and, to some extent, speaking a common machine language. But the defining feature of interoperability which has surprised many analysts is that it does not always come from common standards imposed from without, for example by governments or regulatory bodies. Interoperability is evolving from a series of partnerships and alliances between users and manufacturers, and depends less on who controls their development. In open, network-based systems, the creation of common standards comes from what George Shaffner calls 'the systematic elimination of low value differentiation' (Tapscott, 1996: 110).

Compare this situation with the creation of assessment systems in education. Different teams of auditors require institutions to meet varying sets of criteria. University departments are assessed separately on their research, their teaching, their research training, their quality assurance mechanisms. Schools are required to manage complex, shifting sets of performance criteria, all of which matter, but many of which clash. Performance and understanding can be assessed from a number of perspectives, and the various methods and systems for assessing them are rarely able to combine in clear, meaningful ways because they are couched in different languages. Most efforts to clarify and standardise assessment come from above, and are imposed on practitioner bodies. Headteachers preparing for Ofsted inspections often have to rework their financial accounts to fit the format required by the Ofsted framework, which is bespoke rather than standardised. While there is clearly a role for the integration of external standards bodies at the top, as the recent merger of the Schools Curriculum and Assessment Authority and the National Council for Vocational Qualifications testifies, the creation of common standards and formats for the assessment of ability should also come from dialogue and engagement between different groups of experts and practitioners, working horizontally, *across* their different systems, rather than responding to edicts from above.

Achieving interoperability through the systematic elimination of low-value differences should be an urgent priority for all those concerned with developing and assessing the abilities of young people in education.

Ladders of generality

This picture will, I hope, give the outlines of how systems of assessment which truly reflect the achievements of different kind of learning can be created. There is no single blueprint which can be perfectly designed and then imposed upon the amazing range of learning activities already taking place. But it should be possible to work towards a situation where more objective, externally verified systems of assessment flow directly from a culture of context-based disciplines and rigorous evaluation which begins with the perspective of each individual learner. From the unique, richly detailed perspective of an individual performance, we should be able to create layers of assessment which move progressively through orders of generality, incorporating the perspectives of others who have the authority to judge, referring to the performance of others and to common standards, but without losing details or information relevant to the achievements of each learner. Such a system relies as much on internal discipline, rigour and honesty, and on the creation of frameworks and systems which can speak to each other and work together, as it does on high-up authorities defining and applying uniform criteria. The aim would be to combine the richness and complexity of individual achievement with the clarity and transparency of effective general systems, in a framework which is both flexible and rigorous.

11

NURTURING LEARNING
RELATIONSHIPS

One of the most important implications of this book is that learning does not just take place inside institutions which are formally dedicated to education. The projects I have described take place across and between established organisations, bringing together different collections of people and resources to achieve objectives to which all the participants subscribe. Such projects are valuable partly because of the compartmentalisation of conventional education into subjects and contexts which cannot speak to each other. If the boundaries between different ways of knowing things are too high, then knowledge and insight gained by one route or in one context will not be integrated with or applied to others. Maths learned formally in classrooms cannot be used in situations where it might be useful, and scientific methods memorised in order to pass examinations cannot be applied to problems which call for practical scientific understanding. Many active learning projects counteract these tendencies, challenging participants to develop their personal skills and understanding, but also requiring them to apply what they know to real problems in the real world beyond the classroom and the examination hall.

Quality of learning and depth of understanding seem to depend at least as much on the *connections* that people can make between what they know and how it might be applied as they do on their capacity to acquire and retain the knowledge in the first place. The resources available to support learning, as well as the opportunities to demonstrate understanding, are distributed across the whole of society, not contained within the walls of schools and colleges. The projects that we have examined tend to involve a wide range of people. This is one of their strengths; they encourage the broadening of horizons, provide young people with examples of how knowledge is applied and used, how responsible roles are performed, and how collaborative action can produce shared achievement.

But what is it that connects these people together in order to produce such achievements? Surely they do not combine naturally, spontaneously or unconsciously. Learning from others is hard work. Learning from each other in a reciprocal relationship is even harder. It requires attention to discover how somebody else can assist us, and why they might be interested in doing so.

It requires us to think about what we might have to contribute which is useful to them, and to find ways of communicating clearly. It also requires sustained effort over time – learning rarely happens by accident, although sustained and intelligent effort often produces unexpected results. In order to help these things happen, we enter into *relationships*. Relationships come in all sizes and colours. There are many broad categories: teacher/pupil, mentor/ mentee, warder/prisoner and assessor/candidate are just a few which have relevance to our contemporary education system. But each individual relationship is uniquely configured, representing a particular connection between two people.

If we want to enhance people's capacity to learn for themselves in a wide range of contexts and situations, and to be able to transfer knowledge and skills from one context to another, then we need to focus on the kinds of human relationship that promote effective learning. We are moving away from the view that learning takes place only inside people's heads, or inside single institutions designed for the purpose. The reality is much more complex and unpredictable – initially more threatening and riskier, but also potentially far richer and more rewarding.

The analysis of social networks that we used to examine citizenship and employability is helpful here, too, because it offers another way of describing people. Rather than seeing someone as a bounded, isolated individual, whose essential properties or abilities are contained within, social network analysis describes people in terms of their connections to others. Researchers such as Ronald Burt of Chicago Business School and Jo Anne Schneider of the University of Wisconsin (see Schneider, 1997) have developed methods which can map the range of a person's relationships, the frequency of her contact with others and the intensity or depth of the connection. Such analysis produces a unique network signature, representing the person as a cluster of relationships or connections. We have already seen the value of weak, long-range ties for providing information and access to opportunity. Relationships which are distributed across organisations, social groups and geographical areas connect us to a wider range of resources and help to broaden our horizons. From this perspective, it is the most surprising and unconventional relationships which are of most use. If our relationships mirror the formal external structures by which we organise our lives – school classes, tiers of management, offices, families – then our access to information and resources is determined by these structures. So, for example, if the only relationships a person has at work are with his co-workers on the same grade of employment as him and working in his particular office, his access to information about what is happening in the organisation is limited to a small, dense network of connections which overlap strongly. Much of what he can learn from his co-workers will already be common knowledge. However, as soon as he establishes a connection with somebody in a different part of the organisation, perhaps just by striking up conversation in the canteen, there is a connection not just between those two but between the two groups of workers, and the pool of knowledge that is common to each is increased.

We live, of course, in an age of unprecedented connections. More than ever before, we can find connections with people who at first glance have nothing to do with us. More than a billion homes across the world can talk to each other over the telephone. An internet connection allows us to converse with people on the other side of the world who do not even have to disclose their true identity in order to strike up a relationship. Events in a particular place, such as the funeral of the Princess of Wales, can become a near-universal collective experience, distributed across the globe-spanning communications infrastructure. We are increasingly aware of the extent to which we are connected through the natural environment, and the ways in which emissions and fuel usage in one part of the world can produce acid rain, ozone depletion and climate change in another. Not only are we aware of it, but we can collaborate to look for solutions, coordinating environmental action by email and mobile phone, monitoring air and sea temperatures in different parts of the world, and posting the results on the internet.

But such distant connections can be threatening and dissatisfying. Many people complain, justifiably, that communicating electronically is a poor substitute for 'the real thing'. Internet relationships run the risk of being superficial, or even artificial, based on the way participants would like themselves to be thought of rather than the way they actually are. Exchanges and transactions are less likely to be repeated if they are produced from random electronic encounters. Exchanges of email or voice mail are often a very poor kind of conversation. Shared responsibility is weakened when the consequences of neglect seem far away. Similarly, greater mobility and freedom can weaken the bonds of family and neighbourhood relationships, making people less able to comprehend and less disposed to trust each other. The growth of connections, both in number and diversity, poses a challenge. If they are to be useful and not threatening, supporting understanding rather than confusion, harmony rather than cacophony, we must learn how we can use them to create valued relationships.

The idea that education is about developing the capacity for productive and appropriate relationships is, of course, very old. Socialisation, or preparation for the roles and responsibilities which society expects us to fulfil, is at the heart of any conception of educating the young. Any experienced parent or educator knows that managing relationships successfully is essential to achieving the order required to instil knowledge, values and understanding. What is not so clearly accepted, although it is beginning to happen, aided by a rapidly growing pile of scientific evidence, is that developing the capacity for successful relationships is a challenge primarily of nurturing biological predispositions. We are all social animals; the impulse to sociability is in our genes. Other people make up part of the universe into which babies are born, and which they begin to explore and comprehend even from within the womb, where unborn children develop a strong attachment to their mother's voice. One report for the US National Center for Clinical Infant Programmes found that the seven most critical qualities needed in order to do well at school were: confidence, curiosity, intentionality (the wish to have an impact), self-control, relatedness, the capacity to communicate and cooperativeness (NCCIP, 1997). Most of these are directly concerned with relationships, the capacity to form and sustain connections with others.

If such predispositions are inbuilt, they none the less require careful development and refinement. While some children are naturally highly developed in the personal intelligences, others are less able to recognise their own needs and emotions, let alone those of others (see, e.g., Goleman 1996: 118). But the point is that developing these capacities is a question of building on what is already there, rather than imposing alien concepts and external structures. This insight is becoming more widely recognised almost by the day because of huge advances in neuroscience. The fact that brain scanning can now produce images of the brain which depict different emotional states, and that such results can be explained and related to real life in such powerful and accessible ways (Goleman's *Emotional Intelligence* is now Taiwan's best-ever-selling book, outstripping both Confucius and the Bible), means that child-centred conceptions of learning are taking a firmer hold in people's commonplace understanding. The central idea underlying this view, however – that turning connections into meaningful relationships is a process of working from the inside outwards, responding to stimuli, adjusting patterns of activity to fit goals better, and adjusting the goals over time – is yet to take firm root. As adults struggling with the demands that society places on us, we are continually looking both for personal satisfaction and for validation of our actions. The temptation to assume that what we do can be validated by systems and structures which have ultimate objective truth is always strong. The recognition that such systems are created by our own collective patterns of thought and action is harder to cope with, and harder to see if we are used to looking for single causes and linearity rather than for complex patterns of interaction and evolution.

So relationships, from the perspective of each individual learner, are about outward expansion, making and spotting connections and fitting them into our view of the world. If the knowledge or insights that such connections produce clash with our established view, then either we reject them or our view shifts, sometimes subtly and unconsciously, and sometimes radically and stressfully. The external forces and tools that we use to structure and manage relationships: the legal frameworks, contracts, organisational hierarchies, social norms, are important guides; they help to set appropriate boundaries, to shape the connections through which relationships develop, and they are designed to make dealing with one another safer, more reliable, more appropriate. But one way of recognising the need to enhance and strengthen relationships from the inside, rather than simply trying to reinforce the hard, external structures, is to acknowledge that many such structures are weakening and losing their power, especially among younger people.

While socialisation is still vitally important, the challenge of socialisation is not the same as it used to be. Understanding and sustaining relationships is both more important and more complicated than ever before. But the external structures we have used to classify and validate these relationships are of less and less help as guides for finding our way around them. Social class is increasingly irrelevant and rejected as a legitimate guide to how relationships should be structured. Organisational hierarchies, similarly, are constantly changing, because some of the most important relationships are the ones that cross organisational boundaries. The timing of important life events, such as going to university, getting married, starting a job, having children or retiring, is becoming more varied and less predictable, so that we are less able to say what kind of relationships somebody 'should' have just by looking at their chronological age. Added to all these complications is one of the most important of the values of younger people: their desire for *authenticity*. It is not just that the webs of relationships which we build up throughout life are already complex, varied and constantly shifting. It is also that younger people increasingly want to create them *for themselves*.

A good example is the shift away from marriage. It is not that younger people flatly reject the idea of long-term relationships, but that they are less prepared to slot into what they see as predefined structures and expectations. What happens is that, all too often, the partners in a relationship find that they do not have the experience, the reflective capacities, or the tools with which to find their way around a problem. The resources might well be there, but they do not know how to make use of them. And when the external structures and constraints have been lifted, for whatever reason, the result is too often misunderstanding, collapse and damage, rather than problems solved and relationships strengthened.

So relationships, connections between people, are relatively easy to establish, but more difficult to build value into. As connections between people, they are the pathways along which resources for learning can travel. If such connections are enforced rather than jointly established, if they only go in one direction, or if the signals which pass along them are incomprehensible to either participant, good learning is unlikely to take place over time. But if we can fashion them to withstand strain, to grow and change in response to experience and circumstance, and to reflect the values of mutual respect, appreciation and curiosity, they can serve among the most important tools for encouraging understanding and achievement.

The nature of learning relationships

What does a learning relationship look like? Given the conclusions we have already reached, the basic components should not be too much of a surprise.

160

Shared objectives, clearly understood

An effective relationship between learning partners requires a clear understanding of objectives, both immediate and longer-term. People's wider aims might differ, but they will share a concrete first-order objective, for example to complete a maths assignment successfully, to organise a fundraising event, or to make a part of the local neighbourhood safer and more attractive. Such a goal will imply a number of second-order objectives, such as finding appropriate forms of collaboration, securing the consent of others who may be affected, presenting the results in clear, accessible terms. Being more general, such goals rest on top of the specific, concrete aims of an undertaking; they are logically implied by it, but they are often not consciously articulated by participants. Establishing and agreeing objectives is the first step to any shared achievement, in any realm; thinking through and agreeing the steps towards the overall goal, and agreeing on the conditions to be met in order for it to happen, the essential steps which follow through from it. It makes obvious, intuitive sense that identifying and clarifying aims and objectives should be the first stage of a learning process. Teachers and pupils often take it for granted that they know what they are doing, as do millions of adults, both in their personal relationships and in their places of work. But much evidence shows that people who are ostensibly doing the same things often think they are doing them for strikingly different reasons (see, for example, Rudduck et al., 1996).

Clear and high expectations

For learning relationships to achieve their full potential, expectations of what each partner is able and ready to do must be both clear and high. Clear, because confusion leads reliably to failure and to loss of confidence in the partnership; high, because successful learning requires people to go beyond themselves. The process of identifying, clarifying and negotiating expectations, defined in relation to ability, resources and goals, creates the platform from which learning can be launched. Expectations may change over time, as a relationship begins to bear fruit. Refining and developing people's expectations of each other is integral to continued learning. But this process cannot begin until the initial framework is negotiated and agreed. High expectations fit with the principle of 'sufficient challenge', the overall goal of many teachers and the cornerstone of Csikszentmihalyi's theory of 'flow'. If expectations are too high, they produce anxiety, stress and failure. If they are too low, they produce boredom, stagnation and complacency. Expectations must be managed at many different levels of relationship – between two individuals, certainly, but also between individuals, groups and institutions. Some schools, for example, build the negotiation of expectations into their induction for new pupils, to start an ongoing process of refinement and comparison through a pupil's school career. Each pupil sets out her expectations, while a teacher representing the school does the same. At regular periods, these expectations are revisited, performance is compared against them, and they are refined and updated for the next phase of the relationship.

Clear differentiation of roles

Relationships are most often thought of in terms of what people have in common, what they share. But the reason we enter relationships, as Theodore Zeldin (1994) has pointed out, is because we want to be surprised. If we knew exactly what somebody else had to offer, what they were going to do or say, there would be little point spending time or effort with them. The differences between learning partners are actually more important than what they have in common. But these differences, the surprises which can lead us to learn more about the world, can only be uncovered if there is a secure foundation of mutual understanding and expectation.

Just as people's motivation, their reasons for being involved, may differ, so will the roles that different partners perform. These roles will depend partly on what they want to get out of the exercise but, just as important, they will reflect differences in expertise and authority. For example, a teacher may use her authority to direct pupils in observing particular rules of collaboration when they work in groups, but might simultaneously expect pupils to use their own judgement about exactly how to approach a particular problem, or even which specific problem to tackle. For the teacher, who has greater authority in the whole subject, and in the ways that the subject might be learned, there is a clear mandate to shape pupils' rules of engagement, both with the problems and with other learners. But the learner also has a particular kind of authority: he is the person who knows best whether he understands the question at hand, and what the most effective way is for him to learn it. The choices that the pupil makes, and the outcomes that flow from them, will inform the teacher about how to teach the topic more effectively in future. Learning flows in both directions.

The task of any relationship is to find ways of sharing difference; that is, to strengthen the connection by distinguishing between the differences that are of most value and those which are unhelpful. High-value difference leads to meaningful exchange. Low-value difference is distracting and divisive. Authority is often presumed to rest in its outward manifestations – the titles that we use to address people, the list of achievements or length of experience that individuals have in a particular field. But authority is in fact a product of inner value, the value which a person places in her own worth, in relation to a particular domain, and the value which others recognise and affirm from their own perspectives. Authority is not conferred by formal rules of differentiation and status, although it can be reflected by them. Access to external resources – wealth, status, information which can be used to influence others – is power

(Clark, 1996: 108). Authority is the product of communication, recognition and affirmation of the ability of others.

As an illustration, examine the relationship between an athlete and his coach. The coach might direct the types of exercise available to an athlete, the routines in which they might be used, and the factors to bear in mind when doing them. The athlete would then use his own judgement to decide exactly which exercises to use on a particular day and for how long. These judgements would be made on the basis of past experience, of current physical condition, perhaps of the weather, and the number of races coming up in the near future. The athlete, since he is the best person to judge the state of his own body, makes a decision about which exercises to work on, based on a complex assessment of his environment. Observation and discussion of the outcomes of these decisions will affect the ways in which the coach manages the longer-term training regime, and possibly the advice she gives to other athletes in her care. Coach and athlete collaborate to achieve a concrete goal, in this case optimal performance in a specific event, and also continuously to improve both the effectiveness of the partnership over time, and their joint understanding of the factors affecting athletic performance. The roles, power and authority of the partners are different; each will look to the other for specific judgements, information and advice. Together they create norms of collaboration from which both benefit.

This is one reason why active learning projects do not imply the collapse of adult or professional authority. The experience of role differentiation among those with whom you work is one which assists young people in identifying and understanding the different authority which others command in various situations. A successful learning relationship will pay full respect to experience and authority, including that of teachers, parents, peers and other adults, by underpinning their particular importance to the success of the shared project. In an era when automatic deference to professional and institutional authority is increasingly scarce, this is an important fact. Bolstering the authority of adults and professionals in this way requires two things: first, a recognition that authority is a product of relationships, and requires the recognition and affirmation of those who are affected by your authority; second, that power and authority are not the same thing, and that expecting young people automatically to accept someone's authority because they are in a position of power is unrealistic, as well as unhealthy.

Regular review and evaluation

Learning can only take place with regular opportunities for formative assessment, reviewing progress, reformulating objectives and refining the strategies for achieving them. As learning relationships develop, this review becomes embedded in everyday interaction. It involves sifting through specific pieces of information and experience, sorting them into groups that are relevant to particular learning objectives, and applying them to more general problems or obstacles. This cycle of reflection, clarification, distillation and application is an integral part of the learning process. It is most valuable when each learner is an active participant in the process, but value is added if the learner's insights are enriched by the expertise, observations and authority of others. Learning to stand back, assess and incorporate one's conclusions into practice is itself a discipline. It is at the heart of any learning relationship.

Honesty and seeking the truth

In order to develop, learning relationships rely on the exchange of accurate and appropriate information. If relevant information about a project, or about a participant's beliefs, feelings or attitudes, is withheld, the achievements of the partnership will be limited or damaged. A useful way to sum up this require-ment is the principle of 'full and frank disclosure'. Well known to lawyers, following this rule does not mean bringing out all possible information at every opportunity – such an approach would quickly bring the learning process to a halt. Instead, it requires the capacity to search out information which might be useful, to decide which of it is appropriate or relevant to the goals of the project, and to communicate it honestly. Alongside the research, observation and communication skills required to gather and present information, this prin-ciple requires the capacity to make judgements about relevance, and an underlying commitment to seeking the truth. Such commitment is, of course, an important moral characteristic, which we would like all young people to develop. But it does not have to be viewed as a separate condition for estab-lishing learning relationships. If learners are genuinely committed to the objectives of a shared undertaking, then it is in their direct interest to seek and tell the truth, in relation to the achievement of those ends. The more general disposition, while some young people will develop it more naturally than others, does not logically come before the specific cases in which it is expressed. Rather, the disposition can be developed from repeated patterns of successful learning, and cultivating the capacity to stand back and reflect on them.

Celebrating achievement

Learning always involves positive achievement. To have learned something means to be better able to do something – to perform a task, approach a problem, think through an argument, listen to a piece of music. Learning equips us to find our way around more effectively. Such achievement should always be fully acknowledged and celebrated, especially when it involves young people who are learning how to learn for themselves. If education is valued by society at large, then learning achievements at every level should be recorded, acknowledged and celebrated. Such encouragement, of course, is a significant factor in reinforcing the motivation to learn, although when motivation depends entirely on encouragement from others it becomes unsustainable. Celebration at key stages along the pathways of learning is an integral component of success over time, reinforcing the most important message of high-quality education, that learning is intrinsically worthwhile.

Openness

While learning relationships may become intimate and strong, they should never be closed to the ideas, observations or influence of others. A successful learner is one who can make the most of the resources available to her, resources which are distributed unevenly across people, physical things and symbolic systems. While a learning relationship may be founded on a one-to-one exchange, as in the classical apprenticeship, it should possess the strength, suppleness and quality to face outwards as well as inwards, being able to include and respond to resources and stimuli that come from without. When relationships are based on closure and exclusion, they stagnate and restrict.

Dynamism

Learning relationships are generative: they generate answers to questions and solutions to problems. As such they are constantly seeking new ground, new material to work on. This does not mean that every learning relationship is characterised by restless energy and hyperactive excitement. But there is always a dynamic tension inherent in a learning relationship, between the perspectives and aims of partners, and between their current situation and the shared goal that they have set themselves.

Voluntarism

Learning relationships do not work unless all partners choose to be involved in them. One of the repeated refrains of work on pupil motivation, surveys of young people's opinion and evaluations of effective projects, is the value of voluntarism. Choosing freely to participate is an important part of any learning relationship. Young people are more disposed to take mentors and teachers seriously if they know that they have chosen to give their time. A recent MORI survey of 11–16-year-olds in Britain found that 67 per cent agreed with the statement that 'No one can make you learn, you have to want to learn.' Experience of Study Support projects has often found that the motivation, satisfaction and practice of teachers can be transformed by the realisation that pupils are prepared to give up free time to come and learn more from them. Voluntarism does not mean that everything should be 'take it or leave it'; learning requires discipline and commitment. But consent and voluntary commitment help to set the conditions under which meaningful exchange can take place.

Trust

Finally, the bedrock of an effective learning relationship is trust. Trust, the willingness to believe that people will act in good faith and honour their commitments, is what underpins the development of fair, cohesive communities and prosperous, dynamic economies. In a learning relationship, trust cements and sustains the norms of collaboration – communication, shared experience, common purpose and mutual respect. As it grows it eliminates the need for caution; strong, secure ties to parents among young children permit them to experiment more at the boundaries of their experience, to interact with new people and test out unfamiliar surroundings. Trust strengthens our capacity to take purposeful risks, deviating from established patterns or dissenting from the common view for the sake of achieving shared goals more effectively. Detailed and petty rules can be abandoned as the bonds of trust are strengthened, between individuals, and within and across groups of learners. Trust is reflected in the depth of common knowledge and experience, the intimacy and extent of mutual confidence between learners.

As with truth-seeking, it is important to note that trust is not a precondition for isolated instances of either collaboration or learning; we can agree to collaborate on a purely instrumental contract basis if the gains, objectives and roles to be performed are agreed in advance. But as Fukuyama (1995) and many others have shown, self-interest cannot sustain the norms of successful collaboration over time. A successful learning relationship is one which can withstand variation, uncertainty, experimentation and diversion from its original course. This is only possible to achieve if the learning partners can trust each other to remain true to the norms and overall objectives of the partnership, or if not, to communicate this fact honestly. High levels of trust allow us to be risk-takers, to adapt more speedily to changes in our environment, and to experiment with new ways of solving problems. The second reason for noting that collaboration can begin without high levels of trust is that it means there is much greater scope for engaging people in learning than we might otherwise think. Initial experience of successful collaboration, even on a short-term project, can produce a small endowment of trust which then grows into the foundation of a continuous learning relationship. This is why establishing trust with the most distanced and demotivated young people is such a crucial objective for educators, and for society as a whole.

These ten principles offer a general guide for turning raw connections into learning relationships. They are principles based on reflection and observation, and transforming them into educational practice is not straightforward. They will never all be present in the same degree, and there will always be more that could be done on each of them. But paying careful attention to them, thinking about the basis on which each could be achieved, offers a way to transform the relationships we enter and sustain every day.

The capacity to build learning relationships depends on one overall principle: mutuality. Mutuality is a principle guided by reciprocity, recognition of interdependence and willingness to share. What we share depends on the nature and scope of the relationship in question, but in general it will include the willingness to share goals, responsibilities and achievements. It is the basis of any successful collaboration, and the more its norms and spirit are nurtured and embedded in communities and institutions, the less need there is for formalised rules, imposition of control and coercion.

Mutuality requires openness and sensitivity to those around us, the people who make up our social universe, and it also requires us to have a clear idea of ourselves: who we are, what matters to us, and what we have to offer. But these are not just preconditions. It is through learning relationships, our patterns of interaction with society through its members, that we can clarify and extend our ideas about ourselves and our perceptions of others, drawing on resources from both within and without, organising and synthesising them to create actions and communications.

Understanding these relationships is the real key to unlocking the potential for learning throughout society. It requires honesty and courage to open up the space within which learning might occur. It is especially difficult for adults to acknowledge that they can learn from young people. But developing them is a challenge for everybody, because to face the threats and responsibilities of the future, we all need to be able to learn more effectively, to approach our lives with more intelligence.

Recognising the potential of learning relationships translates into a clear set of challenges. For schools, colleges and professional educators, the challenge is to support students in developing the capacity to learn from relationships, and to create learning relationships – meaningful, generative patterns of interaction – with the people around them. As well as facing inwards, focusing on the tasks in hand, students must be able to face outwards, to examine how what they already know relates to what is going on around them, and to apply themselves to establishing, clarifying and sustaining learning relationships. School can do this by creating learning environments in which students can identify and strengthen these connections, where they can learn the application of knowledge as well as its accumulation, and progressively take responsibility for applying it in appropriate ways. Educational institutions must become exemplars of learning relationships, as many already are. They must also find ways of communicating what they know to the outside world, through partnerships, networks, shared projects and transparent practices.

The challenge to young people is also clear. Their nascent capacity to take responsibility for themselves must be recognised and developed from the inside, to show that treating them as young adults is a risk worth taking. They must work hard at making meaningful connections: understanding is not something a teacher or mentor can do for you, however skilled and experienced they are. The generalised personal disciplines of thoughtfulness, self-assess-ment and communication can be applied to school-based projects, but also to the world outside the classroom: to friendships and playground rivalries, family tensions, budding romances, part-time work, community volun-teering, leisure groups, sports clubs and street survival.

But for learning relationships to work, they must be reciprocal. There is little point in schools becoming transparent exemplars, or in young people facing outwards and looking for connections, if the response is indifference, ridicule or hostility. For those of us who have entered adulthood and do not work inside education, the challenge is to open our eyes, to think about what we can contribute and what we might learn, and to respond positively. Without this response there is little point in doing anything.

The mentoring society

If the response is positive, the work can begin. From this point, we can imagine creating communities characterised by the quality of their human relation-ships, progressively building and renewing trust and mutual respect, making our connections work for each other, adding value to our interdependence by recognising, celebrating and learning from it. Knowledge, understanding and wisdom will be transferred, not through single, linear, one-off interventions, but through loops of communication that are recurrent and reciprocal, virtuous cycles of mutual comprehension and shared achievement.

This vision is founded on mentoring, on learning relationships based on mutual care, recognition of the value of experience and authority, and celebra-tion, not just of successful end-states and outcomes – university doctorates, professional status and exam results – but of the successful negotiation of transitions: from childhood to adolescence, from adolescence to adulthood, from dependence to independence and on to healthy interdependence. It is about recognising the ability to establish order and coherence from within, rather than imposing it from without. Looking at education from this perspective shows how it can infuse every section of society through the connections of learning relationships. It is a different way of mapping what happens, illustrating why learning cannot be contained within institutions. It might also be expressed through Charles Handy's suggestion that every young person should have a mentor to support and guide them through their transition to adulthood. This is a goal which the education system should strive to reach as it reshapes itself – a crucial element of a new landscape of learning.

12

THE NEW LANDSCAPE OF LEARNING

Faced with the choice between changing one's mind and proving
there is no need to do so, almost everybody gets busy with the proof.

(J K Galbraith)

The future is not what older people think, but what younger
people do.

(Nicholas Negroponte)

At the end of the twentieth century we have lost many of the great totalising
narratives of the industrial age. These stories sought to give meaning to the
world, and to our lives, by explaining our small part in a historical journey of
destiny. Communism has collapsed, and faith in the power of markets has
been tempered by the recognition that they do not provide the whole answer.
Markets are embedded in social norms, beliefs and cultures, and depend on
them for their effectiveness as systems of exchange. They cannot account for
everything. While religion still plays a strong part in our spiritual lives, in
Western societies it lacks the ability to control and fixate that it possessed
when it was embedded in the steep, tight structures which previously ruled
society. People's search for meaning in their lives often includes a spiritual
dimension, but it is more fluid, more subject to choice and circumstance,
less able to be certain about exactly how we should behave (Demos, 1997).

Do we believe in progress?

There is, however, one overarching story which has proved more enduring.
It is a story of generalised 'progress', driven mainly by economic, technological and scientific development, realised at a personal level through rising
living standards, upward mobility and self-improvement. Because it allows us
to focus mainly on our own lives and the difference we can make to them, this
story emphasises personal freedom, the space within which we can do as we
choose. It may have become more potent as people have lost confidence in
more specific ideological narratives. Learning and education play a powerful

role in this story because of their central role in improving our life-chances, not only giving people greater economic power, but also strengthening our capacity to make meaningful choices. This story of progress is, in many ways, compelling and attractive. Individual freedom and mobility is essential to personal achievement and satisfaction with life. But as a general narrative for society, it is pushing against some powerful constraints.

One of the most obvious is that individual freedom quickly brings us up against the barriers of our interdependence, forcing us to realise that we are shaped, not just by individual will, but by the people, ideas, relationships and collective memories that make up our social environment. As Mihaly Csikszentmihalyi puts it:

> Whether we like or not, our lives will leave a mark on the universe.
> Each person's birth makes ripples in the social environment: parents,
> siblings, relatives and friends are affected by it, and as we grow up
> our actions leave a myriad of consequences, some intended, most not.
> (Csikszentmihalyi, 1997: 129)

In an age of connexity, when so many of the world's people are connected in unprecedented ways – through economies, ecologies, communications networks and common causes – this recognition becomes overwhelmingly important. One of its implications is that collective identity and common meaning are so valuable that they should be nurtured alongside the individual. It has helped to produce a political swing back towards community – an emphasis on responsibilities alongside rights, constraints on freedom that help to protect what we cherish. But ideas of community which only look backwards are dangerous, because communities are constantly changing. Appealing to objectivity of this kind can too easily become a defensive, reactionary measure, controlling the freedom of others in a futile attempt to hold the line against forces of change which no one group can control. David Clark has put it succinctly when he warns of the 'corruption' of community:

> What should be universal becomes parochial, what should be
> ecumenical becomes sectarian, and what should be inclusive becomes
> exclusive. Beliefs, values and feelings are employed to set system
> against system, for the protection of those within and the denigration
> of those without.
> (Clark, 1996: 165)

This is one reason for believing that freedom and 'progress' do not produce enough on their own to achieve the kind of society we might want to live in. But there are other reasons. If we return to some of the challenges outlined in Chapter 2, we can see that allowing the engines of development simply to play themselves out will not solve them. The spread of global markets and the wealth created by a capitalist system are pushing against the limits of the natural environment. Despite a huge growth in material standards of living over the last thirty years, fulfilment and happiness do not seem to have increased, by almost any measure of psychological wellbeing. A large section of society has also effectively been excluded from sharing in this new wealth. Genetic science is giving us the power to do almost unimaginable things in the fields of reproduction and health, including cloning living mammals. But without knowing *how* such knowledge should be applied, it seems to threaten as much as it promises to society. If we look at the hard questions that we face, we can see that simple 'progress' is not enough to ensure that we survive and thrive in the next century.

Another view

But there is a choice. The narratives that have lost their grip seem to be ones which have put too much faith in one source of knowledge. Whether it is an account of history, like Marxism, of the meaning and purpose of life, like Christianity, or the power of an organisational framework like the market, these stories have assumed that they can provide a definitive, closed account of what matters and what that means for our lives. The narrative of progress that we are left with, on the other hand, seems only to give us a collection of stories that make sense for individuals and specific social groups, driven by under-lying forces of change. The ways in which these individual stories combine do not produce a coherent, compelling vision of how society as a whole might be shaped. As a result, it cannot give any meaningful guidance about how we resolve the tensions and collisions that arise from our interdependence – the clash between different forms of social identity, between generations, between economic dynamism and environmental sustainability, between wealth creation and social inclusion.

What is the alternative? Is it possible to find a narrative which balances the need to shape society as a whole with the realisation that no single perspective can provide a whole answer? I believe that there is another view of progress, which is gradually coming into focus: it recognises the uniqueness of each of us and our place in the story, but also recognises the complexity of the systems which govern us and our development. Such a view means that we can believe in progress, without assuming that we know everything needed to achieve it. We can hope that society *can learn to do better*, just as we hope this for ourselves and our children. In short, we can believe in a learning society.

Thriving on complexity

Finding new ways to understand complexity is the major contribution which science is beginning to make to our wider views of society (Kauffman, 1995). In the absence of grand, totalising theories which seek to impose an external order on our social universe, we are moving towards solutions which are *generative*, creating clarity and progress by looking for new ways of combining resources and employing knowledge to further our goals.

This view is gradually infusing politics, spurred by the recognition that the old polarities between left and right are no longer helpful, and that ultimate, goals are inappropriate to the real problems we have to solve. The biggest political challenges are about how to do more with less: how to make government more effective without significantly raising the burden on taxpayers; how to cope with population growth and enable people to provide for themselves while preventing war and famine; how to order economic development without further ransacking the world's natural resources; how to reconcile individual aspirations with our collective needs and resources. Solutions to these problems require creativity and positive-sum thinking. They require us to find new ways of using the resources that we already possess. The most important resource of all, which is most evenly distributed across all humans, is our capacity to behave intelligently and to learn.

The models which emerge from such approaches are couched in the language of complex systems, seeking a balance over time between clarity and confusion, internal and external, in a state of constant flux and reinvention but simultaneously reflecting deeper, underlying principles of order. Think of the human body, and the constant chaotic change which allows us to live and to feel experience. Think of weather systems and the ease with which their balance over time is upset by the impact of human behaviour. Think of evolution itself, and the ways in which natural patterns adapt over time to environmental change. This way of thinking recognises that we each occupy a small point in time and place, but also sees the importance of our connections to the rest of the world, our place in deeper systems of order, and our unique perspective and responsibilities. It leads to a way of approaching the world which is purposeful and ambitious, but also careful and humble, seeking to maintain and develop systems of increasing complexity so that they support people's needs and interests in appropriate, sophisticated ways. As Csikszentmihalyi has pointed out, this evolutionary view of progress also provides us with a way of thinking about good and evil, given the tendency of complex systems of organisation to fall apart if they are not tended and developed:

> Entropy, or evil is the default state, the conditions to which systems return unless work is done to prevent it. What prevents it is called 'good' – actions that preserve order while preventing rigidity, that are informed by the needs of the most evolved systems. Acts that take into account the future, the common good, the emotional wellbeing of others. Good is the creative overcoming of inertia, the energy that leads us to the evolution of human consciousness. To act in terms of new principles of organisation is always more difficult, and requires

more effort and energy. The ability to do so is what has been known as virtue.

(Csikszentmihalyi, 1997: 143)

Guiding metaphors

Obviously, education systems have a fundamental part to play in a learning society. But how do they fit into the new landscape? If they are to play their part effectively, we have to question some of our underlying assumptions about what they are. Any system of organisation is profoundly influenced by its governing metaphors, the mental images which we use to give overall shape to a system of organisation, and to the goals and dominant methods that we associate with it.

Two guiding metaphors appear most often among thoughtful educational commentators and practitioners. The first is the factory, the second the prison. Both are increasingly inappropriate to the needs and goals of a twenty-first-century education system. The factory metaphor is most clearly explained by the idea that education is the process by which raw materials are transformed into a product which meets standardised quantity and quality requirements. The organisational form of the large secondary school illustrates this metaphor well. Judged primarily by its output, which is assessed through a set of standardised criteria (exam results, attendance rates), the chief goal of such institutions is to come as close as possible to meeting the requirements set by the designers and arbiters of the system. The perspective of the designers and arbiters is detached, objective and abstract, its definitions of quality in output are general and largely uniform.

The second metaphor, the prison, refers to the view that educational institutions are primarily custodial. It has deep cultural and historical roots: the assumption that education is supposed to take young people off the hands of other adults; the association in many people's minds between the reform schools of the late nineteenth and early twentieth centuries and the workhouse; the fact that education to age 16 is compulsory and that for most people there is no real alternative to state provision. It is best expressed in those schools which, in the absence of clear educational or value-based aspirations, and of meaningful support from parents or the wider community, make their dominant purpose the control of pupils' behaviour rather than the cultivation of knowledge, skills and understanding (Hargreaves, 1997).

Each metaphor is increasingly inappropriate, for two main reasons. The first is that the factory image is out of date even as a description of factories. Technology, competition and consumer demand have shifted the organisation of production into a totally different sphere. The prison metaphor is wrong simply because young people cannot be contained in this way; in the end, they will make their presence felt one way or another, however much institutions try to control them. Eighty-five per cent of waking time between birth and age 16 is spent out of school. Since the challenge of education is to support young people in becoming responsible, integrated members of society, segregating them in custodial institutions seems intuitively to be a bad idea.

We could continue to hunt down the origins of these two metaphors and try to update or replace them, but there is a deeper reason for their being misplaced. They are both expressions of one of the most influential metaphors of the twentieth century: the machine.

> Well-oiled, efficient and measurable, the ideal machine had a clear purpose or function which it carried out perfectly. Everything could in principle be conceived as a closed system, consisting of cogs and wheels, instructions and commands, with a boss or government at the top, pulling the requisite levers and engineering the desired effects.
>
> (Mulgan, 1997: 173)

It must be said that thinking in machine-like terms can be highly appropriate. Where external conditions are stable and predictable and the goals of output have been clearly defined, machine systems have proved very efficient. But when external conditions vary unpredictably, machines are incapable of responding effectively, literally because they have been pre-programmed, and the responsiveness required from different parts of the system can only be engineered from the top.

How does education relate to the machine metaphor? We need only look at the language of the current debate to recognise its strength. The implicit goal is to produce a system which works in an orderly, consistent and predictable way, screening out irrelevant or trivial information, evaluating objectively from a distance, judging from above and establishing common standards. Throughout the 1980s and 1990s, much of the emphasis has been on creating systems which give planners and controllers at the top greater leverage over system components further down. The machine metaphor is also at the heart of the visions which built state education systems for the industrial age (Green, 1990). It was implicit in the drive to professionalise teaching and the bureaucratic administration of education.

The educational framework we are left with is one which controls progression through different stages of achievement, and the validation of achievement from above. Entry to and progress through the system is uniform and standardised; pupils typically learn in groups of 20–30, commanded by a teacher who controls both the content and the style of learning, according to criteria which are also increasingly set from above. For pupils and parents, choice is limited to specific junctures, timed to coincide with age rather than individual progress. Schools are chosen at ages 5 and 11, although real choice depends on the resources available to parents to move across different systems and geographical areas. Subject choices are available to pupils at 13, 14, 16 and 18, but once that choice is made the content and delivery of the option are prescribed and directed. Labour and expertise are divided vertically, according to specialised knowledge at each layer of the hierarchy. The common elements, acknowledged to be important by Sir Ron Dearing when he organised them into five cross-curricular themes, are too often subsumed by the pressures of testing, curriculum coverage, and an implicit emphasis on hard, easily quantifiable results. The basic achievements of education are classified in standard, numerical ways. Cohorts of students are released in standardised groups according to age. Failure to fit into the system at any point, for whatever reason, leads to vicious cycles of underachievement, isolation and demotivation.

More generally, the machine metaphor is perhaps most powerfully expressed in the assumption that education is something that happens at the beginning of life, an assumption that proponents of 'life-long learning' are still struggling to counter. The 'front loading' of education in the first two decades of life comes from the assumption that young people are themselves in some way machines, and that if we can get the programming right while they are being formed as adults, they will continue to function efficiently and productively from then on.

The limits of the machine

Systems which cannot respond to radical changes in their environment will always fail in the end. In the short term, there are some productivity gains from working the machine harder, reprogramming more often from the top, tightening specifications and quality standards, and setting ambitious targets. But in the end, if the only response to a new environment is to run the machine harder, the result is that its components break down faster. If the machine system is made of people, they get exhausted, stressed and demotivated, often releasing themselves prematurely from their responsibilities (for example through early retirement), making more mistakes and blaming those around and above them for their inability to produce results.

For education systems as a whole, the limits of the machine metaphor should be clear if we pay attention to the weaknesses, failures and challenges that we have focused on in this book. They include young people who have 'qualifications' but are unable to thrive in the complex environments that they encounter in the world beyond the classroom, and adults who 'know' things, but are unable to use their knowledge productively in challenging or unfamiliar situations, reverting to intuitive understandings based on the world of early childhood, and approaching problem-solving in rigid or unstructured ways. They also include a chronic waste of resources by schools, which for a number of reasons are unable to tap the information, time, skills, tools, facilities, wisdom and talent of the communities in which they sit because the mental, cultural and physical barriers between them are too high.

Transitions

In other sectors of society, especially business, organisations are changing their form and their governing principles in response to a changing environment. Often, although not always, the stimulus for action has been crisis or threat. Usually it has been in recognition of the fact that information can be built into systems in ways which allow intelligence to be distributed across them, rather than just programmed in from the start.

The principles which they have used to transform themselves have increasingly come from new insights into the natural world: the development of complexity theory and systems thinking, the study of evolution, the breakthroughs in understanding patterns of activity in the brain.

At the core of this change is the recognition that order in the natural world is not created by the imposition of pre-existing structures, but through 'relatively simple rules of connection'. In open systems like the human body, which can repair themselves and adapt spontaneously to external change, components are more likely to be self-governing, constantly responding to external environmental changes and internal changes in their own composition. These rules of connection allow them to be far more sophisticated at reading and responding to changes than structures governed by their original design. Such systems are not closed to the outside world, but open. Their component parts are able to create patterns of interaction which impact not just on the external environment, but also on the whole system of which they are a part. They can invent and reinvent their form and patterns of behaviour in direct response to new stimuli, rather than relying on re-engineering from above.

If we look at the changing world of organisations, we can see the impact of biological systems and metaphors in many places: the molecular economy, living organisations, evolving systems, and so on. The dynamism of such organisations flows from their capacity to create flat, responsive structures organised around multiple connections. Effectiveness in an environment characterised by rich and complex information demands two capacities: processing, or transformation of data into knowledge; and connection, establishing links between users and providers of knowledge, and developing common languages and objectives in order to facilitate meaningful exchange. This means that networks, as we have seen in other chapters, are essential to creating value.

Many network-based organisations, like the internet, are literally out of control, developing quite spontaneously and subject to few, if any, controls (Kelly, 1994). In some contexts this is appropriate. But simply running out of control is no solution to the challenges of education. In biology, cell systems which run out of control and develop too fast become cancerous. Schools which run out of control, like the infamous William Tyndale primary school of the 1970s, or more recently The Ridings (neither of which are now anything like they once were), can end up doing immense damage to their pupils and staff. The challenge is to manage a dynamic balance between order and chaos, between the predictable and the surprising, between internal order and the patterns and stimuli of the surrounding environment. In such a scenario, control is shared between partners, not monopolised. Responsibility is distributed and achievement is shared.

The parallels with education should be obvious. The main task of a contemporary education system is to prepare its students for a world in which there is less order, less predictability and more chaos, where old solutions are running up against complex, apparently insurmountable challenges. Such challenges will not be met simply by internalising the rhythms, disciplines and predefined order of conventional education, but by using the resources that education can give access to and applying them to problems in every sphere of life. If we take a look at what happens in schools, we quickly realise that it doesn't matter how hard those in charge might push; unless those at the end of the process, teachers and students, are prepared to play, there will be little progress. The power of teachers at the front line to stymie the plans of those at the top is obvious, because in the end they control the way in which priorities and objectives are delivered. In the early 1990s teachers brought the pilot phase of National Curriculum testing crashing down. Similarly, unless a student is prepared to accept the way in which teaching is delivered, she will make little progress. In the end, you cannot be forced into learning, and the number of young people currently floating in limbo, outside schools and colleges, off the official unemployment registers and resistant to any approach from those with institutional authority, is another testament to the inability of controlled systems to create genuine learning relationships.

The seeds of change

Many of the initiatives we have studied in the course of this book have characteristics which can also be found in these newer kinds of organisation. They are project-based, bringing together people and resources for time-limited periods to develop and achieve shared objectives. They are, to a significant extent, young-person-led, distributing responsibility and power across their various participants. They often set objectives which relate directly to the challenges and complexities of their local environments, rather than to a more abstract set of requirements imposed from above. In doing so they face outwards rather than inwards, engaging horizontally with the people and institutions that they can affect, and that can help them to achieve their goals. Their use of resources is more creative and varied than straightforward dependence on professionals and taxpayers' money. They emphasise communication, collaboration, evidence and forward thinking, building them into the achievement of more concrete objectives.

Their partnerships and alliances are either dissolved at the end of a project, or else reformed in response to new or further objectives. Flows of information, membership of teams, and formulation of goals are triggered in response to time-specific and context-specific targets, not to pre-classified, pre-timed, standardised periods or targets.

As a result, the projects are often more chaotic than the standard educational model. It is less easy to predict what people will be doing at what time, who will be involved and exactly what the outcomes will be. They are therefore more challenging for those responsible for governing the whole system, and there may be more risk involved in permitting them to happen. But the benefits when things are done well more than outweigh these risks. The satisfaction, motivation and shared achievement which flow from them, and the experience of applying skills and knowledge in messy, real-life situations, generate huge value. The experience of achievement flowing from responsibility, observation of the positive impact that structured, collaborative action can have, and attention to the processes and relationships which create such achievement, are precious educational resources.

In terms of organisation and administration, effective active learning projects also meet the requirements of the new world of organisations: horizontal integration, effective communication, trust, distributed responsibility, and high-quality management of information. Active learning projects are not simply 'creative chaos'. They depend for success on clear and rigorous planning, collection and examination of evidence, demonstration and presentation of results, reflection on problem-solving approaches and close attention to how the gains of such work can be applied to other contexts. Achieving success often requires greater clear-headedness, determination and rigour than are necessary to jump through the standard hoops. The difference is that the rigour is in bringing together resources – human, physical and informational – which are distributed across a complex environment rather than contained within one context or institution.

Transforming the mainstream

The projects and programmes that we have examined, and many more that are beyond the scope of this study, therefore represent the seeds of change, sown at the margins of the formal education sector. They are often a product of local, grassroots collaboration, a dynamic interaction between parents, schools, businesses and the voluntary sector. Many of them have already achieved significant results. But they still operate largely on the edges of the mainstream system. What would be required to develop their scope, impact and effectiveness?

The answer, at the most general level, is that we need to reconceptualise education as an open, living system, whose intelligence is distributed and shared across all its participants and whose aims and applications go far beyond the achievement of formal, standardised qualifications, numerical targets and occupational grades. Schools and colleges must become network organisations, not in the fullest sense of collapsing their structures and rules into formless, over-connected webs, but by establishing themselves as hubs at the centre of diverse, overlapping networks of learning which reach out to the fullest possible range of institutions, sources of information, social groups and physical facilities.

Access to such educational hubs should be as open as possible, available in response to diverse needs and requirements at different times. As often as not, engagement with such a hub by a prospective learner would involve the brokerage of a learning opportunity with another provider, rather than simple incorporation into the institution itself. But the institution would, through its connections, be part of the package, providing a base from which to organise learning, perhaps an assessment and validation specialist, and a series of other learning support services.

There are many different kinds of external connection which schools and colleges already support, from shared financial management with other schools to informal social networks and information technology support systems. As an organisation, the profile of a school can be mapped in many different ways. But the primary kind of network which schools would nurture and sustain would be human. The traffic to be managed and directed would be contact, exchange and collaboration between learners, and the connections along which such traffic would travel would be the norms and ties of learning relationships.

Such ties cannot be grafted into place from a standard blueprint. They would be built up, broadened and deepened by the experience of collaborative learning, supported by information technology whose primary function would be to facilitate reciprocal communication rather than to crunch data. Such ties would not become permanent through their content, or the fact that they organise standard, recurring programmes, but through the norms and principles which they help to establish. These norms would shape the culture of learning, the ethos, which is the essence of any learning organisation or community. Many of the spokes radiating outwards from the hub would be open-ended, serving as sensors and feelers rather than as strong, formal ties. Such connections serve to alert the centre to changes and opportunities on the outside, and contain the potential for stronger activation, laying the foundations for future collaboration.

As a result, the life of the learning system is more organic, less mechanical, less regulated, more chaotic, less predictable, more creative. It is composed of many individuals with hugely varied characteristics and interests, who join together at different times and for different purposes, but who create and sustain the whole network through their various activities. Those with an overview and a strategic responsibility, such as local education authorities (in whatever form), government departments, universities and employers, should provide a steering function, rarely intervening directly but generalising important lessons, looking for new ways of releasing resources for specific projects, calling for and disseminating evidence of quality and achievement. The focus would not be on imposing order from without, but on stimulating the continuous creation of excellence from within.

Such a system would begin to forge new kinds of interface between the three major strands of learning identified by Michael Barber (1996): in school, at home, and in organised out-of-school settings. At the moment, the connections between these strands are still weak, left too much to chance and the unrewarded effort of teachers, parents, young people and volunteers. Good parents with the time, money and motivation will help young people gain access to a wide range of learning activity, but this is not the case for ignorant, deprived or preoccupied parents, who are to be found in all social and economic classes. Similarly, teachers are too often unable to relate learning experiences within school to the wider experiences and cultures in which young people participate.

Such a system would be challenging to create and develop. But the encouraging thing is that many of its basic components are already in place. We already spend a lot of public and private money on education. We are already seeing the creation of a new information technology infrastructure. We already care, as a society, about the quality of education, although one can hope that we will come to care more. We already live in communities rich in human and social resources, full of experience and aspiration, often bursting with unfulfilled potential. What we need to do is to reconfigure the resources we already have, to establish new connections, and to create an educational infrastructure which is genuinely open to the range of experience, ability and aspiration which surrounds it.

In such a molecular structure, learners would be conceived as *intelligent agents*, applying internal and external resources to find their way around. They would be surrounded by networks of support, with whom they would share responsibility for negotiating the objectives of their learning. In creating such a system, we would be releasing ourselves from over-dependence on taxation and public spending to provide resources for education which are filtered through an expensive and slow-moving bureaucratic system. This is not to say that public spending is not essential, but that the resources available to support learning can be understood on many different levels.

Such a system would be based on principles of organisation which truly meet the demands and needs of a knowledge society, and would represent a major sector in the knowledge economy on which we increasingly depend.

Fear and hope

The world into which young people grow has become more complex and confusing, more uncertain, more risky, but also potentially more rewarding. The volume of information with which they have to deal continues to grow.

But the tragedy is that, in an age when knowledge and information are more widely accessible than ever before, they can still create deep, damaging divisions between people. Knowledge workers are becoming the new global elite. People who are best at learning how to create and manipulate knowledge are the winners by default in a global economy where, increasingly, winners take all. This is not just because of their superior access to formal educational opportunities. It is because they can connect to informal, distributed networks of intelligence which enable them to move faster, to adapt more effectively, and to grab opportunities before the majority have even noticed them.

The growth of the knowledge economy has the potential to create social divisions just as deep as those of the nineteenth and twentieth centuries. It is manifest in education, where, despite growing participation and rising public expenditure, many schools can do no more than contain and control their pupils, lacking the support, the wider resources and the vision to connect young people with any capacity for self-directed learning or any meaningful longer-term opportunity. In a bleak scenario for education in the UK, David Hargreaves has predicted that one of the four major sectors of education to emerge over the next twenty years will be custodial schools, effectively 'serving the function of containing and reproducing the underclass. . . . For most of these schools, learning continues to be an event and a place, whereas for the other sectors it is a culture' (Hargreaves, 1997: 16).

We are entering an age in which we cannot organise the principles of learning and education around fixed social hierarchies, fixed occupational or industrial divisions, or fixed totalitarian ideologies. Diversity and innovation are becoming defining features of the economies and societies in which we live. But such change does not lessen the danger that the knowledge society could leave many people out, heightening the need for the rest to protect themselves more heavily, raise the barriers to joining their ranks, and seek to control the unfortunate more closely.

We can already see some of the features of such a scenario: rising school exclusions, greater social polarisation, rising achievement among the majority while the minority withdraw into isolated, fatalistic enclaves, suspicious of external intervention and hostile to educational opportunity. Hundreds of thousands of young people are already on the margins, not in formal education or training, not even on the unemployment registers. Their life-chances have been drastically reduced by the failure of public services to motivate and educate them and the failure of their communities to establish connections with anything that offers hope or meaningful opportunity. Yet the projects we have examined seem to have characteristics which are very different from those we tend to associate with good educational performance: trust, a focus on relationships, a readiness to start at the point where young people are rather than where we think they should be, entrepreneurial use of financial, social and cultural resources, reflection of local circumstances and genuine sharing of responsibility. Research from the USA confirms that the neighbourhood youth organisations which thrive in some of the most disadvantaged urban areas have similar characteristics to these, rarely identified among formal policy objectives (McLaughlin *et al.*, 1994).

If we want to avoid this scenario, we must see radical change in education as one of the central routes to reducing social exclusion. But it is just as important to recognise that failure to use new opportunities for learning affects us all. The evidence of misunderstanding and distress examined in Chapter 2 is not restricted to the most disadvantaged. It ought to be possible to envision an education system that would truly serve the needs of everybody, providing learning opportunities and relationships which nurtured the talents, interests and needs of every individual learner. Creating a system of networked learning, connecting neighbourhood learning centres with a wealth of learning resources and opportunities, seems to me to offer the most effective way of doing this.

Back to the future

Almost thirty years ago, Ivan Illich proposed a similar idea: that we should 'de-school' society, using existing technologies to create a series of 'learning webs' through which learners could find peers to learn with, objects and contexts in which to learn, people prepared to share particular skills, and educators at large, professionals and para-professionals who would offer their services and be judged by their reputation among past students. His argument was that 'we can provide the learner with new links to the world instead of continuing to funnel all educational programmes through the teacher' (Illich, 1971: 73). This revolutionary vision was quickly dismissed, but, as David Hargreaves has also said (1997), Illich may have been right in principle but wrong in projected timescale. Learning is now more diverse and heterogeneous than ever before. Government already contributes less than half of the total spent on education and training in the UK, and this excludes the voluntary, informal effort put into learning by millions of people who do not gain officially accredited qualifications. Businesses such as Rover and Unipart are inventing universities without qualifications, where distance learning enables people to incorporate what they learn into their on-the-job performance. Skill and opportunity exchanges are flourishing, unregulated by the formal educational sector. A striking example is Creative Activity for Everyone (CAFE) in Ireland, a network which lists people interested in being involved in learning and helps to broker connections between them. The burgeoning Study Support movement follows a similar principle, creating environments and relationships which encourage voluntary, self-directed learning.

This, surely, is the basis of a learning society. But it will not happen spontaneously. Complex systems require hard work and commitment to sustain them. As the failures of child-centred education in the 1970s and 1980s showed, encouraging creative spontaneity alone is not enough to facilitate genuine understanding. Achieving high-quality learning is more challenging and rigorous than simply viewing learning experience as a stream of consciousness. Similarly, the networks which function most effectively are not those where everybody is connected to everybody else, because too many connections are sluggish, amorphous and unresponsive.

But rigour is not rigidity, and clarity is not control. Clinging to structures in education which are being transformed or thrown away elsewhere is a guaranteed way of making sure that young people will be ill-prepared to safeguard our futures.

Learning in the twenty-first century

This vision implies that schools will progressively transform themselves to become the hubs of learning networks, centres of learning excellence which aid the development of understanding by brokering learning opportunities with people and organisations in the communities around them. They would be staffed by learning specialists of different kinds. One group might be responsible for developing a long-term mentoring and guidance relationship with their students, helping to plan and review activities and assist each individual in shaping their goals for the short, medium and long term. Others would be specialists in assessment, observing and recording progress and ability, not just within the school but in the range of contexts where young people are learning. From the earliest age, students would be jointly responsible for planning and assessing their learning, discussing what they can do with a range of others, including parents, peers, professional educators and adults from the surrounding community.

Rich and coherent information on attainment

From the age of four or five, records of progress would be collected in an integrated, IT-based portfolio of achievement, regularly updated and reviewed, which would stay with the student right through into adulthood. As well as expert assessments, it might eventually include self-assessment, video recordings of project presentations, written work and a number of more standardised assessment results. Over time, this portfolio would provide detailed evidence of progression and attainment, able to offer complex, sophisticated and clear evidence of what a student has and has not been able to do.

An active learning partnership

As a student's career progressed she would take growing responsibility for planning, organising and assessing her work and for playing a part in decisions about the running of the school. Practical, team-based projects would become an integral part of the learning experience, but careful reflection on its

How an active learning curriculum can work in practice

To take a specific example from the United States, let us consider Carl, in his second year at high school, who has built a foundation for the transition to work. He attends a career academy that operates within a large comprehensive high school. The close-knit school-within-a-school has strong support and involvement from industrial and post-secondary partners. Carl has the same team of teachers for his academy classes, which include English, maths, science and social studies, computer applications and health occupations. Several of the classes are linked with local community colleges as part of a 'Tech Prep' partnership. Carl and his classmates are 'block-scheduled', facilitating special interdisciplinary curriculum, group projects, and field experiences. In addition Carl keeps a portfolio documenting his work. This year, Carl will perform 100 hours of volunteer service in a hospital, earn CPR and first aid certification, attend health career conferences, and frequently go on field trips to health and science facilities. Also, he will maintain weekly contact with an adult mentor, who works in either a healthcare or bio-science profession. As a junior, he will explore careers by rotating through a series of medical and business departments in healthcare facilities, and he will be trained as a health peer educator. He will have paid internships in the summers following junior and senior years, and during the second term of his senior year. As an intern, he will also keep a journal, attend weekly workplace reflection seminars, and participate in community-based projects.

As a senior, Carl will produce a major health-related project, with teachers and industry partners as his coaches, and complete a portfolio of his work in the academy. After graduation, Carl can enter community college programmes in allied health, biotechnology, nursing or physical therapy, continue his education at a four-year institution, or get a skilled, entry-level job. 'I feel I am more prepared and more knowledgeable than any of my friends preparing for college. I work in a real hospital, with real patients and real employers. I have hands-on experience. . . . My job is important and people rely on me to do it well.'

(The National School-to-Work Learning and Information Centre, Washington DC, quoted in White, 1997) outcomes, and integration into a growing body of text-based, propositional knowledge, would also be a core part of the learning programme. Placements in voluntary organisations, neighbourhood projects, manufacturers, offices, newspapers and other organisations would become an integral part of each student's package of learning opportunities. Interpersonal intelligence would be nurtured, not just through timetabled lessons, but through the continuous practice of learning relationships based on mutual respect and reciprocity. Young people's sense of themselves, their emerging identity, would evolve in tandem with their growing capacity to understand the perspective of others and to take responsibility.

IT as an environment and a tool

Students would use IT resources, not just to gain access to information, but to analyse, synthesise and present it in a range of contexts. Computer-based environments could be used to learn about how complex systems work, for example in biology, the natural environment, city planning and a host of other applications. They would learn to apply systematic perspectives to every sphere of life, learning a 'meta-curriculum' of thinking strategies and techniques by paying attention to the importance of good thinking in all the learning activities they undertake.

Learning to be an intelligent agent

This would be an education characterised, not by the accumulation of knowledge whose applications are predictable and standardised, but by a series of intelligent encounters with the problems and resources of different learning environments. Such encounters are far closer to the challenges that we actually face in the adult world. They would help to uncover the gaps and cracks in our ability rather than encouraging the view that there is an answer to everything, to be found by making linear progress through the external structures that society places around us.

Real power, real responsibility

From the age of 14, compulsory schooling might come to an end, to be followed by a number of different community-based learning packages which continued for five years or more. Enrolling in a school would no longer mean entering an institution that would educate within its walls, but entering into a covenant to find the most appropriate, challenging combination of learning opportunities, students undertaking to apply themselves to making the most of them and giving back some of what they learn to others, the school undertaking to broker opportunities and support learning relationships. Young people would have power to choose what they did, but this choice would be guided by a rich network of resources, guidance and support contexts for learning. The student's education would step outside the classroom, integrating diverse perspectives and experiences into a rounded, disciplined, individual view of the world.

Neighbourhood learning centres

Schools and colleges would become neighbourhood learning centres, welcoming learners of all ages to contribute to and learn from their range of learning activities. With core public funding, they would evolve into a variety of forms, becoming the focus for social, health and careers services alongside a range of educational programmes. Such centres would work to combine the social, cultural, financial, informational and human resources of their local communities with those of a publicly funded, professionally staffed education system.

Common standards

Such diversity does not preclude the specification of commonly understood measures of achievement. Common frameworks for assessment are important to ensure rigour and transparency. But it does mean that we must give up on the assumption that standard, text-based individual tests are the only and most accurate instruments for assessing understanding. Benchmarks, targets, some standard frameworks and shared measures would underpin the coherence of the learning system as a whole. But learning is conducted and demonstrated in thousands of different ways, and a standard framework that is too strong and too inflexible will constrain and damage our prospects for creativity and achievement.

Learning to think

Infusing the whole of a student's learning career would be a strong emphasis on the disciplines of thinking, learning and managing information. This 'meta-curriculum' would overlay the specific content of all learning and teaching, developed and consolidated through reflection, recording, assessment and performance. Alongside the qualifications and achievements of a student's first extended spell in education should be a set of disciplines and dispositions which provide a true foundation for lifelong learning. The frameworks and categories for the meta-curriculum are still not clearly defined, although we have many promising pointers: from Geoff Mulgan's (1996) 4 Ss – skills for the information age – to specific programmes such as CASE (Cognitive Acceleration in Science Education; see Barber, 1996: 180) and theoretical frameworks such as David Perkins's work on reflective intelligence (Perkins, 1995).

The road to the learning society

These elements would combine to produce an overarching framework for learning in the twenty-first century. Over time we might create a curriculum for lifelong learning, to replace a series of frameworks which in the past have helped to fix people into their own social and economic status. Such a curriculum for young people would organise learning around a series of themes, rather than simply around basic skills and academic subjects. Subjects, projects, placements and assessment would combine around the individual, who would be actively involved in making their combination coherent and generative, paving the way for effective learning throughout life.

This vision involves shifting the way we see education from a separate sector of society to a culture which infuses every sector, linking together individuals, communities and institutions through diverse, overlapping networks of learning relationships. Education is no longer the one-way transmission of information and knowledge, but the patterns of interaction which allow us to acquire new information, develop the disciplines which can lead to greater understanding, and discover shared meaning through mutual comprehension. The task of those who take on young apprentices in the different realms of life is to nurture the development of judgement, the capacity to take in all relevant and appropriate information, including an assessment of one's own skills and abilities, and to work out the best response.

When the external structures and controls on our behaviour are weakened, internal discipline and strength of character are even more important to achievement and responsibility. But such discipline is not best acquired by becoming accustomed to the imposition of external control, or through repetition of standardised tasks. These might have been valid goals for education when they characterised the working lives of most of the population, but the world is no longer like that. If we want young people who are able to be both rigorous and flexible, who can be creative about serious problems rather than just superficial forms of expression, we must enable them to use intelligently the full range of resources that a knowledge society puts at their disposal. These resources are far too widespread and complicated to be collected, standardised, replicated and injected into education through a chain of institutional command and control. They are distributed across our whole environment. Teaching young people to use them well requires us to allow young people the opportunity to practice with them *in* society, and to make an impact on the rest of us in doing so.

For adults, this is perhaps the most difficult and challenging dimension of the learning society. Continuous learning involves forgetting as well as remembering. To solve new problems, we must be able to cast aside assumptions and models that no longer serve us well. All of us have a deeply ingrained set of assumptions about what education is, some positive, many negative, because it is an experience that all of us have been through. This is

187

why most people have strong views on education. But if we want our learning to reflect current reality, we must be able to question these assumptions, and to understand what it is really like to be a young person growing up now. This involves a fundamental shift of power between older and younger generations. It means recognising that we do not have all the answers, and that we can learn from the young as well as teaching them. It means taking them seriously, putting time, effort and care into our dealings with them, providing secure, fertile social environments in which they can learn their way around, and becoming actively involved in their learning. Such a shift has to be voluntary. As adults and guardians, we have the power to control much of what young people are allowed to do. But we do not necessarily have the authority, and when power and authority come apart, the result is eventually alienation, hostility and rejection.

If we do make the shift, we will be able to measure our learning, not by the amount of money we spend on it, or by the number of certificates we have, but by our success in solving real problems, the time and care that we put into our own learning, our health and wellbeing, and the extent of our mutual understanding and shared achievement. Then, and only then, will we be on the road to the learning society.

BIBLIOGRAPHY

Alexander, T (1997) Family Learning, Demos, London

Barber, M (1996) The Learning Game: Arguments for an education revolution, Victor Gollancz, London

Barley, S (1996) The New World of Work, British–North American Committee, London

Bentley, T (1996) Angry Young Men? A study of the habits, aspirations and opinions of unemployed young men in Britain, unpublished manuscript

Biggar, N (1997) Good Life: Reflections on what we value today, SPCK, London

Bloom, A (1987) The Closing of the American Mind, Penguin, London

Cambridge Econometrics (1994) New Sources of Employment Growth, Cambridge

Carnegie UK Trust (1997) Years of Decision: The Carnegie Young People's Initiative, Youth Work Press, Leicester

Catan, L, Dennison, C and Coleman, J (1996) Getting Through: Effective communication in the teenage years, Trust for the Study of Adolescence, Brighton

Ceci, S J (1996) On Intelligence: A bioecological treatise on intellectual development, Harvard University Press, Cambridge MA

Centre for Successful Schools (1994) Young People and their Attitudes to School, interim report of a research project, Keele University, Keele

Citizenship Foundation (1997) Citizenship and Civic Education, Citizenship Foundation, London

Clark, D (1996) Schools as Learning Communities: Transforming education, Cassell, London

Cole, M (1996) Cultural Psychology: A once and future discipline, Belknap Press, Cambridge MA

Coles, R (1997) The Moral Intelligence of Children, Bloomsbury, London

Csikszentmihalyi, M (1988) 'Society, culture and person: a systems view of creativity', in R Sternberg (ed.), The Nature of Creativity, Cambridge University Press, New York

—— (1997) Living Well: The psychology of everyday life, Weidenfeld and Nicolson, London

Cumming, J and Carbine, B (1997) Reforming Schools Through Workplace Learning, National Schools Network, New South Wales

Dearing, R (1996) Review of Qualifications for 16–19 Year Olds, summary report, SCAA, London

de Bono, E (1983) 'The cognitive research thinking program', in W Maxwell (ed.), Thinking: The expanding frontier, Lawrence Erlbaum, Hillsdale NJ
—— (1986) Six Thinking Hats, Viking, New York
Demos (1997) Keeping the Faiths: The new covenant between religious belief and secular power, Demos Quarterly 11, Demos, London
—— (1997a) The Wealth and Poverty of Networks: Tackling social exclusion, Demos, London
DfEE (1996) Statistical Bulletin 3/96, HMSO, London
—— (1997) Labour Market and Skill Trends (1997/98), HMSO, London
Dorling, D (1996) A New Social Atlas of Britain, John Wiley, Chichester
Drucker, P (1993) Post-capitalist Society, Butterworth-Heinemann, Oxford
Ermisch, J and Francesconi, M (1997) Family Matters, Paper No. 97–1, ESRC Research Centre on Micro-Social Change, Colchester
Fukuyama, F (1995) Trust: The social virtues and the source of prosperity, Hamish Hamilton, London
—— (1997) The End of Order, Social Market Foundation, London
Gardner, H (1983) Frames of Mind, Fontana, London
—— (1991) The Unschooled Mind: How children think and how schools should teach, Basic Books, New York
—— (1993) Multiple Intelligences: The theory in practice, Basic Books, New York
Goleman, D (1996) Emotional Intelligence: Why it can matter more than IQ, Bloomsbury, London
Goodwin, P A (1988) Efficacy of the Formal Education Process in Rural Alaska, vol. 1, Applied NeuroDynamics Corp., Honolulu
Granovetter, M S (1973) 'The strength of weak ties', American Journal of Sociology 78, 1360–80
Green, A (1990) Education and State Formation: The rise of education systems in England, France and the USA, Macmillan, London
Hall, P A (1997) Social Capital in Britain, Centre for European Studies, Harvard University, Cambridge MA
Handy, C (1995) Beyond Certainty: The changing worlds of organisations, Hutchinson, London
Hargreaves, D (1994) The Mosaic of Learning: Schools and teachers for the next century, Demos, London
—— (1997) 'A-roads to the learning society', School Leadership and Management 17(1), 9–21
Harris, A (1996) Evaluation: A curriculum framework and management tool for schools, London Enterprise Agency, London
Hechter, M, Nadel, L and Michael, R E (eds) (1993) The Origin of Values, de Gruyter, New York
Henley Centre (1994) Brook Street/Henley Centre Organisation Change Survey, Henley Centre for Forecasting, London
—— (1997) Planning for Social Change 98, Henley Centre for Forecasting, London
Huskins, J (1996) Quality Work with Young People, Bristol, distributed by Youth Clubs UK
Illich, I (1971) Deschooling Society, Calder and Boyars, London

Industrial Society (1997) Speaking Up, Speaking Out! The 2020 Vision Programme Research Report, Industrial Society, London

Industry in Education (1996) Towards Employability: Addressing the gap between young people's qualities and employers' recruitment needs, London

Inglehart, R (1990) Culture Shift in Advanced Industrial Societies, Princeton University Press, Princeton

Jarvis, V (1995) Smoothing the Transition to Skilled Employment: How can school-based vocational guidance be improved?, NIESR, London

Jupp, B (1997) Saving Sense: A new approach to encouraging saving, Demos, London

Jupp, B and Lawson, G (1997) Values Added: How emerging values could influence the development of London, LPAC, London

Kauffman, S (1995) At Home in the Universe: The search for laws of complexity, Penguin, London

Kelly, K (1994) Out of Control, Fourth Estate, London

Kidder, R (1995) How Good People Make Tough Choices: Resolving the dilemmas of ethical living, William and Morrow, New York

King, Z (1997) 'Towards greater involvement of employers in key skills learning in the 16–19 curriculum', unpublished paper

Leadbeater, C (1997) Britain: the California of Europe? What the UK has to learn from the West Coast, Demos, London

—— (1997a) The Rise of the Social Entrepreneur, Demos, London

Leadbeater, C and Goss, S (1998) Civic Entrepreneurship, Demos, London

Lipman, M, Sharp, A M and Oscanyan, F (1980) Philosophy in the Classroom, Montclair State College, Philadelphia

MacBeath, J (1996) Times Educational Supplement, 29 November

McLaughlin, M W, Irby, M A and Langman, J (1994) Urban Sanctuaries: Neighbourhood organisations in the lives and futures of inner-city youth, Jossey-Bass, San Francisco

Mulgan, G (1996) 'The new 3Rs', Demos Quarterly 8, The New Enterprise Culture, Demos, London

—— (1997) Connexity: How to live in a connected world, Chatto and Windus, London

Mulgan, G and Bentley, T (1996) Employee Mutuals: The 21st century trade union?, Demos, London

NCCIP (1997) The Emotional Foundations of School Readiness, National Center for Clinical Infant Programs, Arlington, VA

NCH Action for Children, Fact File (1996/7)

Park, A and Jowell, R (1998) Young People, Politics and Citizenship: A disengaged generation?, Citizenship Foundation, London

Parsons, C (1996) 'Permanent exclusions from schools in England in the 1990s: trends, causes and responses', Children and Society 10(3), 177–86

Perkins, D (1992) Smart Schools: Better thinking and learning for every child, Free Press, London

—— (1995) Outsmarting IQ: The emerging science of learnable intelligence, Free Press, New York

Power, A (1995) Area-based Poverty, Social Problems and Resident Empowerment, Discussion Paper WSP/107, Suntory-Toyota International Centre for Economics and Related Disciplines, London School of Economics, London

Putnam, R D (1993) Making Democracy Work: Civic traditions in modern Italy, Princeton University Press, Princeton

Roberts, H and Sachdev, D (eds) (1996) Young People's Social Attitudes: The views of 12–19-year-olds, Barnardos, Ilford

Roker, D, Player, K and Coleman, J (1998) 'British young people's invovement in volunteering and campaigning', in J Youniss and M Yates (eds), Community Service and Civic Engagement in Youth: International perspectives, Cambridge University Press, New York

Rudduck, J, Chaplain, R and Wallace, G (1996) School Improvement: What can pupils tell us?, David Fulton Publishers, London

Rutter, M and Smith, D J (eds) (1995) Psychosocial Disorders in Young People: Time trends and their causes, John Wiley, Chichester

Salovey, P and Mayer, J D (1990) 'Emotional intelligence', Imagination, Cognition and Personality 9, 185–211

Schneider, J A (1997) 'Welfare-to-network', in Demos, The Wealth and poverty of Networks: Tackling social exclusion, Demos, London

SCPR (1997) British Social Attitudes, the 13th Report, Social and Community Planning Research, London

Senge, P (1990) The Fifth Discipline: The art and practice of the learning organisation, Century Business, London

6, P (1997) Escaping Poverty: From safety nets to networks of opportunity, Demos, London

—— (1997a) Holistic Government, Demos, London

Smith, G, Smith, T and Wright, G (1997) 'Poverty and schooling: choice, diversity or division', in A Walker and C Walker (eds), Britain Divided: The growth of social exclusion in the 1980s and 1990s, CPAG, London

Stone Wiste, M (ed.) (1998) Teaching for Understanding: Linking research with practice, Jossey-Bass Publishers, San Francisco

Strebler, M (1997) 'Improving employee capability', Training Tomorrow 11(6), MCB University Press, Falmouth

Tapscott, D (1996) The Digital Economy, McGraw Hill, London

Taylor, M (1995) Unleashing the Potential: Bringing residents to the centre of estate regeneration, Joseph Rowntree Foundation, York

Tower Hamlets (1993) Learning to Achieve, Education Department, London Borough of Tower Hamlets, London

—— (1997) Getting Results: Study support in Tower Hamlets, London Borough of Tower Hamlets, London

Warwick, D (1994) The Thinking behind the Linking, Middlesex University, Middlesex

—— (1995) 'Schools and businesses', in A Macbeth, D McCreath and J Aitchison, Collaborate or Compete? Educational partnerships in a market economy, Falmer Press, London

White, J N (1997) Schools for the 21st Century: Educating for the information age, Leonard Publishing, Harpenden

White, M (1971) 'The view from the student's desk', in M L Silberman (ed.), The Experience of Schooling, Holt, Rinehart and Winston, New York

Wilkinson, H (1996) 'New kids on the block', in The Return of the Local, Demos Quarterly 9, Demos, London

Wilkinson, H and Mulgan, G (1995) Freedom's Children: Work, relationships and politics for 18–34-year-olds in Britain today, Demos, London

Wilson, W J (1996) When Work Disappears: The world of the new urban poor, Alfred J Knopf, New York

Young, M and Wilmott, P (1962) Family and Kinship in East London, Penguin, London

Zeldin, T (1994) An Intimate History of Humanity, Minerva, London

INDEX